Symbol, Story,
and
Ceremony

Symbol, Story,
and
Ceremony

*Using Metaphor in
Individual and Family Therapy*

GENE COMBS, M.D.
AND
JILL FREEDMAN, M.S.W.

W. W. NORTON & COMPANY • *NEW YORK* • *LONDON*

Material excerpted from the following sources:

Excerpts from STEPS TO AN ECOLOGY OF MIND by Gregory Bateson. Copyright ©
1972 by Harper & Row, Publishers, Inc. Reprinted by permission of Harper & Row,
Publishers, Inc.

Reprinted with permission of Macmillan Publishing Company from ANGELS FEAR:
TOWARDS AN EPISTEMOLOGY OF THE SACRED by Gregory and Mary Catherine
Bateson. Copyright © 1987 by The Estate of Gregory Bateson and Mary Catherine
Bateson.

UNCOMMON WISDOM: Conversations with Remarkable People. Copyright © 1988 by
Fritjof Capra. Reprinted by permission of Simon & Schuster, Inc.

Erikson, M. H. THE COLLECTED PAPERS OF MILTON H. ERIKSON ON HYPNO-
SIS. 4 volumes. Edited by E. L. Rossi. New York: Irvington, 1980.

Text from "The Wishing Well," from MOUSE TALES by Arnold Lobel. Copyright © 1972
by Arnold Lobel. ISBN: 023941-7. Reprinted by permission of Harper & Row, Publishers, Inc.

Library of Congress Cataloging-in-Publication Data

Combs, Gene.
   Symbol, story, and ceremony : using metaphor in individual and
family therapy / Gene Combs and Jill Freedman.
      p.   cm.
   ISBN 0-393-70092-5
   1. *Metaphor—Therapeutic use.*   2. *Psychotherapy.*   3. *Erickson,*
Milton H.   4. *Bateson, Gregory.*   I. *Freedman, Jill, M.S.W.*
II. Title
RC489.M47C66   1990   *616.89′14—dc20*   *90-32847*

W. W. Norton & Company, Inc., 500 Fifth Avenue, New York, N.Y. 10110
W. W. Norton & Company, Ltd., 37 Great Russell Street, London WC1B 3NU

   3   4   5   6   7   8   9   0

*To my parents, Rosie and Milton Freedman,
whose blend of loving optimism and loving
pessimism has always been a tremendous
source of motivation for me. This accomplishment wouldn't be the same without their
excitement and delight.*

J.H.F.

*To my mother, Bennie Caudill Combs, and to
the memory of my father, Gene N. Combs.
His hard work, foresight, and generosity
made possible the long and wonderful sabbat-
ical in which this book was conceived.*

G.N.C.

ACKNOWLEDGMENTS

WE WOULD ESPECIALLY like to recognize our clients, who are the real developers of all the attitudes, approaches, and techniques that we address in this book.

Many other people helped and supported us throughout the endeavor. Steve Freedman gave ready help and enthusiasm, beyond the call of brotherhood. He did last-minute typing and editing without which we couldn't have made it on time. Milton Freedman attended to our bills and mail while we were off writing in Europe. Dave Clark, Jennifer Andrews, and Monica Andrews shared resources, recommended books, and tracked down articles. Charlie Johnson and Yvonne Dolan gave support and encouragement at several important junctures, as did Bill O'Hanlon, who magically seemed to turn up with just the right words whenever we were most discouraged. Debby Tolmach and Jeff Sugarman listened to and encouraged us at a time when we thought the book would never be finished. John Walter and Jane Peller were unfailingly enthusiastic. *Vogliamo ringraziare particorlarmente la famiglia Rossi per la sua costante amicizia e l'aiuto offerto.*

Maxine Shear and Virginia Simons read portions of the manuscript and offered suggestions. Christie Turner participates in a kind of long-distance team with us and in that capacity was involved in several of the cases described. Dot Feldman and Kay Grask opened up opportunities and provided us with a variety of teaching experiences in which we developed our presentation of many of the ideas in this book. And special thanks to Susan Barrows, our editor, who helped to make this a delightful experience. If she ever wants to change professions, she has all the qualities of a good therapist, and she tells a great story.

CONTENTS

INTRODUCTION

What We Mean By Metaphor

IN DORIS LESSING's story "Out of the Fountain," Ephraim, a master diamond cutter, is summoned by a wealthy merchant to cut a diamond for the merchant's daughter, Mihréne. When the job is completed the merchant invites Ephraim to join his family for dinner.

At dinner, Mihréne sits by her fiancé's side, wearing a string of costume pearls, as is the fad of the time. The diamond cutter is struck by her beauty and grace and dismayed by the costume pearls. Twice he asks in a voice "rough with complaint" why she wears them. After the dinner, Ephraim spends days searching for a single perfect pearl. When he has found it, he returns to the merchant's home and, after a second dinner, presents the daughter with the pearl, saying in a harsh voice that she shouldn't wear false pearls. Soon after the dinner, the daughter breaks her engagement. Against her parents' wishes she marries a revolutionary with no money, whom she considers a hero.

Ephraim and Mihréne do not meet again for many years. They have both survived the war, but Mihréne's hero and her first child have died. She is pregnant with the child conceived during her husband's final leave, living with an aunt of her husband " . . . with no resources at all but her pride. . . . " Many times she has been hungry, yet sewn into her slip, retained through all misfortune, is the pearl.

A metaphor is something that stands for something else. In this story the pearl is valued not as treasure, but as a metaphor for the jeweler's appraisal of the daughter. One can infer that, whenever the daughter looks at the pearl or feels it in her slip, she replays the scene in which she got it or the new way she began to think of herself upon receiving it and feels good about herself. The pearl stands for such important things to the daughter that even in times of severe deprivation she retains it as a symbol rather than cashing it in for economic comfort.

The symbol is especially effective because it is given by someone whose special skill is to recognize the best characteristics of a gem in the rough and bring them out in a single well-chosen tap. The diamond cutter's occupation is metaphorically his role in the story. He identifies and values the daughter as a "gem," bringing out in a single encounter characteristics that even she does not know she has.

From a different perspective, the story is a metaphor for the ideas it expresses. For example, it may symbolize the idea that a single encounter can change the entire meaning and direction of a person's life. Alternatively, it might remind us that a sense of one's own value is more sustaining than physical comfort.

From still another vantage point, we are using the story as a metaphor for metaphors. In placing it at the beginning of a book about metaphor, we are using the pearl as a symbol of all symbols. We are also using the story as a representative of all stories and the presentation of the pearl as a metaphor for all ceremonies.

A metaphor always communicates on at least two levels: the level of pearl as pearl and the level of pearl as symbol. Doris Lessing's story has many more than two dimensions, each one adding richness of meaning. It is this multiplicity of dimensions that distinguishes metaphorical from "straight" communication.

Symbol

We use the word "symbol" to refer to the smallest units of metaphor—words, objects, mental images, and the like—in which a richness of meaning is crystallized.

INTRODUCTION xv

I(JF) once worked in an agency that had a very moody director. On certain days, when staff members were on their way to ask him for something, their colleagues would say, "Don't ask today. He's wearing a suit." Those suits had become a symbol to the whole staff that the director was in a bad mood.

Words are in and of themselves symbols of experience. Sometimes a word can become a more explicit and multidimensional symbol. For instance, a man who had been out of work for some time was listless and unhappy. He emerged from a guided trance addressing these issues with the word "spunk," which accompanied an energetic feeling of resolve about doing something. On his own initiative, when he reached home he wrote *spunk* on some 3×5 cards and posted them throughout his apartment. He reported that, no matter what his mood, when he saw one of those cards he would feel a surge of energy and the resolve to do something.

Whether it be a word on a card, a suit, a pearl, a swastika, or a star of David, a symbol is a discrete thing that sets off powerful associations.

Story

Everybody knows what a story is. And everybody has had the experience of learning a lesson from a story. We consider a story to be metaphorical when it is used to communicate something more than the events of the story itself. You can use any story as a metaphor. Just as a pearl can be either simply a pearl or a symbol of self-worth, a story can be either simply a story or a metaphor. The distinction emerges in how you tell it and how your listener hears it.

People tell stories as metaphors all the time. For instance, my mother-in-law, Rosie, once told me(GC) the following story when I was upset because I thought that a shirt that I'd just unpacked was too wrinkled to wear: "Last week when I was having a party, I took a tablecloth out of the closet" (Rosie has a closet full of tablecloths, each on its own special tablecloth hanger) "and I fully expected it to be perfect. I had already picked out all the other things for the party to match the embroidery on that tablecloth. But it was really wrinkled. I had to go ahead and use it anyway, because the guests were coming soon. I was worried, but I shouldn't have been; when I got everything on top of it, you couldn't tell that it was wrinkled at all."

Rosie was using the story to illustrate a simple idea. She knew I was going to wear a coat and tie and thought the shirt would look fine once I had them on. The Doris Lessing story that opens this chapter is an example of a more complex metaphorical story.

Whether it be simple or complex, a story is a bigger unit of metaphor than a symbol. It relates several elements through time rather than being a discrete "bit" of communication. It may, in fact, be the substrate within which several discrete symbols are embedded and interrelated.

Ceremony

By "ceremony" we mean a set of actions, often called a ritual, that has symbolic importance for the people performing it. The diamond cutter presents the perfect pearl along with the harsh judgment that the daughter shouldn't wear false pearls. When she participates in this ceremony by accepting the pearl, Mihréne engages in symbolic action that changes the course of her life.

Ceremonies are an important part of life. Whether as simple as the hand wave villagers use in greeting when they pass each other on the road or as elaborate as the coronation of a British monarch, they metaphorically highlight various aspects of what Gregory Bateson (1979) called "the pattern that connects." The phrase "the pattern that connects" is itself a metaphor, one that Bateson used to refer to the fundamental pattern of relationships that connects the cell with the body, the person with the family, the starfish with the star, the universe with itself. One important function of ceremony is in highlighting and affirming the continuity of certain valued aspects of this pattern of relationships.

Another function of ceremony is in marking changes in relationships. We traditionally symbolize important changes of relationship with ceremonies such as weddings, baptisms, bar mitzvahs, and funerals. In therapy we do likewise by constructing ceremonies to symbolize important changes of relationship, both of people with each other and of people with themselves. In such therapeutic ceremonies we offer people the opportunity to participate in new patterns. When successful, the ceremony both creates a context in which change can occur and metaphorically marks the change.

A simple ceremony that we once used with a husband and wife who were doing more than their share of fighting was to have them spend 15 minutes after work each day in total silence. We suggested that during this time they sit next to each other and hold hands. At the most basic level this was a symbolic way for them to experience their connection differently. Moreover, when they accepted our suggestion, they symbolically said to each other that they were willing and able to change their behavior.

For us, the notion of ceremony can include many kinds of activities: homework assignments, enactments, role-playing, rehearsal, etc. The thing that makes such activities ceremonies is their significance to clients on the symbolic level. For a socially isolated man, enrolling in a scuba diving class might or might not be a ceremony. If in suggesting that he enroll in such a class the therapist intends the act of enrolling to stand for other kinds of reaching out, if the therapist interacts so as to create an aura of importance, perhaps even of mystery, about enrolling, then the man may begin to experience it as something more than signing up for a class. It may stand for something other than a small step toward social involvement. When a person has such an experience, the actions of enrolling become a ceremony, a rite of passage into a fuller and more rewarding way of living. Scuba diving comes to stand for a client's willing exploration of deeper and less well-known worlds of experience.

The Intent and Structure of this Book

This book describes a set of strategies for using metaphor in psychotherapy. These strategies were inspired by the life and work of two men, Milton Erickson and Gregory Bateson.

Erickson pioneered the use of symbols, stories, and ceremonies to pursue therapeutic goals indirectly. The creative use of indirection is essential in allowing for newness and evolution in psychotherapy.

One of the knottiest problems therapists face is how to influence psychological evolution without becoming either too directive, thereby not allowing clients freedom to find their own way, or too random, thereby having no useful influence. Bateson believed that successful evolution requires a balance of purposive and random elements. Metaphor, with its multidimensional and inexact nature, allows psychotherapy to be purposive while leaving room for "the random." This is important because, as Bateson (1979, p.163) wrote, "without the random there can be no new thing."

Two points that we wish to make in this book are that indirection is a useful source of the random in psychotherapy and that metaphor, which we consider to include symbols, stories, and ceremonies, is an excellent tool for indirection. At a more specific level, we hope to acquaint therapists with the various uses of metaphor in psychotherapy, to provide instruction in how to construct metaphors, and to give examples of a wide variety of metaphors.

Many more people use metaphor than know they are using metaphor. We have enjoyed sitting behind one-way mirrors and watching therapists unknowingly make wonderful metaphoric interventions. Luckily, metaphor can be just as effective without a therapist's conscious appreciation as with it, although it is more personally gratifying for people to be aware of their abilities.

There are some therapists who use metaphor in some contexts of their lives but not in doing therapy. Perhaps it's because their clinical training didn't include it or because their attitude about "work" demands more linear and direct kinds of thinking. Still others haven't developed the metaphoric genius that lurks within, only indulging in it in their dreams. If you are somewhere on the continuum we have just hinted at, this book was designed specifically for you.

If you are already terrific at generating metaphors and know it, you probably are reading this book because you enjoy a good story. So we'll do our best to include a few of those too.

Section I, *Fundamentals*, consists of three chapters. The first chapter gives an overview of principles we consider to be characteristic of Ericksonian psychotherapy. Chapter 2 gives a condensed look at some of Gregory Bateson's philosophical notions as they relate to metaphor and its use in therapy. Readers who are already using Ericksonian approaches in their work or those who are already conversant with Bateson's writings may want to skip Chapter 1 or 2 and proceed directly to Chapter 3, which shows how to use metaphor in six basic therapeutic processes: developing a relationship, gathering information, accessing and utilizing resources, suggesting ideas, reframing, and facilitating new patterns of thoughts, feelings, and behaviors.

In Section II, *How to Construct Metaphors*, we give detailed guidelines and illustrative case examples that teach the reader just that. Chapter 4 is a compendium of practical exercises designed to develop flexibility, creativity, and confidence in thinking metaphorically. Chapter 5 teaches how to develop symbols, Chapter 6 contains strategies for creating stories, and Chapter 7 gives strategies for constructing ceremonies.

Section III, *The Therapeutic Interaction*, contains a final chapter in which we give our ideas on how to set up a context in which to work metaphorically and how to deliver metaphors effectively.

Symbol, Story,
and
Ceremony

I

Fundamentals

1

AN ERICKSONIAN APPROACH

WE BELIEVE THAT most of our ideas about how to do psychotherapy come directly or indirectly from the work of Milton H. Erickson, M.D. Five of these ideas are so important that we discuss them in detail. They are:

1. A multidimensional perspective
2. Strategy
3. Utilization
4. Indirection
5. Experience

A Multidimensional Perspective

People are complex and contradictory by nature. Any holistic system of psychotherapy needs to accept and address this fact. It is easy to recognize one meaning of a nonverbal expression and build an idea of the "truth" of a situation from it. It is more useful to recognize the various possible meanings of a nonverbal expression and integrate them into an evolving understanding of a person's situation — a situation that almost certainly includes contradictory aspects.

When Erickson worked with people he paid attention to what they said and what they didn't say, what they said in words and what they said in facial expression and body movement, when their breathing changed and when they momentarily stopped breathing, their particular word choice, and whom different family members looked at and didn't look at while speaking. He used the information he obtained in these ways to enrich his understanding of the problems, resources, and goals of the client system.

When we fail in therapy, it often has to do with not using a multidimensional perspective. It is all too easy to become engrossed in a single aspect of a system and fail to connect with other important aspects. This often happens when we unquestioningly accept a client's verbal report of the problem and the goal. Such a report is a valid communication from an important part of the client, but it is not by any means the whole story. Accepting the verbal report of that part of the client most ready to talk is like doing family therapy with only one family member present and accepting her or his description of the problem as the truth for the whole family. It is important to work with the whole client system:* conscious and unconscious, verbal and nonverbal, active and passive, pleased and angry, individual and group.

Erickson attended closely to clients' conscious-level communication and unconscious-level communication and responded in kind. He paid close attention to the words that he used, choosing those that he felt had just the right associations for his purposes. He varied his posture, his facial expression, and all the parameters— rate, rhythm, pitch, timbre, etc.—of his voice in order to communicate eloquently through several channels at once.

In our quest to emulate the multidimensionality of Erickson's work, symbols, stories, and ceremonies are the most reliable tools we have found. Any time we use metaphor we are communicating on at least two levels. Most really good metaphors, whether they be stories, paintings, statues, gestures, or songs, communicate in more dimensions than we can count. When we couch our messages to people in metaphor, we help to insure that those messages are perceived in many dimensions.

---

*We are not suggesting that the whole client system needs to be in the therapy room in order to be addressed.

It is just as important to discover the client system's metaphorical messages to us. Different aspects of the client system may communicate in different ways. If one message is given verbally and another nonverbally, the therapist has to consider both dimensions in formulating a plan. Generally, the most respectful way to intervene in such cases involves different communications at the verbal and nonverbal levels.

In supervising a first session of family therapy, when the family entered the room we noticed that all three children and the mother pulled their chairs together away from the father. Each member in turn, including the father, asserted that everyone loved each other but that they weren't enjoying each other as a family. They theorized that this was due to differing schedules and to diverging interests as the children grew up. They said that they wanted to start having good times together again. Although the family members looked directly at anyone else who talked, when the father talked they looked at the floor.

We don't know the thoughts and feelings that led each family member to draw away from the father and not to look at him when he talked, but we do know that those behaviors were as much a part of what was going on as were the words they spoke. As the therapist responded verbally to the family's wish to have good times together by asking about enjoyable times they had already experienced and what different members would find enjoyable in the future, we wondered about the nonverbal communication.

We called in a request that the father move his chair closer to the rest of the family. Then we watched to see how family members responded to this move as they continued to talk about possible good times together. The father seemed hesitant as he moved. Other members had little reaction that we could see. We watched for any indication that anyone felt unsafe with this closeness or that particular members welcomed it, but saw evidence of neither.

After the father moved, he was more relaxed and talked more easily. By the end of the session, his family looked at him some of the time when he spoke, although still not as much as they looked at each other. In future sessions, we will be curious to notice where people sit and how they respond when other members talk.

We believe that the moving away from and not talking to the

father was part of the situation the family defined as not having a good time together. Therefore, we thought that, if they behaved differently, they might begin to enjoy each other more. Even though we didn't fully understand the meaning of the nonverbal behavior, it included information that was not in the family's verbal description of their problem. It singled out the father. Following the family's example, the therapist's response singled out the father at the nonverbal level and spoke to the family as a unit at the verbal level.

While recognizing and responding to different dimensions that people present is important, believing in and eliciting dimensions that are not presented is even more important. Because the therapist's beliefs influence which dimensions are available in the therapy, it is particularly important to believe that people are resourceful and that they have a wealth of useful experiences. When people are so caught up in their problems that they forget that other dimensions exist, it is particularly important for therapists to remember that people are a lot more than their problems. An experience I(JF) had with a couple when I was a student symbolizes the importance of this belief for me.

Anna Marie and Glenn came to therapy because they were considering divorcing and thought that they should talk with someone about it. Anna Marie described her emotional and sexual frustration throughout their five-year marriage. She believed that Glenn was not as interested in emotional closeness or sex as she was. In the previous year she had become completely numb, and no longer had feelings of love for Glenn. Anna Marie wanted the opportunity to find someone else with whom she might have some closeness, but she had remained in the marriage because of her concern about the effects a divorce might have on their little girl. Glenn spoke little. He felt the inevitable end of the marriage was his fault. Although he loved Anna Marie he just didn't seem to be able to give enough.

After two grim and not very hopeful sessions, I walked into a local ice cream shop one day and saw Anna Marie and Glenn sitting close together eating ice cream, giggling, and giving every appearance of having a wonderful time. I was astounded—what I saw did not match the couple I knew. I had unwittingly stumbled on another dimension.

At the following session I told them that it seemed to me that they were having a great time at the ice cream shop. They agreed that they were, and said that they often had a great time together. I was baffled, and said that usually people who had a great time together felt close. They agreed they did feel close at those times, but that it didn't carry over to intimate contexts. I then discovered that they would both be delighted if it did, and that, if they could have those feelings of closeness and enjoyment in an intimate context, they would want to stay together. With that agreement, the therapy was on a whole new path. I don't know how much sooner we might have found the new path if I had believed in a "lost dimension" in the beginning.

Strategy

At a live supervision session in Chicago, a therapist said to Jay Haley that she often worked with clients on their breathing. She wondered if he did. Haley answered, "I do if they have a breathing problem."

Haley (1963, 1973) has written extensively about the importance of strategy in Erickson's work. The above anecdote illustrates his belief that plans about how to carry out therapy should emerge from the particularities of each client's situation. We agree with Haley that Erickson's emphasis on carefully individualized therapeutic strategies was distinctive.

Generally, the first step in Ericksonian strategizing is to gather enough information to formulate both a reasonable hypothesis about how clients are experiencing their current situation and a reachable goal in terms of what they want from therapy. A plan is then developed about how to facilitate movement toward the chosen goal. Both the plan and the underlying hypothesis are continually modified as more information emerges. The therapist is responsible for developing the plan, continually updating it, and introducing it in a form that works for the particular client system.

Sometimes strategizing is quite simple: Clients clearly and congruently say what they want, we easily find and give some direct suggestions that they follow, and the goal is quickly reached.

Lou had been a bookkeeper with the same company for 37 years. Four months before he came to therapy the company got something that he thought they had needed for a long time, a computer. They also hired someone to run it, Dan. Although Lou's job and salary stayed the same, Dan was made manager of the department, supervising Lou and two part-time college students who had been loosely within Lou's domain. Lou seemed to feel fine about this arrangement. His difficulty was that Dan gave him overly specific instructions, even for trivial tasks that he had done for years, and repeatedly questioned him on what he was doing in a tone of voice that, according to Lou, implied he was a moron. At other times Dan kept to himself and there was almost no social interaction between the two men.

Lou's stated goals were to keep both his job and his sense of dignity. His fear was that he would blow up at Dan and escalate the hostility. After careful questioning, my(JF) understanding was that both Dan and Lou felt threatened and in a one-down relationship with regard to each other. Perhaps for Lou this was because after years of being his own boss Dan was now in charge. For Dan this may have been due to Lou's greater experience.

I needed a plan that would help Lou and Dan develop a better relationship. Since Lou was the one at the session, the intervention had to be through him. The idea I had was for Lou to change the way he responded to Dan. I suggested that he compliment Dan every time Dan questioned him or gave him instructions. If he could find other ways or times to compliment Dan, he was to do that also. He was to give these compliments sincerely, without sarcasm.

I suggested that Dan must feel pretty insecure if he needed to continually put Lou down and that now that Lou had something to do so that he could feel in control of his situation and keep his sense of dignity he could probably even afford to be generous to "someone as insecure as Dan" and sincerely compliment him. If he helped Dan to feel better, Dan probably wouldn't need to put anyone down.

We spent the remainder of the session practicing giving Dan compliments on his thoroughness, on how quickly he understood the details of the job, on how his involvement in every aspect of the job made Lou feel supported, and so on. Lou left the office chuckling; later he reported by telephone that at first Dan became very quiet but within a week and a half he was actually smiling at Lou, who was enjoying his job again.

In this situation, Lou clearly and congruently stated his goals, we developed a plan for achieving them, the plan was carried out, Lou reached his goal, and therapy ended.

Other situations are much more complex. Sometimes the ultimate goal is so far from the present reality that we find it more appropriate to focus in closer and set a series of simple and pragmatic goals, developing plans for them that can be pursued in a stepwise fashion.

When I(GC) first met Jane, she was living on a psychiatric ward. She had been a university student. Over the course of the previous year she had become more and more withdrawn and "weird" in her behavior. She was almost completely mute, so little information could be obtained about what was bothering her. I did know that she had mutilated herself by gouging at her wrists with a broken bottle just before she was admitted to the hospital.

The first goal I set was for Jane to talk during therapy sessions. Once she was talking it became clear that she had difficulty distinguishing between internal and external experience, so our next goal was to learn to tell inside from outside. As work progressed on that goal, she began to have a clearer idea of herself as an entity with boundaries. Jane then began to talk about how empty she felt and how meaningless her actions seemed, so a goal of finding some meaningful and fulfilling activity emerged. After several false starts, that goal was reached when she began doing volunteer work in a hospital emergency room.

Jane and I continued to identify and work toward more goals: finding and making friends, learning to relate to men, finding safe and legal outlets for anger, learning trust in a love relationship, deciding on a career, etc.

Although Jane was seen in a hospital setting where it was customary to identify patients by psychiatric diagnosis, that diagnosis was not really useful in developing an Ericksonian treatment plan. We instead utilized strategic planning, focusing on concrete and pragmatic goals for Jane rather than looking to the generic label "schizophrenia" and letting it dictate a generic treatment plan.

While it is very important that therapists take responsibility for setting goals and devising plans to meet those goals, these actions must be carried out in a way that fully respects and emphasizes clients' resources. A presupposition in Ericksonian psychotherapy is that people already have all the resources they need to live satisfying and meaningful lives. They can be assumed to already know, at some level, what they need to do. All of our therapeutic strategies are aimed at co-creating a reality with clients in which they can discover for themselves the motivation and develop for themselves the confidence to use their particular range of resources, their unique whole selves, in developing and pursuing appropriate goals.

Metaphor facilitates our carrying out therapeutic strategies in multidimensional and flexible ways. Strategies couched in metaphor provide a source of "the random"* that helps insure that clients do something other than blindly follow our authoritarian lead.

To oversimplify for the sake of clarity, suppose we are seeing a couple who have described how disorganized their life is, how they seem to stumble over each other, and how every move they have taken to organize themselves has failed. One of their therapy goals is to learn to organize themselves.

In listening to them, we may get the idea that each is doing a great deal to organize things, but that their plans are not coordinated and often conflict. We may consider suggesting a ceremony of a three-legged walk through a park in which they each tie one of their legs to one of the other's legs. Our idea in this small segment of our plan would have to do with their having a symbolic experience of co-ordinating their movements and learning to work together to reach a goal.

In doing the ceremony, the wife and husband may have discovered instead that in focusing on organization they have missed out

*See description of *stochastic process* in Chapter 2.

on being outside and enjoying the weekends. They might then make and pursue other plans to have fun. When they return they may tell us that their fun has been so energizing that they are getting more done than they thought they could. Instead of learning to co-ordinate their movements, they would have learned that if they balance work and play they will get more done and feel better in the process.

Although we did not have this particular lesson in mind for the hypothetical couple, it could be crucial in meeting their goal. Because metaphor involves multiple dimensions and random elements, people often find different, but relevant, meanings than therapists intend.

Metaphor provides a safeguard against becoming inflexible in pursuit of a goal. It lets clients be full collaborative partners in the creative process. A key element in successful strategizing is the willingness of the therapist to abandon any plan as soon as she or he perceives that it doesn't fit. In order to do this we must constantly attend to the systemic effects of our actions. The worth of a strategy can only be measured by how well it works in moving toward a goal. If a client is not interested in following the ideas suggested or moves no closer to a chosen goal, either the strategy is not a good one for that client or we need an additional plan for helping the client discover the motivation to follow the original strategy. Luckily for us, we have Erickson's example to follow. He was a genius at motivating people to do all sorts of things. His ideas on utilization are a big part of that genius.

Utilization

Erickson was particularly noted for his ability to utilize symptoms and so-called "resistant" behaviors as stepping-stones to therapeutic goals. Ericksonian utilization is based in the philosophy that a client's every uniqueness is a resource that can be used positively. This philosophy is in turn based in two beliefs: that each person is unique, and that every thought, word, and deed has some positive value. These beliefs lead us to study each new client carefully so that we can learn his or her values, beliefs, and styles of relating. Each new bit of information gives us something we might utilize in tailoring our treatment plan. Even the problems that bring people to treatment can be utilized in moving toward their solutions.

There are important fringe benefits to utilization. It enhances the therapeutic relationship by encouraging a therapist to be curious about how each and every aspect of a person can make a positive contribution to the therapy. It gives people a sense of competence and success when therapists respond to them in this positive manner. Since it is a therapist's responsibility to utilize clients' beliefs, jargon, and world views, clients don't need to go through an "initiation" phase of learning therapists' jargon and theories before they can be "good" clients.

Utilization is a very practical way of working. It is much easier to use a behavior that already exists as part of the plan than to get someone to do something completely new. It is much easier to base a strategy on a client's current belief system than to convince her or him to adopt different beliefs. It's relatively easy to find things to utilize. It only requires attending to people in such a way that we can begin to discover the things that are already there.

Erickson (1965, p. 213) wrote the following on the subject:

Since whatever patients bring into the office is in some way both a part of them and a part of their problem, the patient should be viewed with a sympathetic eye appraising the totality which confronts the therapist. In so doing therapists should not limit themselves to an appraisal of what is good and reasonable as offering possible foundations for therapeutic procedures. Sometimes—in fact, many more times than is realized—therapy can be firmly established on a sound basis only by the utilization of silly, absurd, irrational, and contradictory manifestations. One's professional dignity is not involved, but one's professional competence is . . .

Erickson probably came to value utilization so highly (and to be so good at it) through his long years of experience as a hypnotist. He discovered early on that it was limiting for a hypnotist to follow a memorized induction, expecting a client to follow a standardized and predictable route into trance. For example, if a trance subject opened his eyes and started talking, many hypnotists would have interpreted it as "resistance" or "being a poor hypnotic subject."

Erickson presupposed that open eyes and talk were just what that person needed, and utilized them to lead that person into trance. His extension of this idea into nonhypnotic psychotherapy is inspirational. What started as the simple-seeming presupposition that whatever the subject did could be used in a positive way became one of the most important advances in hypnosis and psychotherapy in this century.

In the following case history, Erickson (1965) takes a rather unusual presenting problem and, instead of working to abolish it, utilizes it, building his therapy around it.

A woman came to see Erickson after she had been divorced three times. She blamed herself for not having had a satisfactory sexual relationship in any of her marriages. The first marriage was to an alcoholic who attempted consummation of the marriage while he was intoxicated and blamed the failure on her, describing her as "having a refrigerated derriere" [quotations are Erickson's]. The second and third marriages were brief and equally disastrous, especially sexually.

Since the first evening of her third marriage, her buttocks, in line with her first husband's suggestion, felt continually cold. She was now in love with someone of whom her family and friends approved, but she did not want to bring him unhappiness. All she wanted from therapy was to have the coldness in her "derriere" removed. She thought that hypnotherapy could be of help in this regard. She would not listen to Erickson's thoughts about her difficulties in general. She emphatically insisted that once the coldness was removed all would be well.

Erickson devised his strategy in accordance with her understanding of the problem. He gave her the assignment of filling her bathtub with increasingly hotter water and then submerging her legs until they were covered with goose bumps. (You may wish to check this out—sufficiently hot water can indeed cause goose bumps.) After she accomplished this, Erickson gave her " . . . a laboriously detailed explanation of how an overloading of the thermal receptors by excessive warmth would overflow into the cold receptors of the skin, thereby resulting in gooseflesh. The success of this venture, in [Erickson's] opinion, played a large part in the successful therapy. It supplied her with indisputable visual proof that heat can produce the concomitants of coldness, and that this could be done in a definitely limited area of the body. From that point on there existed for her no doubts or fears of [Erickson's] understandings or competence." In other words, Erickson showed the woman that the physical signs and symptoms of coldness could be brought on by great heat.

In a subsequent session, in hypnosis, Erickson gave the woman a series of carefully worded, repetitive suggestions: She could privately take great pride and delight in her secret knowledge that she could experience heat by having a cool response. Her thighs, buttocks, and abdomen could respond to heat as her legs had. During a number of sessions he repetitively alluded to positive past experiences that had to do with sensations of cold: "tingling delights of sledding down hill on a tinglingly cold day," "the rapturous joys of a cold, cold dish of ice cream on a hot summer's day," etc.

Erickson knew that therapy was complete when " . . . in completely vulgar terms, with many blushes, she stated in essence, 'I like being a frozen-posteriored creature.'"

The therapy centered on a bathtub ceremony that utilized a client's presenting problem and her circumscribed understanding of that problem.

Utilization needn't always be so dramatic. Once it becomes part of a therapist's philosophy, it begins to pervade his or her work in subtle, but very useful ways.

Lynn came to therapy because she didn't feel good about herself. At the first session she described her job selling real estate in an office run by her family. "I know I could make some money if I worked 40 hours a week," she said, "and I know I would feel better about myself if I made some money. But I only seem to be able to do things for other people, not for myself."

As I(JF) began to plan an intervention toward the end of the first session, two things stood out in relation to Lynn's goal:

1. She would feel better about herself if she worked 40 hours a week.
2. She believed that she could only do helpful things for others.

(Therefore if I asked her directly to work 40 hours a week for herself, I was courting failure.) I utilized both these things in designing the following ceremony for Lynn:

She was to keep careful weekly records of how much time she spent selling real estate. Each week, she would make up any time short of 40 hours by doing volunteer work at a local hospital. Because it utilized the two above beliefs, ones that she already held, the ceremony made sense to Lynn. I hoped both that Lynn's self-esteem would improve as she actively helped others and that she would get some practice with a 40-hour work week. If she did no volunteer work, she would be working 40 hours a week at her job, which should improve her income and lead her to feel better about herself.

As it turned out, she chose the second alternative and her success in selling real estate did increase. An unanticipated development was that, once she was working regularly and was more confident, Lynn landed a part-time salaried job with regular hours that provided structure and supplemented her income in a more stable way than working for commission had. Her first experience allowed her to feel confident about her skills, and that made it possible for her to seek employment outside of the family business.

In the above example, I designed a ceremony to utilize two beliefs in a rather straightforward way. However, it is not necessary that utilization take place on the direct and literal plane. Metaphor broadens the scope of possible utilizations. When we strategize at the metaphorical level, we can perceive more possibilities for utilizing a given value, belief, style of responding, or problem. Metaphorical thinking frees us from the strictures of having to utilize literally and logically.

At an introductory talk on Ericksonian approaches, Sheila volunteered to be a demonstration client. She was very poised and self-confident in front of the audience and immediately began describing her problem in an earnest and frank manner.

It seems that she had purchased a computer several months before. She considered herself to be a pretty bright person and had studied the instruction manual, but every time she sat down at that "damn computer," within a few minutes it would make this horrible mechanical beep and print "Response not valid." Not being very experienced with mechanical things, she had no idea what to do next. For a while, she called friends who had computers and asked them what to do or went back to the instruction book, which was no more helpful than the damn computer. Sometimes she could then go on for several minutes before that damn computer would make that horrible mechanical beep and print "Response not valid" again. At the time of the demonstration she was not attempting to use it at all.

She had decided to buy the computer because several of her friends advised her that it would be very helpful to her in her work as a teacher and consultant, especially since she was compiling a book of exercises to go along with her consultations, but now she felt awful about the amount of money she had invested in this worthless machine. Her goal was to somehow get some use out of it.

In listening to Sheila's description of her problem, there were two things that stood out as utilizable:

1. She seemed to feel positively about humans (whom she worked with and mentioned as friends) as opposed to mechanical things.
2. She presented her problem in a very frank and earnest manner and probably valued these characteristics.

If I(JF) were to utilize these features in a straight way of thinking, I might have told Sheila that it was true that a computer can be an efficient tool in teaching and consulting, freeing more work time to interact with people, but lots of people found themselves in Sheila's position with computers, and what they really needed was an instruction manual that was frank about the problems novices encounter and clear in explaining possible solutions.

I might then have suggested that Sheila take on the project of writing "Frank Talk About Computers: A Beginner's Guide." Sheila could learn to work at the computer (so that she eventually would have more time to work directly with people), while gathering information for her book (which would fill a big human need and probably make her some money).

In this hypothetical approach, I would have utilized Sheila's positive attitude toward people to motivate her to use the computer. The valued characteristic of frankness would have been utilized by including it in the proposed book's title.

Instead, I used metaphoric thinking. I said to Sheila, "You strike me as someone who values directness and frankness. Am I right?" Sheila agreed. "Then it seems to me you should value that frank communication your computer gives you when it beeps, instead of pussyfooting around when you've done something wrong. To think that after such straight talk you turn your back and walk away! You don't seem like that kind of person to me. If a friend gives you frank criticism do you turn your back and walk away without a word?"

"Of course not," Sheila answered.

"Well, I think such an earnest helper as you have deserves better. And to remind you that that beep is just his way of speaking frankly, I suggest you name him. Any ideas on a name?"

Sheila, grinning, said, "I'll have to think about a name."

"How about Frank?"

"I love it. Frank Ernest Wang. That's what I'll call him," she announced and laughed.

Sheila kept in touch and told me that she started using Frank Ernest Wang immediately. When he beeps she shouts and curses. The two of them have since developed a frank working relationship.

Metaphorical thinking produced the idea of utilizing "frank" as a name and having the computer become a "person" with whom Sheila could have a relationship.

Another way of combining metaphor and utilization is by attending to the metaphors already used by a client and finding a way to utilize those metaphors as part of a treatment plan. The first way involves taking something that is already there and finding a way to use it as a metaphor. The second involves finding a metaphor that is already used by a client and using it for some purpose.

In the following example, a client's metaphor is utilized to make it smoother and easier to talk about difficult things.

Jack had been in and out of several psychiatric hospitals. He began abusing psychedelic and psychostimulant drugs in his mid-teens, then started running with "the wrong crowd," and was hospitalized for the first time when he intentionally set fire to his apartment after a week of accusing everyone around him of being demons or agents of the devil.

He came to see me(GC) just after being released from a year-long stay at a well-known residential treatment center. His goals were to get a job, stay straight, and learn to live independently of his parents. His main problem was that he had learned to use craziness as a refuge. When things got hard, like when his car broke down and he needed it to get to work but didn't want to ask his parents for a loan to fix it, he would start smoking marijuana and staying up all night, which soon had him looking weird and talking pretty strangely.

Things culminated in a brief hospitalization, during which he talked wildly about a dragon having been released from the lower depths and how he was under its control. After that episode, he tended to get very upset and angry if anything about the hospital was mentioned or if his psychotic behavior was directly commented on. He would, however, talk calmly and lucidly about the dragon and whether or not he felt he was in danger of being under its control again. For example, if Jack came in talking rapidly and irritably, instead of asking, "Have you been feeling like you did before you landed in the hospital?" or "Have you been hearing voices again?" I could say, "Is the dragon threatening to bother you again?"

The dragon soon became a therapeutic ally. Jack began to have internal conversations in which he asked the dragon what he needed to do to keep it content and got answers like "Go to bed before 3:00 in the morning." When we worked in this metaphorical way, we were able to develop plans that allowed him to avoid the dragon's influence. Jack never succumbed to its clutches again.

When we listen for the metaphors that people habitually use and utilize them directly, without reducing them to logic or consciously focusing on their meaning, therapy is enriched. If a client says several times "as peaceful as Bantry Bay," we don't have to know anything about Bantry Bay to begin mentioning it to that particular client when we want her or him to feel peaceful.

When we directly utilize a person's metaphors, rapport is enhanced. A person can't help but feel more at home. It's like walking into a stranger's house and finding your favorite music playing.

Indirection

In life, the shortest distance between two points may not be a straight line. It's easier to open the passenger door you forgot to lock than to call a locksmith when you've left your keys in the ignition. It's quicker to get most kids to bed by saying, "Let's have a bedtime story," than by saying "Go to bed." And everyone knows that the way to a man's heart is through his stomach.

The above are examples of *indirection*. It's nice when people bring in well-delineated goals and we can offer direct suggestions or behavioral tasks which they then follow, but there are many times when direct approaches don't work. People frequently respond to a well-meant direct suggestion by saying something like, "If I could do that I wouldn't be here!" At these times it's good to have a toolbox full of indirect approaches.

Erickson didn't invent indirection (folklore is full of it—think of Brer Rabbit saying, "Please don't throw me in that briar patch!"), but he championed its use in psychotherapy in a way that has inspired two subsequent generations of psychotherapists. His case reports are full of examples of the artful and inventive use of indirect approaches to strategic goals.* He believed, as we do, that insight is often irrelevant to change, that people don't have to understand consciously how or why or even what they've changed in order to change. This belief lets us feel free to approach change through unconscious, nonverbal, and indirect channels when clients aren't responding to direct approaches.

The freedom to approach goals indirectly does not, however,

*See *Hypnotherapy: An Exploratory Casebook* (Erickson & Rossi, 1979) or *The Answer Within* (Lankton & Lankton, 1983) for an overview of indirect language patterns. See any of the collections of Erickson's cases for inspirational examples.

give us permission to be sneaky, tricky, or otherwise disrespectful of clients. While insight may not be relevant to change, integrity is. It may be possible to trick people into doing something that doesn't really fit with their overall values, but in the long run such a use of indirection seldom produces lasting change and often produces a rift in the therapeutic relationship.

An indirect approach is any approach that moves toward a goal in something other than a straight line. It might deviate only slightly from a straight line, such as asking, "Do you think you know what might be useful in that situation?" rather than, "What would be useful?" It might appear to move directly away from the goal, as in telling a child who is sucking his or her thumb that it's unfair to leave out all the other fingers and repetitively saying that each finger should get equal time. Indirect approaches may combine any number of moves in any direction as long as the goal is eventually reached and there is some deviation from the straight and narrow path.

The skilled use of indirection facilitates therapy in several ways:

1. It allows therapists to bypass reflexive objections of clients.
2. It allows therapists to test clients' responses to ideas without calling attention to them.
3. It allows therapists to build a careful foundation before being direct.
4. It encourages active mental search on the part of clients, which in turn:
   a. develops access to forgotten resources,
   b. stimulates new associative pathways,
   c. gives clients a greater sense of creativity in and responsibility for the therapy process.

Metaphor is the handiest and most versatile tool we have for indirection. Any time a direct approach is not working, we need only to find a way to do the same thing metaphorically and we've devised an indirect approach. Every example of metaphor is an example of indirection; therefore, each of the points listed above applies to the use of metaphor in therapy.

Metaphoric approaches tend to bypass reflexive objections a

person might have if we stated things "straight out." Since ideas are not presented directly, it is harder for people to object to them. For example, remember Jack, who could talk about "the influence of the dragon" when he couldn't talk directly about his psychotic behavior.

Metaphoric approaches allow us to test a client's responses to an idea without calling direct attention to it. If we want to suggest a ceremony to a family but are unsure if family members are motivated enough to perform it, we might tell a story about another family who performed a similar ceremony. The more interest family members show in the story, the more likely we would be to suggest they do the ceremony. Some families would become interested enough to do it without being assigned. If family members seemed bored, antagonized, or intimidated by the story, we would need to rethink our strategy.

In much the same way, metaphors can be used to build a careful foundation before we directly approach an idea. If we want an extremely shy client to tell us details about his sex life, we might start by talking about "certain basic needs we all have," such as hunger. If that produced neither discomfort nor the desired information, we might tell anecdotes from some of our own early dating experiences. If that produced neither shock nor an immediate flood of sexual information, we might mention "the birds and the bees" in an apparently unrelated context. We would proceed to use metaphors that more and more directly approached the desired subject matter until we either got the information we wanted or got cues that a different strategy might be more successful.

Because it is indirect, metaphor encourages more active involvement on the part of a client. He or she must search through a number of stored or imagined experiences in order to find personal meaning in a general symbol or story. In watching movies and videotapes of Erickson's work, we have been impressed by the high proportion of time his clients seem to have spent in this type of internal search. The searching stimulates mental associations and thereby makes the lessons of therapy more memorable. The creative work involved in searching through and reorganizing experiences makes clients active collaborators in the process of therapy.

Experience

Following Erickson, we believe that experience is the best teacher and strive to design experiences that allow people to learn how to set and reach their own goals. By experience we mean not only doing things (external activity), but also thinking and feeling (internal activity). The more a person is actively experiencing something, the more associative pathways tend to be stimulated.

Here is a typical quote from Erickson (1948, pp.38–39) on this subject (he happens to be talking particularly about hypnotherapy with chronic alcoholics):

> It is [the] experience of reassociating and reorganizing his own experiential life that eventuates in a cure. . . . The chronic alcoholic can be induced by direct suggestion to correct his habits temporarily, but not until he goes through the inner process of reassociating and reorganizing his experiential life can effective results occur.
>
> In other words, hypnotic psychotherapy is a learning process for the patient, a procedure of reeducation. Effective results in hypnotic psychotherapy, or hypnotherapy, derive only from the patient's activities. The therapist merely stimulates the patient into activity, often not knowing what that activity may be, and then guides the patient and exercises clinical judgment in determining the amount of work to be done to achieve the desired results. How to guide and to judge constitute the therapist's problem, while the patient's task is that of learning through his own efforts to understand his experiential life in a new way. Such reeducation is, of course, necessarily in terms of the patient's life experiences, his understandings, memories, attitudes, and ideas; it cannot be in terms of the therapist's ideas and opinions.

While we're quoting Erickson, we'll let him illustrate what he means with an example (Erickson, 1954a, pp. 99–102):

> A young couple in their early twenties, much in love and married for a year . . . , sought psychiatric help. Their problem was one in common—lifelong enuresis. During their 15-month courtship neither had had the courage to tell the other about the habitual enuresis.
>
> Their wedding night had been marked, after consummation of the marriage, by a feeling of horrible dread and then resigned desperation, followed by sleep. The next morning each was silently and profoundly grateful to the other for the unbelievable forbearance shown in making

no comment about the wet bed. [This pattern continued with] . . . an ever-increasing feeling of love and regard for each other because of the sympathetic silence shown.

Then one morning, neither could remember who made the remark, the comment was made that they really ought to have a baby to sleep with them so that it could be blamed for the wet bed. This led at once to the astonishing discovery for each that the other was enuretic and that each had felt solely responsible. While they were greatly relieved by this discovery, the enuresis persisted.

[They sought an appointment with Erickson, saying they couldn't pay for therapy but earnestly wanted help. Erickson agreed to accept them for "experimental therapy."]

They were then told that the absolute requisite for therapeutic benefits would lie in their unquestioning and unfailing obedience to the instructions given to them. This they promised. The experimental therapeutic procedure was outlined to them, to their amazement and horror, in the following fashion:

"You are both very religious, and you have both given me a promise you will keep.

"You are to receive experimental therapy. . . . This is what you are to do: Each evening you are to take fluids freely. Two hours before you go to bed, lock the bathroom door after drinking a glass of water. At bedtime get into your pajamas and then kneel side by side on the bed, facing your pillows, and deliberately, intentionally, and jointly wet the bed. This may be hard to do, but you must do it. Then lie down and go to sleep, knowing full well that the wetting of the bed is over and done with for the night, that nothing can really make it noticeably wetter.

"Do this every night, no matter how much you hate it—you have promised, though you did not know what the promise entailed, but you are obligated. Do it every night for two weeks—that is, until Sunday the seventeenth. On Sunday night you may take a rest from this task. You may that night lie down and go to sleep in a dry bed.

"On Monday morning, the eighteenth, you will arise, throw back the covers, and look at the bed. *Only as you see a wet bed, then and only then* will you realize that there will be before you another three weeks of kneeling and wetting the bed.

"You have your instructions. There is to be no discussion and no debating between you about this, just silence. There is to be only obedience, and you know *and will know what to do.* I will see you again in five weeks time. You will then give me a full and amazing account. Goodbye!"

Five weeks later they entered the office, amused, chagrined, embarrassed, greatly pleased, but puzzled and uncertain about [Erickson's] possible attitude and intentions.

They had been most obedient. The first night had been one of torture. They had to kneel for over an hour before they could urinate. Succeeding nights were desperately dreaded. Each night they looked forward with an increasing intensity of desire to lie down and sleep in a dry bed on Sunday the seventeenth. On the morning of Monday the eighteenth, they awakened at the alarm and were amazed to find the bed still dry. Both started to speak and immediately remembered the admonition of silence.

That night, in their pajamas, they looked at the bed, at each other, started to speak. . . . Impulsively they "sneaked" into bed, turned off the reading light, wondering why they had not deliberately wet the bed but at the same time enjoying the comfort of a dry bed. On Tuesday morning the bed was again dry, and that night and thereafter Monday night's behavior had been repeated.

Having completed their report, they waited for [Erickson's] comments. They were immediately reminded that they had been told that they would give an "amazing account" in five weeks time. Now they knew that they had, and that [Erickson] was tremendously pleased, *and would continue to be pleased*, so what more could be asked?

. . . A year later they introduced [Erickson] to their infant son, amusedly stating that once more they could have a wet bed but only when they wished, and it would be just "a cute little wet spot." (Emphasis in original)

Erickson had people do many things. Intentionally wetting the bed is only one "amazing and horrifying" example. They all involved vivid experiences of one sort or another. Although in the quotation at the beginning of this section Erickson is talking specifically about activity and experience being important in hypnotherapy, you can see from the example that he applied the same principles even when he wasn't using formal hypnosis.

One of the first things that Erickson did at a particular teaching seminar was to look through the papers on which seminar participants had written identifying data. He then said that one of his daughters was invited to a party at a professor's house. She went, and there were white carpets. They were served red wine, and very early on Erickson's daughter spilled her glass of wine all over the white carpet. Then he said, "There's always one in every crowd," and leaned forward, looking piercingly at one of the participants, saying as he handed her paper back, "You forgot to put the date."

Later, the participants found that hardly anyone had put the date. When Erickson followed his story of a social blunder by saying, "There's always one in every crowd . . . you forgot to put the date," they were all *immediately* in the experience of not knowing what was the right thing to do—wondering, searching for the meaning in Erickson's communication. What did he mean by "there's always one in every crowd"? One what? He was talking about his daughter, whom he obviously loved, but he was revealing an uncomfortable experience she had. So there was both a positive and negative dimension in identifying with her. Since each of the seminar participants thought he or she was the "one" in the crowd, they had a number of layers of experience: identifying with the daughter spilling wine on the professor's carpet, reliving their own individual versions of and associations to social blunders, searching through their memories of standing out in a crowd (perhaps in good ways), and the immediate experience of being Erickson's students and wondering about the significance of not dating their papers.

There's always an element of ambiguity in metaphorical communication. There is always a number of ways it can be taken. People tend to want to resolve ambiguity. They listen closer, think harder, and become more experientially involved in therapy when there is a certain amount of ambiguity in a therapist's utterances. Not knowing can lead to a very active kind of participation, and a major thing that happens in that participation is that people are reassociating and reorganizing their internal experiential lives.

There are a number of variations of the cartoon in which one character points out a food advertisement to a second hungry character. The hungry character snatches the ad and devours it, confusing the metaphor for the real thing. As with all good comedy (and some bad), there is truth in this cartoon. People's proclivity to experience the reality of metaphor explains both tears at a movie and the effectiveness of metaphor in psychotherapy. In their associations to and identification with metaphorical experience, people make it real. The ad in the cartoon is not real food, but as a therapeutic metaphor is experienced and owned, it is transformed so that real and nourishing new ways of thinking, perceiving, and being emerge.

In offering a client a metaphor, a therapist offers a *choice*. The client must choose how to respond; even not responding is a response. The therapist can then utilize the client's response, perhaps to offer another metaphor. In this way both are constantly active in the dance of therapy, collaborating in an evolving experience.

And remember . . . there's always one in every crowd.

2

A BATESONIAN PERSPECTIVE

IF MILTON ERICKSON is our symbol of *what to do* in psychotherapy, Gregory Bateson represents *how to think*. Actually, as we begin to understand his patterns of thought, we see that Bateson provides a model for how to think about thinking. No overview of his work can really do justice to his ideas, so we highly recommend that you read his books if you haven't already. We especially draw upon the ideas in *Mind and Nature*.

What we offer in this chapter is an introduction to Bateson's way of thinking as it relates to the use of metaphor in psychotherapy. In making such a selection, we can't help but make distortions and deletions, so be warned that these are only our understandings of a small portion of Bateson's work.

Bateson's Style of Teaching

From time to time we have each believed that Bateson explicitly made some point or other. In searching his books to find exactly where he stated it, we have discovered that he didn't. Sometimes we would find a place where it seemed he was just about to, perhaps in the next paragraph; but he didn't.

In trying to teach other people his way of looking at the world,

Bateson rarely attempted a straightforward description of the whole picture; he preferred instead to present interrelated ideas in the form of stories, seemingly scattered observations, jokes, and symbols such as seashells or whole cooked crabs, trusting that his audience would make meaningful connections.

Fritjof Capra (1988, p.76) has described how in his conversations with Bateson, "Bateson would lay out his web of ideas and I would check certain nodes in this network against my own understanding with brief remarks and quick questions. He would be especially pleased when I was able to jump ahead of him and skip a link or two in the network." The following conversation, reconstructed by Capra, illustrates Bateson's preferred interactional style. The participants are Capra and Bateson, who are sitting on the deck outside the lodge at Esalen. We include it here so that you can get a feel for Bateson's style of communicating.

"Logic is a very elegant tool," he [Bateson] said, "and we've got a lot of mileage out of it for two thousand years or so. The trouble is, you know, when you apply it to crabs and porpoises, and butterflies and habit formation"—his voice trailed off, and he added after a pause, looking out over the ocean—"you know, to all those pretty things"—and now, looking straight at me [Capra]—"logic won't quite do."

"No?"

"It won't quite do," he continued animatedly, "because that whole fabric of living things is not put together by logic. You see, when you get circular trains of causation, as you always do in the living world, the use of logic will make you walk into paradoxes. Just take the thermostat, a simple sense organ, yes?"

He looked at me, questioning whether I followed and, seeing that I did, he continued.

"If it's on, it's off; if it's off, it's on. If yes, then no; if no, then yes."

With that he stopped to let me puzzle about what he had said. His last sentence reminded me of the classical paradoxes of Aristotelian logic, which was, of course, intended. So I risked a jump.

"You mean, do thermostats lie?"*

Bateson's eyes lit up: "Yes-no-yes-no-yes-no. You see, the cybernetic equivalent of logic is oscillation."

---

*Capra is here referring to the Epimenides Paradox, in which Epimenides, a Cretan, says "all Cretans are liars." If the statement is true, then the speaker is a liar, so the statement is a lie. If the statement is false, then Epimenides is not a liar, so his statement is true.

He stopped again, and at that moment I suddenly had an insight, making a connection to something I had been interested in for a long time. I got very excited and said with a provocative smile:

"Heraclitus knew that!"

"Heraclitus knew that," Bateson repeated, answering my smile with one of his.

"And so did Lao Tzu," I pushed on.

"Yes, indeed; and so do the trees over there. Logic won't do for them."

"So what do they use instead?"

"Metaphor."

"Metaphor?"

"Yes, metaphor. That's how this whole fabric of mental interconnections holds together. Metaphor is right at the bottom of being alive."

Metaphor as the Logic of Nature

You may have heard the following story. It was a favorite of Bateson's.

> A man wanted to know about mind, not in nature, but in his private large computer. He asked it (no doubt in his best Fortran), "Do you compute that you will ever think like a human being?" The machine then set to work to analyze its own computational habits. Finally, the machine printed its answer on a piece of paper, as such machines do. The man ran to get the answer and found, neatly typed, the words: THAT REMINDS ME OF A STORY. (Bateson, 1979, p.14)

In this anecdote, Bateson is elaborating on his notion that metaphor is the logic of nature. He believed that metaphor was inescapable in living systems, as every thought that we have is *about* something. In Bateson's words, "When we think of coconuts or pigs, there are no coconuts or pigs in the brain" (1979, p.32).

Start with a real pig "out there" in the world. In order for us to perceive the pig, some news of the pig must impinge on our sense organs. In the case of vision, light must first strike the pig, where it is differentially reflected, refracted, and absorbed, and then strike the rod and cone cells in our retinas. What strikes our retina is not the pig, but light which stands for the pig, so it's not the pig, but a *metaphor* for the pig, that first brings news of the pig to our bodies.

The light is then transformed into an electrochemical reaction which travels along a nerve, so we have a metaphor (changes in electrochemical activity in the nerve cell) for a metaphor (changes in the light striking the retina) for a pig. At each synapse as it travels through our nervous system the news of the pig is transformed—from a pattern of electrical impulses to a pattern of chemicals (neurotransmitters) flowing across the synapse and again to an electrical metaphor. Through processes that we don't yet understand very well, the neurochemical news is transformed into "consciousness" as the idea of a pig.

But it is not a pig. It is a pattern of neurochemical symbols that we have learned to associate with the thing in the external world that the phonetic symbols "p" "i" and "g" represent. You may further note that the letters must be combined in a certain sequence, a certain story if you will, before they represent a pig.

In this way, Bateson argued persuasively that in mind all is metaphor. Of course it is incredibly cumbersome to carry around a conscious awareness of the transformations involved in our moment-by-moment perception, but it is not a trivial exercise to remind ourselves occasionally what's going on outside of consciousness.

We can never definitively know anything about external reality. The best we can do is to seek more and more workable metaphors for it—ones that work across more contexts and in communication with more people. Since everything is metaphor, skill in working with metaphor is essential for effective communication.

The Name Is Not the Thing Named

Bateson was very fond of Korzybski's statement, "the map is not the territory." He found it useful in sorting out all sorts of mental confusion. As the metaphor of the pigs and the coconuts illustrated, we can never know any territory directly. All we can know are various "maps" of it or metaphors for it.

Any map (or any type of description, for that matter) exists on a different logical level than what it describes. It is "meta" to what it describes, and confusion can occur if the description is treated as a member of the class it describes. In other words, the word "pig" is not a pig. You won't get much nutrition from the word, no matter how you cook it.

Bateson found Whitehead and Russell's theory of logical types useful in understanding and working with such potential confusion. This theory was developed to deal with the occurrence of paradox in classical logic. It asserts that no class can be a member of itself. In other words, a name is of a different logical type than the thing that it names. While this assertion may seem trivial and even obvious, Bateson found that it was not at all unusual for theorists in the behavioral sciences to commit errors of logical typing.

If we are to avoid such errors when we use metaphor, it is important to remember that the metaphor is not of the same logical type as the idea it represents. A metaphor can point to an idea, but it can never BE the idea. It is in the room between the idea and the metaphor that multiple meanings are possible.

Learning Through Abduction

Bateson used a multiplicity of metaphors to illustrate the usefulness of multiple descriptions. A simple example is binocular vision. Each of our eyes gives us a description of the world. When the images from each eye are combined in our mind, a new description, one with a much more vivid sense of depth, emerges.

> It is correct (and a great improvement) to begin to think of the two parties to the interaction as two eyes, each giving a monocular view of what goes on, and together giving a binocular view. This double view *is* the relationship. (Bateson, 1979, p.147, emphasis in original)

Bateson coined the term *abduction* to describe the type of reasoning (of the same logical type as deduction and induction) in which you place two or more systems, models, or metaphors in conjunction and look for patterns that connect them.

In drawing any distinction, you distinguish some sort of difference. If this page were uniformly white, with no variation in color, it would contain no information. Black must be distinguished from white before letters and words can be noticed. The possibility of reading emerges through the drawing of many distinctions—one letter from another, one word from another, one meaning of a word from other possible meanings, etc. — and each of these distinctions is a relationship. Black has meaning *in relationship* to white; "a" has meaning *in relationship* to "e," "i," "o," and "u." So, even at this simple level two or more things must be related in some way before any of them can have meaning.

Bateson learned about the natural world by distinguishing patterns of relationship in one complex system and examining other complex systems for the presence or absence of the same patterns. By mapping back and forth across systems, he could refine his understanding of relationships within each system. At the same time, he would begin to distinguish patterns of relationship between the two complex systems, patterns that described a larger connection. At times he described his life's work as a search for "the pattern that connects" the entire biological universe.

In psychotherapy, metaphor is a wonderful tool for double description. It allows clients to learn through abduction. If a therapist, for instance, tells members of a family a story about people in a situation similar to theirs, they then have the possibility of looking at their situation in relation to the people in the story. They might see patterns in their situation that they have never seen before. Once they have perceived a new pattern, they can apply it, and in the application they will distinguish further patterns.

Any single metaphor is a particular version of a particular part of the world. When people have only one metaphor for a situation, their creativity is limited. The more metaphors they have to choose from for a given situation, the more choice and flexibility they have in how to handle it. Finding multiple metaphors expands the realm of creativity.

A Different Definition of Mind

Bateson gave us a new way of thinking about what constitutes a mind. Most people in Western culture think of a mind as something that occupies an individual brain. Bateson's concept was larger.

In illustrating his definition of mind, Bateson (1972, pp.458–459) asked people to consider the set of events most people would describe as "a man cutting down a tree with an axe." He described the tree, the enlarging notch in the tree, the axe head, the axe handle, and the man wielding the axe.

As the axe flies through the air it progressively modifies the shape of the notch in the tree's side, and the changes in the shape of the notch modify the man's decisions about how to swing the axe the next time. Bateson asserted that anyone explaining this set of phenomena would need to attend to how "news of difference" was communicated at each step of the way around and around the circuit. Change in the shape of the notch in the tree is received as news of difference by the man's retina, changes in the retina bring news of difference to the central nervous system, the central nervous system passes the news along to the muscles, the muscles send information to the axe handle, the axe handle "tells" the axe head how to move, and the axe head continues to change the shape and size of the notch.

Any explanation of the mental processes involved needs to include all parts of the circuit and the transformations of the message at each interface. Therefore, the mind involved in cutting down the tree doesn't stop at the boundaries of the man's body.

For Bateson, mind was more a process than a thing, and the boundaries of a given mind were defined functionally and pragmatically. Each element involved in the dissemination of news of a particular difference was part of the mind that was distinguishing the difference.

> I suggest that the delimitation of an individual mind must always depend upon what phenomena we wish to understand or explain. Obviously there are lots of message pathways outside the skin, and these and the messages which they carry must be included as part of the mental system whenever they are relevant. (Bateson, 1972, p.458)

> Thus, in no system which shows mental characteristics can any part have unilateral control over the whole. In other words, *the mental characteristics of the system are immanent, not in some part, but in the system as a whole.* (Bateson, 1972, p.316, emphasis in original)

When Bateson was considering matters like global ecology or the arms race, he considered the entire natural world to be interconnected in this way. He believed that there was *a necessary unity* between mind and nature.

When we use Bateson's notion of mind, we might draw distinctions concerning a part of a person, a whole person, a couple, a group of fellow workers, a nation, or some other entity. The question of where to draw the distinction becomes important, and the answer is always somewhat arbitrary and relativistic. We know of no rule by which to determine the most appropriate size of map to select, but we do believe it is essential to respect the arbitrary nature of any boundaries we establish.

Again, Bateson's way of thinking about things impels us to remember that all thought is based in metaphor and that it matters which metaphors we use. The "mind" we distinguish can co-vary with the metaphors we use. If we examine a situation through the metaphor of "family," we will draw one set of distinctions, and news of those distinctions will flow through one set of elements— one mind. If we examine the same situation through the metaphor of "community," we will draw other distinctions, news of which will flow through a different mind.

Coevolution

When Bateson turned his attention to the process of evolution, his interest in relationship and his penchant for finding new patterns led him to a new description of that process. He talked about the evolution of the horse in the context of grassy plains to illustrate his view.

> The evolution of the horse from *Eohippus* was not a one-sided adjustment to life on grassy plains. Surely the grassy plains themselves were evolved *pari passu* with the evolution of the teeth and hooves of the horses and other ungulates. Turf was the evolving response of the vegetation to the evolution of the horse. It is the *context* which evolves. (Bateson, 1972, p.155, emphasis in original)

> We should not think of [evolution] just as a set of changes in the animal's adaptation to live on the grassy plains but as a *constancy in the relationship* between animals and environment. It is the ecology which survives and slowly evolves. In this evolution, the relata—the animals and the grass—undergo changes which are indeed adaptive

from moment to moment. But if the process of adaptation were the whole story, there could be no systemic pathology. Trouble arises precisely because the "logic" of adaptation is a different "logic" from that of the survival and evolution of the ecological system. (Bateson, 1972, p.338, emphasis in original)

So Bateson saw the whole prairie ecosystem as one mind in which different elements (horses, grass, horse manure, bacteria, cougars that prey on the horses, etc.) exist in an evolving relationship to one another. All evolution is *coevolution*. Any change in one element is perceived as news of difference in relation to the other elements. The "news" proposes changes in the other elements if the relationship among them is to be maintained.

For Bateson, change (of which evolution is one example) was never a one-sided proposition. The grass changes *in relation* to the horses' hooves. The horses' teeth change *in relation* to the grass. And change itself exists *in relation* to its complement, which is stability.

This idea of coevolution is important in the client-therapist system. Clients don't unilaterally change. They change in relationship with changes in therapists and with other elements of the therapeutic context. A therapist chooses a particular metaphor in relation to what clients share, and clients choose what to share in relation to metaphors chosen by that therapist. Also, it is important to consider the evolution of the client system and the many systems of which the client is part, as well as the news of difference that will be communicated to those systems from the therapeutic work.

Ecologies of Ideas *

Bateson used the above model—horses and grass and all the other interdependently coevolving beings that make up something like a climax prairie ecosystem—as a metaphor for the way ideas interrelate in a mental system.

---

*Much of this section is a paraphrase and condensation of Bogdan's (1984) article, "Family organization as an ecology of ideas."

The relative constancy—the survival—of the relationship between animals and grass is maintained by changes in both relata. But any adaptive change in either of the relata, if uncorrected by some change in the other, will always jeopardize the relationship between them. These arguments propose a new conceptual frame for [various ideas. They] cease to be matters of individual psychology and become part of the ecology of ideas in systems or "minds" whose boundaries no longer coincide with the skins of the participant individuals. (Bateson, 1972, p.339)

In mind, ideas live side by side and from time to time rub up against one another, sometimes supporting each other and sometimes coming into conflict. Over time, they wax and wane in vigor, develop protective coloration, prey upon each other, lie dormant, migrate, copulate, become extinct, and differentiate into new species of ideas.

They coevolve in a process of communication and mutual adaptation over time. In the mind of a client-therapist system, the ideas that thrive are those of the clients and those of the therapist that tend to confirm and support one another over time. The therapist's communications somehow relate to, and are part of, a pattern that includes the communications of the clients, and vice versa.

Just as horses and grass govern or restrain each other, facilitating certain possibilities and minimizing others, ideas, in the mind that constitutes a therapist-client system, restrain each other as they coevolve. The metaphors that we, as therapists, propose in the therapeutic ecology of ideas can have a profound influence on how that ecosystem evolves, just as can our clients' responses and their ideas.

Concepts like "schizophrenia" can become organizing metaphors around which a system of reciprocal invitations to a schizophrenic lifestyle coevolve. Finding a new metaphor which is acceptable to the larger system can invite the client subsystem to evolve a more satisfying lifestyle. Of course, clients may make different meanings of the therapist's metaphors than the therapist intends. Consequently, it is important to attend to how one's invitation is received in the larger system.

In an ecology of ideas, the processes through which meaning is attributed and constructed are very important. As news of difference travels through the interrelated network, its meaning can change. I can intend to communicate the meaning that I am a reputable, well-trained therapist by hanging a diploma on my office wall, but the effect of the diploma in the ecology of ideas that emerges with any given client will depend on the meaning the client finds. If the client takes my exhibiting of the diploma as a sign that I wish to impress people with my learning, he or she may conclude that I am an insecure, overeducated fool, and drop out of therapy.

A therapist's influence on any client system depends on that system's perception of the therapist and the therapeutic situation. In the same way, the client system's influence on the therapist depends on the therapist's perception. If the therapist is to have any influence on the evolution of the client system, he or she must join sufficiently with that system to function as part of a larger mind that includes both for a while.

We believe that therapists who are able to perceive, understand, and utilize the dominant metaphors of diverse client systems have a better chance of participating in healthy coevolution with those systems than therapists who don't. Essential to such ability is the willingness to be changed by a client system as well as to change it.

Cybernetics

Bateson was present at the birth of the modern science of cybernetics. He is generally given credit for bringing cybernetic ideas into the field of modern family therapy.

The word "cybernetics" is based in a Greek root which has to do with the helmsman of a boat. Thus, the metaphor in which cybernetics is based is one of steering — of noticing and correcting error in order to move toward a goal.

The key notion in simple cybernetics is *feedback*. In steering a boat, the pilot sends a message to the rudder. The boat then responds in some way to the change in position of the rudder. If steering is to be successful, the pilot must then notice whether the response is in line with the boat's destination or whether a new message must be sent to correct the previous one. The pilot's detection, judgment about, and correction of the boat's response to the first message comprise an example of feedback.

Much of the early research in cybernetics was during World War II, where it was concerned with improving the ability of anti-aircraft guns to zero in on moving airplanes. This involved ongoing loops of communication, where each circuit of the loop involved communication of the difference between where the gun was aimed and where the airplane was during the previous loop.

If you think back to Bateson's description of a man cutting down a tree, you can see that he was describing a cybernetic circuit. The thing that we did not focus on when we introduced the man, the tree, and the axe was the notion of *purpose*. While it is true that each element in the metaphor can be seen as part of one mental system, it is also true that the subsystem called "the man" is pursuing a goal. If he does not adequately join with the other subsystems involved, he cannot reach that goal. He must notice the responses of the tree to each swing of the axe. He must be receptive to how the axe responds to the messages his muscles send it. If he doesn't close the circle of feedback, he won't be able to achieve his goal.

Therapists and clients come together for a purpose. We believe that it is the therapist's job to be an experienced guide for clients, attending closely to feedback from them and from the larger context in suggesting a safe route to their goal and offering new suggestions based on feedback along the way. Being a really good guide is tricky business. If we stick slavishly to what we believe to be a direct path, striving not to vary from it at all, and guide clients in an authoritarian manner, they may reach their destination, but they may not be able to continue on their journey without the continued use of a guide. The therapist and client systems may become so closely joined an ecology of ideas that one can't thrive without the other. They may, in fact, become addicted to each other. If we take little responsibility for setting a direction, preferring to co-drift with our clients, we may have an interesting journey in which all parties learn a lot but never get anywhere in particular.

The questions of how aggressively to act on feedback, how tight a course to steer, and how much responsibility to delegate as a good guide are interrelated, and they are important to answer. Bateson's notion of *stochastic processes* is useful in this regard.

Stochastic Processes

Bateson (1979, p.165) talked of evolution and learning as the "two great stochastic systems." The word "stochastic" comes from the Greek word *stochazein*, which means to shoot with a bow at a target. Bateson used it to refer to processes in which events are scattered in a partially random manner, such that some of them achieve a preferred outcome. Any sequence of events that combines a random component (like an archer's imperfect aim) with a selective process (like the act of shooting at a target) so that only certain outcomes of the random are allowed to endure is said to be *stochastic* (Bateson, 1979).

Because metaphor is indirect, multidimensional, and multimeaningful, it is a communication form that incorporates some randomness. When we as therapists have a particular idea and use metaphor to express it, the communication can be thought of as scattered in a partially random manner. We then can note the ideas and metaphors our clients offer in return. Responding to clients' communications and keeping in mind our purpose (which changes as the system changes through communication), we can offer other metaphors. Over time we can note which aspects of our ideas, as they have coevolved with clients' ideas, survive in the ecology of ideas. Using metaphor to join with clients in the larger mind of a therapeutic system lets us create experiences that have some purpose while allowing all parties to learn by trial and error.

When we couch our suggestions to clients in metaphor, we offer spectrums of possibilities that client and therapist can explore together. We can have a clear purpose in our own mind and still allow clients a range of alternatives in how to respond, including the chance that they will understand our metaphor very differently from the way we intended it. Based on the feedback we perceive and our purpose at a given moment, we may offer a different metaphor, again allowing a range of alternatives.

A Respect for Unconscious Processes

Bateson was very fond of a passage from "The Rime of the Ancient Mariner" by Coleridge. At this point in the poem, the ship on which the mariner sails is nearly doomed. Most of the crew has died of thirst, and the ship is unable to move for lack of wind. The mariner has brought on this misfortune by killing an albatross, which now hangs about his neck as a portent of the curse he has engendered.

> Beyond the shadow of the ship,
> I watched the water snakes:
> They moved in tracks of shining white,
> And when they reared, the elfish light
> Fell off in hoary flakes.
>
> Within the shadow of the ship
> I watched their rich attire:
> Blue, glossy green, and velvet black,
> They coiled and swam; and every track
> Was a flash of golden fire.
>
> O happy living things! no tongue
> Their beauty might declare:
> A spring of love gushed from my heart,
> And I blessed them unaware:
> Sure my kind saint took pity on me,
> And I blessed them unaware.
>
> The selfsame moment I could pray;
> And from my neck so free
> The Albatross fell off, and sank
> Like lead into the sea.

Rain came in the wake of this event. Bateson believed that the curative event here was that through the wild beauty of the sea snakes the mariner experienced himself as a participant in the larger mind of nature. This could only happen "unaware." Being aware of what was happening would require a dissociated perspective, which would require a withdrawal from direct participation.

Bateson was a passionate advocate of connectedness. To him, conscious purpose was most useful if connected to and balanced by nonconscious purpose. In our approach to therapy, we believe that purposiveness and planning are essential, but they must be balanced by a respect for nonconscious processes and a willingness to lose ourselves for moments in the larger pattern.

Using metaphor helps assure that we respect nonconscious processes. Bateson talked about this issue in this way:

> What the unaided consciousness (unaided by art, dreams, and the like) can never appreciate is the *systemic* nature of mind.
>
> This notion can conveniently be illustrated by an analogy: the living human body is a complex, cybernetically integrated system. This system has been studied by scientists—mostly medical men—for many years. What they now know about the body may aptly be compared with what the unaided consciousness knows about the mind. Being doctors, they had purposes: to cure this and that. Their research efforts were therefore focused (as attention focuses the consciousness) upon those short trains of causality which they could manipulate, by means of drugs or other intervention, to correct more or less specific and identifiable states or symptoms. Whenever they discovered an effective "cure" for something, research in that area ceased and attention was directed elsewhere. We can now prevent polio, but nobody knows much more about the systemic aspects of that fascinating disease. Research on it has ceased or is, at best, confined to improving the vaccines.
>
> But a bag of tricks for curing or preventing a list of specified diseases provides no overall *wisdom*. The ecology and population dynamics of the species has been disrupted; parasites have been made immune to antibiotics; the relationship between mother and neonate has been almost destroyed; and so on.
>
> Characteristically, errors occur wherever the altered causal chain is part of some large or small circuit structure of system. And the remainder of our technology (of which medical science is only a part) bids fair to disrupt the rest of our ecology.
>
> The point, however, which I am trying to make in this paper is not an attack on medical science but a demonstration of inevitable fact: that mere purposive rationality unaided by such phenomena as art, religion, dream, and the like, is necessarily pathogenic and destructive of life; and that its virulence springs specifically from the circumstance that life depends upon interlocking *circuits* of contingency, while consciousness can see only such short arcs of such circuits as human purpose may direct.
>
> In a word, the unaided consciousness must always involve man in the sort of stupidity of which evolution was guilty when she urged upon the dinosaurs the common-sense arguments of an armaments

race. She inevitably realized her mistake a million years later and
wiped them out.

Unaided consciousness must always tend toward hate; not only
because it is good common sense to exterminate the other fellow, but
for the more profound reason that, seeing only arcs of circuits, the
individual is continually surprised and necessarily angered when his
hardheaded policies return to plague the inventor. . . .

That is the kind of world we live in — a world of circuit structures —
and love can survive only if wisdom (i.e., a sense or recognition of the
fact of circuitry) has an effective voice. (1972, pp.145–146, emphasis
in original)

Coda

Bateson's favorite form of metaphor seems to have been story,
which he defined as "a little knot or complex of that species of
connectedness which we call *relevance*" (Bateson,1979, p.14). In
other words, stories are how a mind connects individual bits of
data.

The following passage, actually written by Bateson's daughter
Mary Catherine, is what Bateson called a "metalogue" — a kind of
made-up dialogue that he used for teaching. We include it here
because we like it, because it ties together many of the strands we
have discussed above, and because it is about stories.

Daughter: So human beings think in stories. . . . So what is a
     story really? And are there other kinds of stories, like sermons
     in the running brook? How about trees, do they think in
     stories? Or do they tell stories?
Father: But surely they do. Look, just give me that conch over there
     for a minute. Now, what we have here is a whole set of
     different stories, very beautiful stories indeed.
Daughter: Is that why you put it up on the mantelpiece?
Father: This that you see is the product of a million steps, nobody
     knows how many steps of successive modulation in successive
     generations of genotype, DNA, and all that. So that's one
     story, because the shell has to be the kind of form that can
     evolve through such a series of steps. And the shell is made,
     just as you and I are, of repetitions of parts and repetitions of
     repetitions of parts. If you look at the human spinal column,

which is also a very beautiful thing, you'll see that no vertebra is quite like any other, but each is a sort of modulation of the previous one. This conch is what's called a right-handed spiral, and spirals are sort of pretty things too—that shape which can be increased in one direction without altering its basic proportions. So the shell has the narrative of its individual growth pickled within its geometric form as well as the story of its evolution.

Daughter: I know—I looked at a cat's-eye once and saw the spiral, so I guessed it had come from something alive . . .

Father: And then, you see even though the conch has protrusions that keep it from rolling around the ocean floor, it's been worn and abraded, so that's still another story.

Daughter: You mentioned the spinal column too, so that the stories of human growth and evolution are in the conversation as well. But even when you don't actually mention the human body, there are common patterns that become a basis for recognition. That's what I meant—part of what I meant—when I said years ago that each person is his own central metaphor. I like the conch because it's like me but also because it's so different.

Father: Hello, snail. Well, so I tell stories, and sometimes Gregory is a character in the story and sometimes not. And often the story about a snail or a tree is also a story about myself and at the same time a story about you. And the real trick is what happens when the stories are set side by side.

Daughter: Parallel parables?

Father: Then there is that class of stories we call *models*, which are generally rather schematic and which, like the parables presented by teachers of religion, exist precisely to facilitate thought about some other matter.

Daughter: Well, but before you go off on models, I want to point out that the stories about snails and trees are also stories about you *and* me, in combination. And I'm always responding to the stories you don't tell as well as the ones you do, and doing my best to read between the lines. But now you can tell me about models or even about Kevembuangga if you want to. That's safe enough—I've heard it before.(Bateson & Bateson, 1987, pp.34–35, emphasis in original)

3

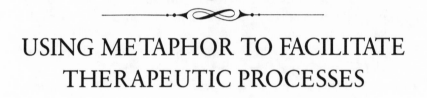

USING METAPHOR TO FACILITATE
THERAPEUTIC PROCESSES

ONCE A THERAPIST believes that he or she has understood the goals of a client system, the task is to develop a plan to help reach those goals. Questions we consider in developing a plan are: What experiences does this person or family need? What has to happen for those experiences to occur? And how can we utilize a client's beliefs, eccentricities, interests, and problems in moving towards those experiences?

Whether and how we use metaphor as part of a plan depends on the therapy goals and the particular people with whom we are working. There are six broad categories of process that characterize what happens between therapists and clients in our approach to therapy:

1. Developing a relationship
2. Gathering information
3. Accessing and utilizing resources
4. Suggesting ideas
5. Reframing
6. Facilitating new patterns of thoughts, feelings, and behavior

These processes are overlapping and occur in no particular order. Not all therapeutic relationships include all of the processes.

44

What is relevant to our purposes here is that metaphor can be used to facilitate each of them.

Developing a Relationship

The quality of the relationship between client and therapist influences everything else that happens in therapy. The most effective type of relationship varies with different client-therapist systems, but focused attention and mutual respect are almost invariably important elements. Additionally, it is important that therapists stay in a flexible position, from which they can facilitate all the kinds of experience that might be needed in the course of therapy.

As we begin any new interpersonal relationship we share symbols. The "sign language" that cowboys and Indians use in the movies is a caricature of the type of symbolic gestures that rapidly evolve between people who don't share the same spoken language. The symbols exchanged by people who share the same culture are more varied and subtle, but equally important.

As therapists, we unconsciously and automatically use certain symbols to obtain information about the mood and intentions of clients and to convey information about our mood and intentions. We note clients' posture, muscle tone, facial expression, voice tone and quality, etc., while introducing ourselves. Only if something seems to require adjustment do we begin consciously to alter the nonverbal symbols that we are sending.

If a person seems unusually anxious about entering the therapy situation, we might start speaking more softly, adopt a more relaxed posture, or share an anecdote. For example, we might ask if he had difficulty parking and then tell an anecdote about our own difficulty parking. In so doing we would use a mutual experience as a metaphor to lay a nonthreatening ground for the relationship. We would also be keeping our image down to earth by characterizing ourselves as fallible human beings. We would alter our symbolic output in different ways if a client seemed angry or withdrawn, but our initial goal would be the same—to establish a relationship of mutual respect in which therapist and client were focusing their attention on the task at hand.

Therapists can pick out any aspect of a client's behavior and utilize it as a symbol of that person's unique way of being in the world. Through this mini-ceremony the therapist demonstrates that he or she accepts and understands that way of being.

What Grinder and Bandler (1981) call *pacing* is one way of doing this. In its most basic form, pacing is mirroring one or more aspects of a person's behavior. * For instance, a therapist might sit in a posture similar to a client's and breathe in synchrony with him or her. When this is done tastefully and respectfully, it is an excellent tool for developing rapport. Most clients don't realize it at the conscious level, but the therapist is nonetheless communicating an acceptance of the client's way of sitting and breathing. The therapist is also becoming more closely attuned to the client's way of being in the world.

We took night classes in Italian in hopes of studying with Luigi Boscolo and Gianfranco Cecchin, whose work in systemic therapy we greatly admire. When we wrote to them we were delighted to discover that they· do some teaching in English. We went to a workshop in Italy where the participants were primarily from European countries and spoke English as a second language. We were impressed with how well they spoke "our" language.

Later, we began to notice that we were speaking English more like the Europeans did: keeping sentence structure simple, using the present tense most of the time, eliminating unnecessary words, and from time to time even waving our hands in the air and saying, "How do you say . . . ?" We had all joined Cecchin and Boscolo in co-creating a common group language.

The relationship that developed among the workshop participants did so through a process of coevolution. In pacing client behaviors, therapists offer clients an invitation to join them in a similar process of coevolution, learning to share and use each other's conscious and unconscious symbols, becoming one Batesonian mind.

All therapists orient clients to the kind of relationship they expect. The words we use in greeting, where we sit in relation to clients, the number and type of questions that we ask, how and

*One can pace many things besides the client's behavior. Beliefs, language styles, preferred sensory systems, and preferred metaphors are examples of other things a therapist might pace.

when we make eye contact, how we interact in scheduling appoint-
ments or handling payments: these and other interactions convey
information to clients about how we expect them to relate to us.
Perhaps it is stretching a point to call these mundane interactions
ceremonies, but they do have some symbolic importance in addition to and apart from their pragmatic significance.

For example, if a therapist routinely begins sessions asking,
"What do you want to accomplish today?" this symbolically ori-
ents clients to a relationship in which they are responsible for
establishing goals. If a therapist routinely begins sessions by asking
what has happened since the last session, clients become oriented
to a relationship in which the therapist expects them to keep track
of and report on weekly activities. If the session begins differently
each time, still a different relationship is symbolically proposed.

It is interesting to look at utilization in the light of symbolic
communication. It can be seen as a ceremony that symbolically
affirms the value of a particular attitude. When therapists engage
in Ericksonian-style utilization, they commit themselves to a process of continually adjusting the relationship in a positive way.
When they come up against a difficulty or stuck place, rather than
being frustrated with the client, they challenge themselves to become curious about how some aspect of the difficulty can be useful. In doing this, they adjust their attitude. Utilization thus
comes to serve as an unconscious ceremony in which therapists
remind themselves of the importance of maintaining a positive
perspective.

Since the act of utilization is so closely linked with positively
valuing people's uniqueness, clients tend to experience it as respectful and supportive, which is certainly helpful in developing a
therapeutic relationship.

The process of coevolution, as therapists and clients learn and
respond to each other's symbols, and the mini-ceremony of positive connotation that occurs each time we utilize attitudes, beliefs,
and behaviors in an Ericksonian fashion continue through all therapeutic sessions; they are not a separate thing that happens at the
beginning of therapy. The therapist-client relationship is constantly changing, and as it changes the metaphors through which it is
expressed shift.

Gathering Information

Gathering information and developing a relationship go hand in hand throughout therapy. On the one hand, a therapist's first move to learn anything about an individual or family begins a relationship. On the other hand, if a therapist consciously thinks of the first move as one of developing a relationship, the client system's response to that move still contains useful information. In fact, at a certain level, all information gathered by any particular therapist is not about how a client system always is, but about how that system responds to the therapist at that time, and it is therefore information about the therapeutic relationship.

The presuppositions of both therapists and clients as to how they are "supposed to" relate to each other shape the information they select to send and the things they attend to in receiving information from the other. Therapists who believe that the therapeutic relationship is one of authoritative expert to uncertain novice will give and get different information from that exchanged by therapists who believe that the therapeutic relationship is one of encouraging coach to talented player or one of person to person in conversation. Clients who believe that what they should do is tell therapists everything they can about what's "wrong" will develop a different therapeutic relationship from that of clients who believe that their role is to tell the therapist about their goals and accomplishments.

The information gathered in any particular relationship shapes the ideas that therapists form. These ideas then guide both the information they gather from that point on and the type of relationship they move toward with clients. As ideas are acted on, they are often modified or new ones take their place. In this way the relationships between clients and therapists, as well as the type of information flowing in those relationships, are constantly evolving.

We believe that therapists should be continuously guided by the answers to such questions as, "What sort of relationship am I currently in with this client?", "How can I utilize that relationship in the service of what the person or family is here for?" and "Do I need to modify our relationship in some way?"

With these caveats in mind, we will proceed to discuss the use of metaphor in gathering information with little further reference to developing a relationship.

Therapist: Is it like _____?
Client: No, it's more like _____.
Therapist: Oh, I see. You mean it's like _____.
Client: Yeah, that's right!

The similes that would be used to fill in the blanks in the above dialogue are a very basic type of metaphor. The entire process of gathering information could be conceptualized as more or less elaborate variations on this simple dialogue, therefore always involving an exchange of metaphors. Sometimes the metaphors are obvious, as in the dialogue. At other times clients offer stories and images that, although they have no conscious symbolic value for them, can be heard by the therapist as a source of metaphoric information.

Clients, too, sometimes hear metaphors in offhand remarks of their therapist, remarks to which the therapist attached no conscious symbolic importance. The meanings made by a client can serve as information to the therapist about what the client wanted or needed to hear at that time or about how the client perceived the therapeutic relationship.

Interacting with people in metaphor allows us to gather information indirectly, thus avoiding much of the awkwardness and defensiveness that can arise when we directly ask for information about personal issues. In a metaphor, more levels of a person can communicate at the same time. For example, metaphors often convey unconscious messages from a person as well as conscious ones.

Two areas in which information is often gathered directly are the nature of presenting situations and clients' goals. As we gather information about the nature of a presenting situation, metaphor is relevant in a number of ways. The stories or memories that people recount as illustrations of their situation are metaphors for it. They are useful to note as such because they may offer cues not available in the specifics of the "actual" presenting situation.

For example, we have a friend who is afraid of flying. Several times when she has told us of her fear she has mentioned that it is like the experience she had of becoming temporarily blinded during pregnancy and the doctors telling her that nothing could be done. In offering the metaphor of her blindness during pregnancy, she is underlining lack of control as important. She is also offering two cues that would be important in the context of therapy: (1) what experts say is important to her, and (2) this can be a temporary experience that could end with a rewarding result. People often unconsciously give information through the use of metaphor in this way.

Both Jay Haley and Cloé Madanes have written extensively about the problem of a child being a metaphor for the situation between the parents. Haley (1984, p.95) writes,

> The description of a child's problem in therapy can often be taken as a metaphor about the problems of mother and father. If a mother says the child is terribly stubborn, one can suspect that later she will say her husband is stubborn. If the husband says his child never does what he asks, one can suspect his wife doesn't do what he asks. The therapist who encourages metaphoric expression about the child, and doesn't point out to the couple what they're really saying, gains a great deal of information about difficulties in the family without having to make them an explicit issue.

Madanes (1981) extends this notion beyond the child, writing that the system of interaction around a symptom of one member of a couple may be a metaphor for a more pervasive system of interaction between the couple. Thus, a wife who felt weak and powerless in relation to her successful and ambitious husband developed a hysterical paralysis that the husband responded to by becoming even more authoritative and "in charge." Madanes saw this as dramatically symbolizing their relative strengths and attitudes in the relationship.

The ways of using metaphor to gather information that we have discussed so far have involved attending to metaphors spontaneously used by clients or to ostensibly nonmetaphoric communications as if they were metaphors. It is also possible to ask people directly to develop metaphors to express their experience of important issues. Art therapists often have clients make a symbol of their difficulties. Other therapists might have people find a fairy tale that symbolizes their presenting situation. Physical movement or descriptions of mental imagery can serve the same purpose.* A therapist is then free to work in the metaphoric realm or to formulate hypotheses based on the metaphoric information given.

It is particularly important to attend to metaphoric descriptions of a presenting situation for information about what may be involved in resolving that situation. Metaphors relating to goals or to what the situation will be like when the presenting situation is resolved can be discovered or developed in many of the same ways as those relating to presenting situations. They may be even more important in the therapy process. When clients develop and fill in details of metaphors that represent how they would like their lives to be, information becomes available to the therapist as well as to the client. Sometimes this is information about difficulties that could result from actually reaching a goal or about a skill a client will have to develop in order to reach the goal. In other cases, developing a metaphor for a goal can provide people with enough information to reach the goal with no further therapy.

By listening for metaphors one can also hear indications about the ongoing client-therapist relationship and how the client perceives that therapy is going. Sometimes therapists can even get information about what sort of metaphors to use in working with a particular person.

As Brenda was leaving the office one day she mentioned that she had bought a Walkman for a man she was dating. Neither he nor his teenage kids, who were supposed to know all about these things, could fit a cassette inside. They concluded that there must be different size tapes and that she must have gotten the wrong type player. I(JF) assured her that there are only regular and mini size tapes, and Brenda left.

At the next appointment she said that once she KNEW, because I had told her, that the Walkman could work, she was able to look at it fresh, as though she had never seen it before, and find a way for it to work. She said that she discovered something that when pushed opened up and the tape fit right in. She had passed it

*See Peggy Papp's (1983, pp.142–143) work on couples choreography.

around to five other people, she said, " . . . but I was the only one who could figure it out."

In this communication Brenda defined my role as one of telling her that what she wanted to accomplish was possible, so that she could then look at things differently and find a way to make them work. She emphasized that she was the one who had to make them work.

It is also useful in gathering information to notice metaphors that are distinctive to a particular client system: words, phrases, or stories that seem central in a client's personal history or model of the world, ceremonies or recurring patterns of events that are special in a given person's or family's behavior. Metaphors that are unique to a system are excellent for pacing that system and for utilizing throughout therapy.

Accessing and Utilizing Resources

Socrates believed that you can only teach people things they already know. The Socratic method, in which a teacher asks students questions that lead them to use their own knowledge in discovering a new concept, developed from this belief. The process of accessing and utilizing resources is similar. It is built upon the belief that in people's stored experience they have emotions, attitudes, behaviors, and understandings that can be drawn on to resolve current difficulties.

The fact that someone is not using a resource in a context in which it would be useful does not mean that she or he doesn't have the resource. The 12-year-old boy who is a whiz at Dungeons and Dragons but can't seem to understand the simplest instructions given in the classroom is a good example. The teenage boy who is tongue-tied with girls does have the capacity to be talkative; just listen to him in the locker room. The woman who has no patience with her mother has tremendous patience with the staff she supervises at work.

One of the circumstances that leads people to consult with therapists is that they are not naturally finding and using the resources they need. The therapist's task then becomes one of identifying and accessing these resources. Resources are already part of people's experience. Feelings, perceptual positions, personal knowledge, attitudes, and behaviors can all be used as resources. They can be elicited simply by bringing forth a context in which a person naturally responds with them. For example, one way of looking at hypnosis is as a ceremony in which a context is created to which people tend to respond with resourceful states, such as relaxation and focused attention. Resources can also be found in the client's imagination. In the movie "Play It Again, Sam," Woody Allen identifies with Humphrey Bogart and imagines that Bogart is coaching him. This imaginary consultation becomes the source of attitudes, behaviors, and feelings that Allen then utilizes as resources.

Past experience and present contexts other than the problematic one are other areas full of resources. Many people who have had positive social experiences automatically draw upon the attitudes and behaviors from these experiences when entering new contexts. They have no trouble being friendly and expecting to be liked. This happens quite naturally.

If you have ever seen someone in the throes of emotionally justifying his or her side of an argument after the argument was over, you have witnessed a demonstration that one can recover a feeling and a perceptual position by engaging in a memory. Teenage girls know that they can relive the romance of the evening before by making an in-depth telephone report to their friends of everything that happened. If there is no telephone available, reliving the evening in a daydream serves much the same purpose.

Both reporting and internally reviewing events are excellent ways to access resources. Creating an imagined event works much the same way. The trick in therapy is creating a context in which a client internally reviews, reports out loud, or imagines an event charged with the resource that would be most helpful in his or her present situation. Since people frequently respond to hearing stories by being reminded of similar events in their own experience or by imagining being one of the characters in the story, telling stories is a natural technique for evoking resources in clients.

For example, Pat came to therapy because she had never been involved with a man, and she wanted to be. She was 40 years old.

She felt scared, as though she was shaking inside, when someone started to get close to her.

In order to access feelings of security and comfort in Pat, I(JF) told a number of stories. Since she was frightened of people, I told stories that didn't involve interaction between people. For example, I told a story about someone staying home in bed with a cold, reading mystery books and drinking tea, and someone else pampering herself with a long bubble bath. Here's one of the stories I told:

"I have two cats who are both sweet in different ways. Sancho is always sweet, and Bolivar is sometimes too busy playing to notice I'm there at all. Sancho likes to put his paws in my hair and I know he's taking care of me by 'grooming' me. Sancho is a cat of peace. When Gene and I first got together, his cat Rosebud and my cat Missy Marple used to have horrible fights. And Sancho would throw himself between them so that they couldn't fight. He'd just sit there in a soft warm ball, and the other cats would settle down.

Now we just have Sancho and Bolivar who are very good friends. Bolivar seems to know when I'm not sleeping well. When that happens, he gently comes over and lays his head very softly on my neck. He feels like warm, soft feathers. And he just stays there and purrs gently and evenly, and lulls me to sleep."

There were two indications that the stories were successful in accessing security in Pat. The first was that she said the stories reminded her of the wonderful snug feeling she had in bed late at night when she was a child and believed that nothing bad could happen to her because her parents were downstairs. The second was that, after several sessions laced with this kind of story, Pat reported with relief that the jumpy, burning feeling in the pit of her stomach, which had been there as long as she could remember, was gone. With a feeling of security, we could begin to more directly address her fear and shakiness inside when others started to get close.

Another way to access a resource is to develop a context in which a person directly responds with a resource rather than accessing it through imagination or memory. Ceremonies often elicit resources in this more direct way. From Paul Carter we learned a ceremony for couples who are having sexual difficulties. This involves having them lie nude in each others' arms and do nothing but breathe at the same rate for five minutes. Coordinating this basic life-maintaining rhythm can symbolize "becoming one." The couples with whom we have used this ceremony have all experienced a renewed connection with each other. For a few, it was the only "sex therapy" necessary.

Sometimes simply helping people find flexible and reliable access to a resource may be enough. As happened with Pat, once the resource is accessed, many clients begin to use it in the appropriate contexts without the therapist's doing anything specific to link the resource to those contexts. I(JF) never connected the stories I told Pat to any particular context, but in the months following the sessions in which the stories were told Pat reported feeling more secure and comfortable in many different settings, both at work and in her personal life.

However, some people require a bridge from the resource to the appropriate contexts (O'Hanlon, 1986). Sometimes the bridge is built directly into the metaphor. For example, in Paul Carter's ceremony in which couples breathe together, instructing them to lie naked in each others' arms connects it to a sexual context.

If a bridge is not built into a metaphor, the therapist can use a metaphor that evokes the resource while the client is experientially involved in the context where the resource is needed. Once it was known that the feeling of being snug in a bed when she was a child evoked security for Pat, it could have been used as a symbol in working with contexts where Pat needed security. For example, her talk about a particular problem area could have been interrupted by saying, "Take a moment to slip into that feeling of being snug as a child in bed. Now, keeping that feeling, consider the problem." Another way to do this would be to ask, "If you felt snug as a child in bed in the problem context, what would be different?" Since Pat began to feel secure in problem areas through her own process of generalization, this was not necessary.

Here is a simple example of utilizing a symbol to contextualize a resource:

Linda wanted to pass a typing test in order to change positions within her company. She could type fast enough when she prac-

ticed at home but each time she took the test she failed. She attributed this to "nervousness." The desk where she always practiced at
home faced a window. By repeatedly reminding Linda of the sense
of ease she felt looking through the curtains above that desk, I(JF)
helped her establish the pattern of the curtains as a symbol of the
sense of ease she had at home.

I suggested that Linda carry a small square of the curtain material with her and that she practice typing in a variety of settings
other than work, each time preceding the typing by focusing on the
square of curtain and feeling the ease associated with being by her
window. When she felt at home typing in a number of different
places, Linda began practicing at work, during her lunch hour,
continuing to use the square of curtain material. It was an easy step
to then feel at home when she took the square of cloth to the
typing test.

The sense of ease was a resource that Linda already had. I linked
it to the square of cloth and then utilized the cloth as a symbol in
the problematic context of typing by asking Linda to look at it in
that context. For many people, simply imagining the curtain pattern would have been enough. Linda felt more secure with a concrete symbol. Eventually, the symbol became so associated with
typing that typing itself became a task of ease.

Many kinds of symbols can be used as cues or "anchors"
(Bandler & Grinder, 1979). In fact, one of the most important
ways that we use symbols in psychotherapy is to stand for, provide
easy access to, and stabilize resources. We discuss this process in
more detail in Chapter 5.

Many times the resource that people need is a new perceptual
position. Because it is very natural to identify with a character in a
story and perceive things from that character's position, stories are
ideal for giving people the experience of a new perceptual position.
Ceremonies can also be very effective. One in which each member
of a couple "tries on" his or her partner's side of an argument may
begin with a wooden mouthing of words, but as it progresses most
people have the experience of seeing things the way their partners
do and therefore understanding their partners better. However, a
different perceptual position does not necessarily entail seeing
through someone else's eyes. It may involve a more abstract posi-

tion, such as a woman seeing a relationship she is in from the perspective of the feminist movement. It could also involve seeing through one's own eyes but from a different perspective. One way to create a different time perspective is through the hypnotic process of pseudo-orientation in time (Erickson, 1954b). Leslie Cameron Bandler has developed a more consciously oriented ceremony to accomplish this; she calls it "creating a compelling future" (Cameron Bandler, 1984). A central feature of the ceremony is having people create an image of their future selves. They then adopt the perceptual position of that future self and look back at the present self. Through the switching of perceptual positions they identify what it is important for the present self to do to assure the well-being of the future self. Often in the course of this ceremony, people develop a symbol of their future self, which then becomes a guide to the perceptual position of the future. For many people, this perceptual position is a naturally built-in resource. For others, its discovery makes all the difference in their ability to do things that will pay off in the long run, such as career planning and quitting smoking.

Perhaps the two most therapeutically significant perceptual positions are objectivity and subjectivity. From the objective perceptual position, people can "look at themselves." They can dissociate from their immediate concerns and examine things in a detached, even-handed way. In the subjective position, people can become immersed in their immediate perceptions and emotions. Both positions are valuable for different activities; to be trapped in either position is limiting. In hypothesizing about situations that lead people to come to therapy, we often consider whether they can flexibly move between objective and subjective positions. In many cases, a key part of our strategy is to help people develop more flexible access to one or the other of these positions.

Al had been having impotence of the "performance anxiety" type ever since his divorce. He had played the field for two years, only recently beginning to date someone about whom he thought he could become serious. But he was worried about his inability to be a good sexual partner.

Al was trying to resolve his situation from a completely objective, dissociated position. Every time he attempted to have sex, he started watching himself as if he were outside his own body, and coaching that body as if it were someone else. The strategy he was using is an excellent one for pain control. It makes it very easy not to feel. For that very reason, it is disastrous for making love. Al didn't have much chance of becoming aroused until he could make love from a more subjective position.

Al's hobby was woodworking. He had won prizes for furniture that he had designed and built. I(GC) knew from previous discussions that he was currently building a guitar for one of his friends. I asked Al to describe his approach to woodworking. He said he did it by "feel." He elaborated, "It's a process of feeling each piece of wood as a living thing, of feeling how the grain runs, where it's stiff and where it's willing to bend. Each type of wood has its own special character, and no two pieces of the same wood are exactly alike."

He went on to say, "I've learned to extend my feelings into my tools, so that as I'm sanding and shaping I can sense the subtle variations and work with them, incorporating them into the design of the finished project."

Al obviously had access to a subjective perceptual position when he was working with wood, so it was possible to utilize his approach to woodworking as a symbol of the resource that he needed in his love life. We had to go to a very different context to find the resource. Certainly no woman would enjoy being thought of as a block of wood. Nevertheless, Al was definitely associated to his feelings in the context of woodworking, so I elected to utilize it metaphorically.

In the beginning, I didn't talk directly about sex with Al. Instead, we talked about the process of getting to know the wood he was using for a particular project. I asked him how he developed the ability to feel how the grain ran, where it was stiff, where it was flexible, etc., and had him describe in detail all the physical and emotional sensations involved. I listened intently and, by eye contact, nodding, and leaning forward, communicated that these were very important discussions. Later, I began to intersperse more direct discussions of sex as he continued to educate me about the fine points of woodworking. Al's expectations of therapy and my increasingly frequent references to his love life were all that Al needed to apply the resource in the appropriate context.

The metaphor we utilized would have been somewhat mechanical for most people. However, it had just the right meaning for Al, and through it he began to put his heart as well as his head into making love. He was wise in his timing, having given his heart time to heal before really becoming involved with a new woman.

Suggesting Ideas

People's ideas are principles through which they organize and make sense of their memories, their ongoing experience, and their future plans. A person's rationale for any action is supported by some idea or set of ideas.

"I shot him because he was a bad man" is supported by at least two ideas: that the person shot was bad, and that bad people should be shot. When our goal is to change an attitude or behavior, it is often necessary to help clients develop ideas that support the new attitude or behavior. For instance, a lonely woman can rehearse various social behaviors until she's blue in the face, but she may not use those behaviors in a social context until she accepts the idea that she is likeable.

We think of a well-chosen idea as functioning in one of two ways. One way is by filling a gap. When a certain idea is added to a person's other ideas, he or she may then have everything needed to reach a goal.

At an initial session with a woman who wanted to lose weight, we told her, among other things, to eat only when she was hungry. She came back the next week, having lost four pounds with ease.

She had never before considered the idea of linking eating and hunger. This idea made such a difference for this particular woman not only because it is a basic one in reaching and maintaining an appropriate weight, but also because she already had the other tools she needed.

The second way a well-chosen idea can function is by precipitating a reorganization of memories, ongoing experience, and future plans. This kind of reorganization occurs when a new idea both cannot coexist with and supersedes some part of a person's previous understanding. In accepting the new idea, the person is accepting a new organizing principle.

Brian had been out of work for a year and a half. When I(JF) discovered that during a number of job interviews he had lost interest in what seemed to me to be acceptable jobs, I said, "You know, Brian, you can take a job without its being the perfect one you want to keep for life." It was only when he paused thoughtfully for a long time and then said, "You CAN?" that I realized this idea might be new and important for him.

In fact, using this idea, Brian took a job within the next two weeks. When he found a better one, he switched jobs. He was able both to look back at past job opportunities in a more positive light and to have more flexible goals in present job interviews.

Many times simply stating an idea, even if it's a needed one, is not effective. Often people have already been given lots of good advice, frequently by themselves, and it has made little impact. Metaphor offers a way to present ideas at a more experiential and indirect level, making them easier for some people to accept and use.

I(JF) was asked to consult about Dan, a 13-year-old boy who was afraid of the dark. My colleague seeking consultation was usually quite successful in working with people with phobias. This time she was having difficulty. Since Dan's parents were recently divorced, she thought that his fear might be a symptom of family difficulties, but the parents were not willing to participate in family therapy.

Dan was very open in talking with me about his fear. He said that he was scared in the dark because he couldn't see what was there and he was worried that sometime something awful would be there that would do something horrible like kill him. He had a resigned air, saying that, no matter what he did, he was ultimately helpless and nothing would work out.

Apparently, the marital difficulties had gone on for quite a while. Dan had watched the most powerful people he knew be repeatedly helpless, by his perception, in their most important relationship. When they finally decided to get divorced, Dan's parents confirmed the idea that people have no control over their lives by telling him that the divorce was no one's fault. It was just something that happened. It didn't surprise Dan at all that even with expert assistance he was helpless against his fear of the dark.

This is what I told him: "Let's say that you're right. Let's say there's this guy with a big rock who will be waiting out there in the dark, and he'll hit you in the head and kill you when you're 80. Until then, you can stay at home leaving the light on at night, never sleep at a friend's, not go away to camp or college, and worry every day about what is going to happen and when it will happen and if it's possible to protect yourself. (Dan nodded throughout this discussion.) And when you are 80, after living a miserable life, one night you'll find yourself in a scary, dark place, and you'll be killed.

"Or, you can decide that's not how you want to live. You can spend the night with friends, go away to camp, go away to college, enjoy whatever you want to at any time of night or day. And when you are 80, after living a happy life, one night you'll find yourself in a dark place, and this big guy will be there and he'll hit you over the head with a rock and you'll be killed."

Dan asked, "Do you mean you can choose how you feel?"

I answered, "Yes."

Dan considered that and nodded his head. That was essentially the end of the session.

At first I thought that Dan's notion that people are helpless would have to be changed. This idea seemed like it would be extremely difficult to change, because children are helpless in many ways. Instead, I decided to utilize the idea of being helpless and define it, as Dan did, in terms of being helpless to deal with outside forces.

The new idea I offered was that you do have a choice about how you live in the face of helplessness. I also suggested that this choice can determine the quality of your life. You don't have to stay in the dark about how to live even though you can't control everything. Dan understood this idea as, "You can choose how you feel."

Dan's therapist discovered at the next session that Dan had already started participating in new activities and was no longer afraid of the dark. These changes lasted.

We don't believe things would have turned out the same if Dan had simply been told that he could choose how to feel. The symbol of "a guy with a big rock" helped Dan accept the idea in several ways. It gave him something concrete to focus his fears on. A guy with a big rock is less scary than the multitude of monsters a child can imagine in the middle of the night. Accepting his fears and giving him a symbol for them enhanced my relationship with Dan; he gave me more of both his attention and his respect. Once Dan's attention was focused by "the guy with the big rock," the symbol could be moved farther away in time, allowing Dan room to think without having to collapse into terror.

Once Dan had room to think, he was presented with two possible versions of his future life. Presenting each alternative as a story of Dan and "the guy with the big rock" made each more compelling and less frightening than his fear of the unknown. In listening and comparing, Dan was able to discover for himself that we may not be able ultimately to control our destinies, but we certainly can choose how we feel. Discovering the idea for himself let him feel more in control of his destiny.

In Dan's case I took a general fear and narrowed its range by creating and using a symbol. Broadening the range of an idea a person already has by using it as a symbol for a whole class of ideas is equally effective.

Susan was the granddaughter of a very successful and dynamic farmer, whom she greatly admired. Her father had followed in his father's footsteps. Susan felt a deep attachment to the land where she was raised, the crops, the particular way the seasons turned there, and especially to the spirit of her grandfather.

She came to therapy when she was in her senior year of college. She had a decision to make, and it seemed that, whatever she decided, she would lose something important.

Part of her wanted to go to graduate school in English. She loved reading poetry and she had received encouragement from her professors about her skills as a critical and analytical writer. She was excited about the prospects of an academic career.

Another part of her wanted to go back to the farm. Her sister had no interest in working the land, so Susan was the last remaining descendant of her grandfather who might continue his work. She loved the idea of a continuing direct contact with what remained of her grandfather, and she genuinely enjoyed the farm work. At the same time, however, she felt that family traditions were forcing her destiny.

Susan thought that if she went to graduate school it would be an act of insolence and rebellion toward her grandfather's memory. She thought that if she went back to the farm it would be in capitulation to a loving, but pervasive, family tyranny.

It seemed to me(GC) that there were several options that she wasn't seeing—options such as going to graduate school and then deciding what to do about the farm, or going back to the farm and continuing to study and write while there—but Susan wanted a more definitive and immediate solution to her dilemma. When attempts to directly suggest alternatives met with failure, I began searching for indirect approaches. One idea I wanted her to entertain was that she could integrate her grandfather's values into her life and still be an independent adult.

One day, as Susan was reminiscing about her grandfather, I was struck by the poetry of her description. I encouraged her to continue and copied down her words as she spoke. Before the next session I laid out her exact words in verse form, then added a first and a last stanza:

> A girl,
> fresh from the family farm,
> bright,
> virginal,
> "the sweet one with common sense,"
> remembers her grandfather:

> Peach trees.
> A cloud of pink,
> faint rose as the blooms start to open,
> then it's just a patch of pink.
> A patch of yellow over there
> where the turnip greens
> are blooming.
> Turn a little further and there's
> white
> from the cherries.

The old man
made these plantings.
Shaped this land.
Walking among the blossoms with
his icy blue eyes,
he belongs in the wind
of bright blue
spring days.

At first we thought he was
just tired,
worn out from traveling.
He'd been to a meeting,
teaching how he pruned his peach trees.
He was talking about what was to be done
in the fall
and next spring.
Then he just sat by the fire and stared.
Not talking.
Not planning.

For fifty-nine years he recorded the weather
every day.
Would go out in the worst of storms.
Fearless.

We would always watch
the fronts coming in.
Long lines of
dark clouds
moving across the blue.

Wintertime at five o'clock
he would always build a roaring fire.
There was always
bourbon and water for everyone.

In spring he watched his peach trees bloom.
He died in spring.
I never saw things

as clear
as I saw them that day.

Having spoken,
she bites her peach
and walks away.

At the next session I gave Susan a typed copy of the "poem" she had spoken. She was moved as she read it. Although she never said anything specifically about the added stanzas, within a month, with essentially no further psychotherapy, she made her decision. She decided to go back to live on the farm—as soon as she had finished graduate school.

I utilized both Susan's interest in poetry and her own poetic speech in this intervention. Since she already associated her grandfather with peaches, I used the peach to stand for all her associations to him. The act of eating the peach and walking away symbolized the idea that Susan could integrate everything that she loved about her grandfather and move on with her own life. The image was meaningful for Susan in a way that direct explanation of the same idea was not.

A ceremony in which people can discover ideas for themselves through actual experience can also have great impact.

Phil wanted to quit smoking. One of the interventions we suggested for him was a ceremony. We said that he could probably learn more about what kept him smoking if he turned the act of choosing and lighting each cigarette into a ritual. The act that would make it a ritual was to pause before he took the cigarette from the pack and to deeply and thoroughly consider whether he really wanted it.

In our own minds, we thought that the act of thinking about each individual cigarette would stand for a continuing contemplation of smoking in general. Thus, we were suggesting that Phil symbolically assess his commitment to not smoking each time he found himself starting to smoke.

What Phil discovered through the ceremony was different. He discovered that he had been smoking many cigarettes that he didn't especially want. Since this was his own discovery through the ritual, he was excited about it. The idea would have been much less impressive if we had stated it to him directly.

Reframing

A young woman came to see Erickson complaining of feelings of inferiority. She had a small scar at the right corner of her mouth, but in her mind it was a horrible disfiguration. She used one hand or the other to keep it covered at all times, so that she never had both hands free. Her "compulsive" need to cover the scar made it impossible for her to drive a car, swim, or do many other things unless she was absolutely alone.

She had been to see three plastic surgeons about corrective surgery, but each had joined her parents in saying that it was only a little scar that required no correction.

She wanted Erickson's help in adjusting to her affliction, but was not interested in changing either her behavior or her understandings about the scar and its significance.

In the first interview Erickson learned that she liked to sketch and was proud of her artistic abilities, so he gave her the assignment of producing and bringing in a life-size drawing of her face showing the exact size, shape, and position of the scar.

Then Erickson told her he wanted her to find out everything that she could about "beauty patches." She could consult the library, ask fashion experts, or find any available source of information on this old-time practice. She was then to make a series of life-size sketches of women's faces showing different locations and shapes of beauty patches.

When she brought the sketches in, Erickson, under the guise of hastily scanning all the drawings, slipped her self-portrait into the pile. Then he asked her to spread them out and go through them one by one and tell him about the various shapes and the reason that each one was in its particular location.

She became so absorbed in the task that when she came to her self-portrait she didn't immediately recognize it. She began describing a beauty patch in the shape of a six-pointed star that was placed so as to attract attention to the mouth as this particular person's most attractive feature.

When she finally recognized herself, she was shocked. She could hardly speak as she struggled to reconcile two sets of conflicting ideas—the old ones about her awful disfigurement and the new ones about a "beauty patch."

As she sat there, Erickson said:

"Your parents, your brother, your friends were all so 'unreasonable' as to think that your scar was just a beauty patch. The plastic surgeons thought so, too, and brushed you off as a silly girl who refused to recognize the scar for what it was. I, too, am sufficiently unreasonable as to see that scar as a little white star-shaped beauty patch at the corner of a very pretty mouth. *And you yourself—in fear, distress, abhorrence—drew your portrait accurately and well, and without knowing it you portrayed that scar for what it was, a beauty patch which, unguardedly, you recognized correctly.* (All italics in this quote are Erickson's.)

"Now, let's be scientific about this. Beauty patches are intended to draw attention to the most attractive feature. You have pretty eyes, you have a pretty dimple in your left cheek, you have a pretty mouth. You like to be kissed, and a number of boys have kissed you. Go out with them again, one by one. Let them kiss you goodnight under the porch light. Make a mental note of where they kiss you, on the left side of your mouth, full face, or on the right side. I think they will kiss the side with the beauty patch. *You will find out.*"

Erickson said that she later reported to him that she was always kissed on the right side of her mouth, but he doubted the objectivity of her report (Erickson, 1927, pp.465-469).

In this case history Erickson gives a vivid example of using metaphor to reframe. Many people had tried directly to convince the young woman that her scar was not ugly, but to no avail. Erickson developed a rather elaborate plan based on the metaphor of "beauty patches." Only after the young woman had thoroughly educated herself about beauty patches did he strategically place her in an experience where she could discover for herself the perceptual frame through which her scar could symbolize things other than disfigurement.

In reframing, the emphasis is not on offering the client new facts; it is on offering the client a new way of perceiving facts that he or she already knows. Reframing is a specific form of suggesting ideas. It is useful when people already have an idea that is hindering evolution. The task is to compellingly offer an alternative idea in the form of a new perceptual frame that will facilitate the free interaction of fresh ideas.

Erickson knew there was already a long list of people who had failed in getting the young woman to accept the fact that her scar was not disfiguring, so he opted for a different strategy. He accepted the fact of a noticeable mark on the young woman's face, then arranged things so that she could see that, instead of a scar, it was a beauty patch.

Any metaphor offers at least two perceptual frames. In one frame, a beauty patch is literally and only a patch of some material that is cut out and applied to the face for cosmetic purposes. In another frame, "beauty patch" stands for any unusual mark on a person's face, allowing a scar to become a beauty patch. This multidimensionality of metaphor makes it a particularly apt tool for reframing.

The indirectness of metaphor allows clients to try out a new perceptual frame without having to decide consciously whether to accept or reject it. The young woman had already unconsciously accepted the new frame that Erickson offered before he began the ceremonial speech that formalized and sealed that acceptance.

A reframe does not have to be as dramatic as the one in the example above to be useful. Sometimes the goal of a reframe is as simple as getting a little more energy flowing in a therapy session. The following example shows how a story can be used for this sort of reframing.

Things were getting pretty grim. We were working with a family in which both brothers, independently and with little or no conscious knowledge of what the other was doing, had carried on an incestuous relationship with their younger sister. They were a very conventional upper-middle-class family, and when the news finally surfaced the parents brought the family to therapy to minimize the psychological harm that might come from this upsetting set of events.

This was the first time the whole family had been together in therapy. Everyone was working earnestly to say what was on his or her mind, but people were beginning to get tired and tense. The sister began to look withdrawn and discouraged.

I(GC) asked her if she'd ever been to one of those science exhibits where they have eggs in an incubator. When she said that she hadn't, I began to describe what it was like.

"At first you can see the egg moving, but there's no crack in it. Then a crack appears. After a while there's a tiny hole through which you can see a beak slowly but determinedly pecking away at the shell. It takes a long time . . . and it's hard work. The chick has to stop and rest from time to time. After a while you can see its whole wet and bedraggled head as it pecks, but it's still not out of the shell. Finally the hole is big enough, and it flops out. It's wet all over, kind of bloody and very tired. It has to lie still for many minutes before it can begin struggling to its feet, but it makes it. In a few hours more it's a clean, dry, energetic, yellow chick peeping and crowding around the food like the rest of them."

The daughter sat forward and beamed, saying "that's really beautiful," and the family returned more energetically to the hard work of effecting their own transformation.

I told the story to change the family's frame of reference about the therapy situation. They had begun to approach it more and more as an ordeal, as some kind of punishment for their "sins." Since this attitude was beginning to sap their energy and enthusiasm, I wanted to offer them the frame of transformation, in which hard work brings happy results.

In both of the above examples, metaphors were created based on a therapist's ideas of useful alternative frames. A different way of using metaphor for reframing is to set up a situation in which clients can find both the metaphor and the new perceptual frame.

Laura and Peter came for therapy because their relationship was deteriorating and they both felt that if things didn't change they wouldn't stay together. They loved each other and had had periods of time in which they were very happy together. They hoped they could find a way to have a good relationship again.

It seemed that, although they had established a good foundation for their relationship, each had subsequently gotten involved in things that the other experienced as threatening. They each felt neglected and taken for granted. They were both hurt and angry. In fact, they were so hurt and so angry that our initial attempts to focus on the positive aspects of their relationship and enhance communication met with failure.

Deciding that we needed more thoroughly to pace their doubts and fears, we offered them a way for each separately to consider exactly what about the partner stood in the way of a better relationship. We suggested that each of them find or create something that represented the obstacles he or she perceived and bring it to the next session.

Peter brought a rock, which he explained represented Laura's always being one way. He said she was inflexible and always did things her way, as if there were no other.

Laura brought a picture of a closed, locked door. She said that it represented the way that Peter closed off large portions of his life from their relationship. He rarely discussed his work with her. He insisted on a strict separation of their finances. He literally closed the door to his study and disappeared behind it all evening several nights a week. Although he often looked pained and worried, he wouldn't talk about what was going on inside.

After they had thoroughly discussed the obstacles that their symbols represented, we asked Laura and Peter to engage in a ceremony. We suggested that they carry these symbols with them everywhere they went for two weeks. During that time, if they were willing, they were to wonder how the symbols might stand for *valuable* things in their relationship.

When we saw them next, Peter told how the rock represented Laura's stability and organization. He remembered how those qualities had originally attracted him to her. He found them very complementary to his spontaneity and realized that he really counted on her being there in such a solid and dependable way.

Laura had a similar experience. She realized that she had always liked Peter's independence and self-reliance. He never burdened her with more than her share of responsibilities. He was very clear about what he would and would not do. He was not jealous of the time that she spent on her work and her hobbies.

Peter, who had been vehement in his belief that Laura's qualities were insurmountable barriers, decided he really liked the rock. He continued carrying it in his pocket and feeling it there all the time. Laura's love of the locked-door qualities in Peter was not as deep and abiding, but she did have a new appreciation that they had positive aspects.

The overall effect of the two-part ceremony was that Peter and Laura had new perceptual frames for each other's behavior. They were aware of positive intentions and meanings underlying what they had once seen as purely negative traits.

The first assignment, establishing a symbol to represent a quality, allowed Peter and Laura each to isolate a specific quality in the other and in so doing narrow and delineate the scope of their difficulties. The second assignment, carrying the symbols with them and wondering how they could represent something useful, enabled them to consider positive meanings of their partner's behavior, but at a distance created by focusing on the symbol rather than on their partner. Since their partner's particular behavior had been repeatedly associated with frustration and disappointment, it would be difficult to examine it without re-experiencing some frustration and disappointment. A rock and a picture were easier to approach with fresh eyes.

After their assignment, Peter and Laura switched back and forth from talking about the symbols to talking about each other. They utilized the symbols when they were helpful and quickly applied their learnings in their relationship. Through this ceremony of symbols they reframed their difficulties in a way that allowed them to take a leap ahead in therapy and in their relationship.

Facilitating New Patterns of Thoughts, Feelings, and Behavior

It can be useful to think about patterns of thoughts, feelings, and behavior, both in understanding presenting situations and in strategizing for change. One cue that it might be useful to think about such patterns is the feeling that something is happening over and over again. Occasionally a repetitive pattern calls so much attention to itself that it would be hard not to address it. This happens most often when the client system is composed of more than one person, because the parts of a pattern are more obvious when they happen between people, rather than inside one person's head.

A family we saw had two daughters. Patsy, age 14, was outgoing and playful, while Rebecca, age 13, was serious and more self-contained. The parents, George and Ruth, argued with Rebecca, saying that she spent all her time in her room and never came out to join them. Rebecca more and more angrily said things like, "What's the use of my coming out and trying to be with you guys? You never agree with what I say. You're not interested in what I want to talk about."

It seemed that the parents, especially George, were more at ease with Patsy, who was affectionate with both parents, and that Rebecca's griping and withdrawing were ways she responded to feeling left out. George and Ruth tended to respond to Rebecca's gripes in awkward and ambivalent ways that led either to more griping or to Rebecca's withdrawing to her room.

We perceived the pattern shown in Figure 1. The pattern can also be expressed in a linear fashion by arbitrarily picking a starting point:

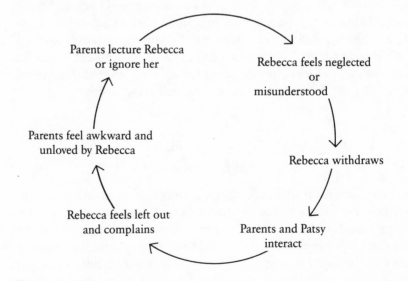

Figure 1.

1. The parents and Patsy interact, not noticing that Rebecca has withdrawn.
2. Rebecca feels neglected and complains.
3. The parents feel awkward and unloved in the face of Rebecca's complaints.
4. They handle these feelings by either lecturing Rebecca or ignoring her.
5. Rebecca feels neglected and/or misunderstood and
6. withdraws, which brings things back to "GO."

The family demonstrated part of the pattern in the waiting room. They sat down together and began talking, with both parents leaning toward Patsy and Rebecca sitting on the edge of the group. Only Ruth occasionally looked toward Rebecca. A few minutes later Rebecca was across the room looking in the fish tank as the others talked on.

Now, during the session, she was griping. As the argument got louder, I(GC) asked George if he would be willing to go over and hug Rebecca. George looked puzzled, but got up and gave Rebecca a very nice hug. I then suggested that any time Rebecca began to gripe, George could give her a hug. Not wanting to restrict its possible range of meaning, I gave no reasons for this suggestion. After the hug Rebecca stopped complaining and the family got back to work on the larger goal that had brought them to therapy.

Later in the session, Patsy and George began to talk more exclusively to each other, and Rebecca soon started complaining. As soon as he noticed this, George, of his own accord, got up and hugged Rebecca. Rebecca pushed him away and squealed "No!" When he persisted, she was clearly delighted.

We used the hug as a symbol simultaneously to disrupt an old pattern of family interaction and to suggest a more rewarding emotional tone. When George began using the symbol of his own accord, its use became a ceremony in which the family practiced a new way of relating. We hoped that this ceremony would soon lead to Rebecca's feeling so warmly included in the family that she would feel no need to complain and to George's having something positive to do instead of feeling awkward and unloved by Rebecca.

We chose the hug intuitively, but our intuitions would not always lead us to use a hug as a pattern-interruption symbol. It seemed that Rebecca felt most rejected by her father and that he, in turn, was most at a loss for how to relate to Rebecca. A hug was clear, dramatic, and easy to do. We hoped that hugging in the presence of other family members would help both George and Rebecca over their awkwardness about how a father could show warmth to a 13-year-old daughter.

When they interrupted the old pattern with a hug, which symbolized emotional, rather than intellectual, attention, the family was free to find a much more open-ended pattern. The new pattern allowed the family members to grow and evolve naturally rather than to stay stuck in the old unsatisfying circle. In this example, we simply interrupted the pattern, trusting that the family would find useful new ways to interact on its own.

Mark made an appointment for himself and his wife Janet that Janet canceled at the last minute. Several weeks later she made another that they kept. The goal for therapy they each had stated over the phone was to stop fighting and have a less rocky relationship.

In the first session, they sat leaning away from each other and toward us. Each complained of anger about the stormy arguments and sullen withdrawals that the other caused. The arguments were about opinions, such as whether a job one of them had was really a good job, not about decisions, which they said they made well together.

They both seemed to want the same thing—for us to see things their way and to declare them right and their partner wrong. They tried to describe several of their arguments, but couldn't agree at all on what either of them had said. In fact, they argued heatedly about what had really been said during past arguments. They ended up talking over each other loudly and simultaneously. The only thing they could agree on was that eventually either Janet stormed into the bedroom and bolted the door or Mark left the house, slamming the door.

After a typical argument, they avoided each other for several days and then "tried to be nice." Being nice meant smiling, talking softly, and agreeing even if they disagreed.

It seemed to us that Mark and Janet were each feeling very misunderstood. This led each of them to focus on asserting their own position to the exclusion of listening to the other, thus unwittingly making things even worse. We suggested that they bring accurate descriptions of each person's position in every disagreement they had to the next session.

If they accepted our suggestion, each time they started to fight, they were to stop and gather detailed information about each of their positions so that they could tell us exactly what each of them thought. If they had a fight on Monday, Wednesday, or Friday they would concentrate on Janet's position first. She would say a sentence and then Mark would paraphrase that sentence, telling her his understanding of what she meant. She would then explain further if necessary and he would restate what he thought she meant. Only when they agreed on one sentence should they go to the next, and they were to continue until they both agreed on what Janet's position was. Then they would do the same thing with Mark's position. When they agreed that they understood each other's positions, they were to stop.

On Tuesday, Thursday, and Saturday they would concentrate on Mark's position first. It was up to them what they did on Sunday. They would have the opportunity to settle the fights in our office at the next session.

The next appointment was set for two weeks later, but Mark canceled that appointment, so we didn't see them for a month. Looking back on it, a month was a more appropriate interval, as it gave them more time to use the ritual.

They came to their second appointment very puzzled. They had notes on their positions in different arguments, but they didn't seem very interested in them. We offered them the opportunity to have an argument in our office, but other things seemed more important to them. They couldn't get into it. There was nothing they wanted to argue about. And in fact, they engaged in the simultaneous, loud talking that characterized the first session, only in brief spurts.

We invited them to continue with the ceremony of understanding each other's positions. At the next session they still didn't want to fight in the office but they were still concerned about their fights between sessions. We offered the assignment a third time. This time they had few disagreements between sessions and did not argue during the following session.

This was not the end of the therapy, since there were several other issues that emerged. However, the ceremony provided a way that they could begin to understand each other. Once they could understand each other they could work out most anything.

Several months later they said that on the infrequent occasions when they began to have fights they stopped and used the exercise. But they also noticed they had evolved their own ways of understanding each other's opinions, and therefore were rarely fighting.

Our understanding of the pattern that Mark and Janet originally used when they came to therapy was something like Figure 2. First they disagreed about something. Then they simultaneously explained why they were right in louder and louder voices (without listening to each other). At some point (this may have been determined by the intensity of feeling, the volume of the argument, how long it had been going on, how many times they had repeated the argument, or some other factor), one or the other of them ended the argument by walking out. They then avoided each other for several days. Then they "tried" to smile, talk quietly, and agree even when they disagreed. (For two people who cared so much about being right, agreeing when they disagreed probably created enough inner conflict that they needed the next argument to discharge it.)

In the ritual, they had the chance to interrupt the pattern as

DISAGREE
↓
SIMULTANEOUSLY AND LOUDLY EXPLAIN
↓
WALK OUT
↓
AVOID EACH OTHER
↓
"TRY" TO AGREE

Figure 2.

soon as they noticed that they were having a disagreement. We believed, from the intense demonstration in the office, that during an argument both Janet and Mark lost track of their stated goal: to have a less rocky relationship and stop the fighting. We invited them to turn their attention back toward their goal by working to understand each other's positions when they began to fight.

When they accepted our invitation, they repeatedly practiced a new pattern, as shown in Figure 3. When they disagreed about something, they distanced themselves enough to identify that they were disagreeing and remind themselves that they wanted to learn to do it differently. Then they cooperated in remembering whose turn it was to talk first. One of them stated what he or she thought, then the other paraphrased it until the person whose position it was felt understood. Then they switched positions and did the same thing. The result was that they understood what each other thought.

Once they understood each other there was no longer a need to decide who was right. The ceremony provided a symbolic experience of discovering that it didn't matter who was right. With mutual understanding under their belts, they were free to evolve new patterns of communication or incorporate some of the experience of the ritual into their communication patterns.

In our examples, explanations of patterns can seem very simple

DISAGREE
↓
BACK OFF
↓
DECIDE WHO WILL TALK FIRST
↓
ONE PERSON STATE A THOUGHT
↓
OTHER PERSON PARAPHRASE IT
↓
REPEAT UNTIL FIRST PERSON
FEELS UNDERSTOOD
↓
SWITCH

Figure 3.

and straightforward. Actually, a habitual pattern of responses is a very complex set of processes. Distinguishing a pattern of behaviors, thoughts, and feelings involves selectively attending to some parts of the pattern as if others didn't exist. Using this type of artificial punctuation involves choosing a starting point and acting as if processes occur in a linear way, with one leading to another.

Even while using the concept of patterns, it is important to keep in mind that other distinctions could be drawn. One could identify aspects of habitual patterns other than thoughts, feelings, and behaviors, and could map the patterns in other than linear ways.

In using this concept, there are several dangers. One is believing that a particular description of a pattern is an objectively accurate and complete map of something that really exists. Bill O'Hanlon calls this kind of error "hardening of the categories." Another danger is perceiving a process that is always changing, at least in small ways, as a fixed thing. Many a therapist is several steps behind the client because he or she fails to notice ongoing changes.

Still another danger is believing and communicating to clients that a complex systemic process is a linear one with each step causing the next. Particularly in working with families, this kind of explanation can become the basis for assigning blame rather than facilitating change. One way of avoiding this difficulty is by dealing with a problematic pattern that the therapist has distinguished without describing it to clients. As the examples show, metaphor is ideal for this purpose.

Even though sequential descriptions of patterns of thoughts, feelings, and behaviors are artificial, they still can be very useful. In the above examples, this kind of description allowed us to make useful interventions.

In other cases, there may be no need to interrupt a pattern. Simply adding details to the existing pattern may be enough.

Ronald came to his initial therapy session with a long list of goals. This is a representative third of his initial list:

— to stop stuttering
— to stop breaking coffee pots when washing them
— to improve communication between himself and his brother
— to get a job

— to learn to hold a visual image in his mind more clearly so
that his sketching would improve
— to concentrate more on the road when he was driving.

He didn't care what he started with or how long it took to reach
any particular goal. I(JF) was uneasy about Ronald's expectations
of therapy from the outset. My misgivings increased when Ronald
brought lengthy new lists to the second and third sessions. I was
concerned that for some of the items, such as improving communication, there would always be room for improvement, so work
might continue on them indefinitely.

Since Ronald didn't care which item he worked on at any particular time, and my suggestions to group items under fewer categories of goals had been unsuccessful, I picked getting a job as the
session focus. I thought that if he was working full time he
wouldn't have time to worry about so many things and might be
more satisfied with himself.

Two things happened at the following session that seemed very
important. The first was that Ronald brought in two large loose-
leaf notebooks stuffed with completed written exercises related to
getting a job. One notebook housed the entire collection from
What Color is Your Parachute (Bolles, 1980), and the other held a
similar set of exercises from a course on getting a job that Ronald
was taking in night school. The second thing was that Ronald said
he was now spending three hours a day on tasks related to therapy.
At each session, I had suggested tasks that Ronald might do, but I
hadn't asked him to accumulate them from session to session and I
hadn't suggested that he do them every day. With the exercises
from his night school class and other activities, he was worried
that, if new assignments continued to be given, he wouldn't be able
to do everything. He thought he might divide his tasks in half and
do each every other day.

Because of the notebooks, the amount of time Ronald was
spending doing therapy assignments, and his interminable lists, I
thought that it would be helpful for Ronald to set some priorities.
A year and a half of doing exercises related to getting a job, but
never in that time calling a prospective employer for an interview,
indicated that Ronald was not using time efficiently.

I hypothesized that Ronald followed a pattern something like this (see Figure 4): First he thought that he would like to accomplish something. Then he became motivated to do it. Following that he identified things he could do to accomplish it. Then he did them and continued doing them until the goal was reached.

The pattern sounds pretty good. The difficulties are that it includes nothing about setting priorities or using time efficiently. There is no way to rule out doing something. Therefore, Ronald was just as likely to put his time and energy into not breaking coffee pots as he was into getting a job.

Ronald and I decided to build two new details into the pattern he was using. To do this, we used a symbol of Ronald's own design to represent priorities and time effectiveness. I suggested that he use it in such a way that the two new details would be inserted into the already existing pattern. We utilized another of his goals to do this.

Specifically, I suggested that, as a way of improving his skills in prioritizing and using time efficiently, Ronald might work on his goal of learning to hold a visual image more clearly in his mind. I asked him to make a collage representing the most important things in his life. The size of each element was to be proportionate to its importance, and Ronald could revise the collage from time to time in accordance with changes in his life.

When the collage was finished, each time Ronald hit upon a possible new goal, he was to look at the collage. If he was not at home, he was to visualize the collage in his mind. If the goal he thought of accomplishing was already in the collage, he was to spend an amount of time on it proportionate to the size of its representation. If it was not represented, he was to visualize the

THINK

"I'D LIKE TO ACCOMPLISH [X]"
↓
BECOME MOTIVATED
↓
DECIDE WHAT TO DO
↓
DO IT

Figure 4.

collage with the addition of a symbol representing the new goal. The size of this new addition was also to be proportionate to its importance.

Ronald was then to spend an amount of time on the new goal proportionate to its size in the collage. We talked about the relative size of some things being so small that they couldn't be seen. They were then not to be done. A bonus to this procedure was that in doing this assignment Ronald would have a great deal of practice in holding visual images in his mind. By making the image each time he thought of something he would like to accomplish, he could be sure of that. He could check the accuracy of his image by consulting the collage.

More importantly, each time Ronald did the assignment he was practicing the pattern with the two new steps (see Figure 5): First he thought that he would like to accomplish something. Then he saw a symbol representing the important things in his life and where this goal fit in relative importance. On the basis of the image he decided how much time was appropriate to spend on the goal. If it was not appropriate to spend time on the goal, he dropped it. If it was appropriate, he became motivated to do it. Then he thought about how he could reach the goal. He then did the behaviors he had thought of, spending the amount of time that he had decided was appropriate.

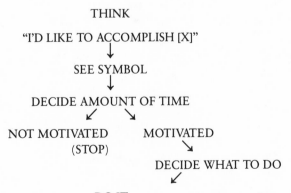

Figure 5.

Ronald had communicated his lack of setting priorities and inefficient use of time through the metaphors of lists and notebooks crammed with completed exercises. Following his lead, I responded to his situation metaphorically, having him create a symbol and engage in a ceremony. The multidimensionality of the ceremony allowed it to stand for both Ronald's directly stated goal of learning to visualize and his indirectly stated ones of setting priorities and using time efficiently.

There were several indications that Ronald was able to see clearly the relative importance of goals and to use time efficiently. He limited his therapy goals and began to ask how long therapy would take. Much sooner than was originally expected, when he was actively engaged in looking for a job and satisfied with changes he had made in both his relationships and his communication skills, he decided to end therapy.

In this example, I used a symbol to represent new steps in an already existing pattern and a ceremony for the client to experiment with the pattern. My hope for Ronald was not that he would continue to go through this elaborate ceremony for life, but that the experience would help him in evolving a natural process.

Because the client was an individual, rather than a family, it was less obvious than in some cases that the presenting situation could usefully be conceptualized as a pattern. My first ideas were about eliciting resources. It was only when Ronald's lists and notebooks seemed similar that I began to think in terms of a pattern.

There is an interplay between the use of resources and patterns. Clearly, Ronald had the resource of setting priorities. If he didn't, he would not have been able to make the collage in which he represented the most important things in his life and showed their relative importance. The problem was that he wasn't using the resource in some contexts. When it came to deciding what to do and how long to do it, he didn't use a pattern that included setting priorities. This became clear when he was overloaded with assignments and, rather than doing the most important things, he did them all.

Sometimes the resource-pattern relationship takes a different twist. The resource is available in the appropriate context, but somehow it's not enough. A person may have all the right stuff at hand but not be able to put it together in an effective pattern. For example, a man may have had very little successful experience socializing. You can help him access feelings of friendliness and confidence, but when he goes to a party he may still have no idea how to interact. The resources need the support of a pattern of thoughts, feelings, and behavior to really complete the job.

The simplest and perhaps most frequent way that we use stories to suggest possible patterns of thoughts, feelings, and behaviors is to tell a story about another person in a similar situation who learned a certain pattern that led to resolution.

Some people become more meaningfully involved in experiencing a new process when they aren't asked directly to do it. Talking about someone else takes the spotlight off them, so that they aren't self-conscious or worried about their ability to do something new. At the same time, they often are aware that the therapist is suggesting a pattern for them. (This is the same sort of strategy that Erickson used in his "my friend John" trance inductions [Erickson, 1964]).

I(GC) was working with Julie, who with increasing frequency was feeling hopelessly overwhelmed by anxious feelings, both at work and in social situations. Whenever Julie noticed an anxious feeling, she began playing movies of past "anxiety attacks" in her mind, said to herself "uh-oh, here we go again," became subjectively involved in the movies, and rapidly spiraled into a state of near-panic.

She wanted to stop experiencing these states and thought that the answer was a prescription for tranquilizers. I thought it would be healthier and more confidence-building for her to learn to handle the feelings on her own. I decided to suggest the pattern outlined in Figure 6 to her: The pattern started with noticing that she felt a little anxious, then moving to an objective perceptual position. From that position she could decide what she needed to do to feel less anxious and imagine actually doing whatever it was. Only when she was certain that she could do that thing would she switch back to a subjective perceptual position and do it.

I knew from previous experiences that directly asking Julie to practice the new pattern would elicit the very anxiety she wanted to transcend, so I elected to tell her about another person who

NOTICE ANXIETY
↓
"GO OBJECTIVE"
↓
DECIDE WHAT TO DO
↓
IMAGINE DOING IT
↓
(WHEN CERTAIN SHE CAN DO IT)
SWITCH TO SUBJECTIVE
↓
DO IT

Figure 6.

learned to "go objective" at the first hint of anxiety, evaluate what she needed, etc. I carefully described several contexts in which the other woman used the pattern, and for each context I went through the pattern piece by piece.

Julie listened to this story with great interest, focused attention, and no anxiety. As she listened she learned the new sequence and began to believe that she could apply it in her own life. At that point I began directly coaching her on how to do so.

With Julie, rather than disrupt the old pattern (as with Rebecca's family), or modify it (as with Ronald), I ignored the old pattern and focused on teaching a new one. This was because the old pattern led so rapidly into an overwhelmed state that working with it, even for modification, would have been quite difficult.

It is possible to interrupt old patterns and practice new patterns of thoughts, feelings, and behaviors without ever using metaphor. For some clients, it may even be best. For others, the use of metaphor makes the work much easier.

In multi-person systems, metaphor makes it easier to work indirectly and avoid the potential for blame that discussion of a "causal" pattern can entail. For people with patterns that lead rapidly into resourceless states, metaphor can enable them to get enough distance from the process to learn how to change it.

Metaphor lets therapists address multiple dimensions of the system, thereby increasing the chances for connection with aspirations and difficulties that are outside of clients' conscious awareness. Directly and consciously practicing a pattern over and over can feel mechanical. Metaphor makes the learning process more graceful and interesting. It leaves people free to respond in ways that feel appropriate for them, including modifying or rejecting a suggested pattern. As it does with the other therapeutic processes, using metaphor in working with patterns allows therapists to adapt the therapeutic experience to fit their clients' needs.

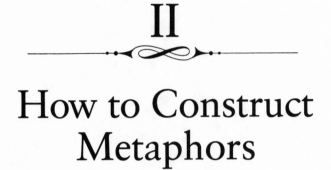

II

How to Construct
Metaphors

4

—————·•·⌒∞⌒·•·—————

LEARNING TO THINK
METAPHORICALLY

THERE IS A CONTROVERSY in the music world about the usefulness of practicing a piano piece each hand alone. Some teachers say that in doing so the student in effect learns three pieces: the left hand piece, the right hand piece, and the piece as written for both hands. These teachers maintain that learning the piece as written is quicker and results in a more fully integrated end product. Other teachers say that learning the two component pieces and then combining them is easier, and the end result is as good.

We don't know the best way to learn a piano composition. We do know that some people are able to approach a piece with both hands and play it. With more complicated pieces it is more difficult, but they begin to sound better with practice. For other people, it doesn't really matter if the best method is to use both hands. When they use both hands with a new piece, it sounds terrible, they feel overwhelmed, and they give up. For these people, practicing each hand alone is the best way, even if it isn't the "best" way, because it works.

As two old each-hand-alone practicers, we offer you this chapter, which consists of one-skill-at-a-time exercises that we believe are useful in learning to think metaphorically. If you prefer the both-hands-together method, proceed directly to Chapter 5.

My(JF) brother Steve used to play his guitar and banjo for hours every day. Once when I commented on his diligent practicing he told me that he rarely practiced. "Practicing," he said "is when you take pieces or techniques you don't know or you have trouble with and do them over and over. When you play tunes you already know, like I do, you're playing, not practicing. It's fun, but not the way to learn very much."

So, we recommend, for learning, that you pick the exercises that work with skills that you would like to improve and repeat them until you're satisfied with your level of mastery, and maybe you'll do some of the others for fun.

Discovering Metaphors

One way to proceed is to take data (ideas, states, attitudes, behaviors, beliefs, etc.) and express them in metaphor. The following exercises provide practice in different ways of doing this. In each instance the central question is, "What metaphor could stand for this particular thing?"

I. Finding Symbols for Emotional States and Attitudes

Even very simple symbols for emotional states and attitudes can be useful in therapy. You can either use them directly or incorporate them into stories or ceremonies.

With this exercise you practice translating states and attitudes into symbols.

1. List a dozen emotional states or attitudes, such as confidence, relaxation, indignation, and compassion, that might be useful in therapy.
2. Take the first item on your list and ask yourself, if that state or attitude were a picture or image, what would it be a picture or image of?
3. Wait for an image to occur to you. When an image has presented itself, make note of it on a separate piece of paper.

4. Then go back to the first item on your list. Ask yourself, if that state or attitude were a physical posture or action, what posture or action would it be? Make a note of the answer that you find.

5. Ask yourself, if the state or attitude were a sound, what sound would it be? List your answer beside your previous answers for this particular state or attitude.

6. Go through the same process with each of the other states or attitudes on your list. Each image, posture, and sound that you discover could be used as a symbol for the state or attitude.

7. Feel free to add other categories (If this attitude were a movie star, which movie star would it be?) to the three listed. These also could be used as symbols.

8. Save your list of symbols for use in exercise IV.

II. Creating Metaphors with Similes

This is an adaptation for individual use of a group exercise we first learned from David Gordon. In doing it, you practice over and over again the central skills involved in one method of translating data into metaphors.

1. Make a list of things you would like to create a metaphor for (presenting situations, resources, patterns, etc.).

2. Say to yourself, "_____ (an item on your list) is like _____," filling in the second blank with whatever image pops into your mind. Don't monitor your answer. Accept whatever image presents itself.

3. Then, elaborate on your simile by saying, "_____ is like _____ in that _____." For example, if I wanted to create a metaphor for "arguments," I might say, "*Arguments* are like *lightning and thunder* in that *they can be very frightening and make a lot of noise. You never know if they are going to cause permanent damage.*" (As you get some practice with this exercise, you will often find that the more far out the initial image, the more you learn in this step.)

4. Disregarding your first elaboration, find another one, such

as "*Arguments* are like *lightning and thunder* in that *they can illuminate things momentarily and be part of clearing the air.*"

5. Go on to the next item on your list and repeat the entire process, finding at least two different elaborations on your simile for each item on the list.

With your similes you have found symbols. Your elaborations could be developed further as the basis for stories or maybe even ceremonies.

III. Body Language as Symbol

Many of the images you found in the previous two exercises were of things that could serve as nonverbal symbols. For example, in the last exercise, if you decided that anticipation is like a yellow balloon, you could use this symbol by talking about it (verbally) or you could actually use a yellow balloon or a picture of one (nonverbally).

With the following exercise you can practice finding ways to use your body (posture, expression, movement) symbolically. In striving to communicate multidimensionally, body language is an important dimension, particularly because you communicate with your body even when you don't intend to. For example, it is important that when we are confident in a person's ability to do something we communicate confidence, instead of allowing an idiosyncratic hand movement to communicate uncertainty.

1. List ten emotional states or attitudes, such as fear, anxiety, confidence, and compassion.
2. One at a time, assume each state or attitude. (You can use memories of times you were in the states, put yourself in the shoes of someone who has the attitude, or just do your best job of *acting as if* you're in that state.)*

---

*We heard the story somewhere of an interaction that supposedly happened between Lawrence Olivier and Dustin Hoffman during the filming of *The Marathon Man*. Hoffman was depriving himself of sleep, running great distances, and otherwise torturing himself in order to convincingly portray his character, a man who was being tortured. After waiting a long while for Hoffman to prepare himself for a particularly gruesome scene, Olivier said, "Dustin, why don't you try *acting* for a change?"

3. As you assume each state, look in a mirror. Ask yourself, "What state or attitude is that person in the mirror communicating?" If it is something different from the state on your list, you need to do some fine-tuning.

4. Fine-tune anything about your body language that doesn't seem to symbolize the state or attitude that you want to express.

5. You may want to be able automatically to assume these fine-tuned body symbols. For some people this is easiest through picking a symbol for the symbol. For example, you can use your weight distribution as a symbol for the whole posture, so that as you balance your weight in a particular way you are reminded of a particular body tension, facial expression, etc. Practice this process. For other people, keeping notes is more effective. Note what your body is doing as you assume each state. Where is your body tense? Where is it loose? Which joints are flexed? Which are extended? Are there noteworthy symmetries or asymmetries? Where are you looking? What else seems important about your body posture and position? Using your notes, you can practice assuming the position.

6. Try each posture out on a friend or colleague, getting his or her feedback about what the posture symbolizes.

7. You may want to do this exercise using only facial expressions.

IV. Trying Out Symbols of States and Attitudes

You can use the list of symbol clusters that you made in exercise I in a reverse exercise to further develop your understanding of how symbols interrelate with states and attitudes:

1. After putting them aside for a week or two, look at the first cluster of symbols. First, visualize the symbolic image.

2. Do and/or imagine the posture or action.

3. Hear or make the sound.

4. What state or attitude is evoked in you?

5. Look back at your first list to see if it is the same as or

different from the state or attitude that originally generated these symbols.

If the state evoked in you is the one you originally created the symbols for, you have experienced a demonstration of the effectiveness of your symbol choice. If a different state was elicited in you, remember that, because of their multidimensionality, symbols can have different meanings. Therefore, flexibility in using symbols is important. In therapy, if a symbol is not eliciting the desired response, be willing to let it go and find another.

Recognizing Clients' Metaphors

The first step in utilizing clients' metaphors is recognizing them. Practicing doing this is easiest when there is no need to attend to other aspects of communication. We recommend using audiotapes, videotapes, and television to provide practice material. Setting yourself the task of noticing metaphors if you have the opportunity to watch sessions from behind a one-way mirror is also a possibility.

V. Recognizing Stories, Symbols, and Ceremonies When You Encounter Them

This exercise can be done with an audiotape or a videotape. Tapes of situation comedies or talk shows will work well. Therapy tapes are also fine. If you use a 20-minute tape, it will take more than an hour to do the exercise all the way through. It doesn't all need to be done at once.

1. Play a tape of any conversation.
2. The first time through, listen only for stories. Stories may be told as examples, memories, dreams, or fantasies. They frequently involve other people and are ways of talking *about* something, rather than talking directly. Listen for sequences of action that you can picture. Phrases like "That reminds me of the time . . . " or "Let me tell you about . . . " or even "A funny thing happened . . . " are common clues that a story is to follow.

3. Play the tape again, this time listening for symbols. Repetitive use of a word may indicate that it has symbolic value. Phrases like "I knew by _____," "it's like _____," "I could tell by _____," "I just kept remembering _____," may also indicate symbols.

4. In the second playing of the tape, stop every few minutes. Are there any images or sounds that are central to what the speaker is saying? These may also be symbols.

5. Play the tape a third time, listening for ceremonies. If the speaker says things such as, "We always _____," "On Sundays I _____, "The way our family does it is _____," he or she may be reporting repetitive ceremonies.

6. In the third playing of the tape, listen for any sequence of activity that the speaker reports. Any time you hear one, switch off the tape and consider whether the sequence has symbolic significance. You probably have already considered these as stories. People will often describe their ceremonies in the form of stories.

7. After some practice with the first six steps, listen to other tapes to identify stories, symbols, and ceremonies in a single playing.

The number of metaphors that different people use varies tremendously. You may want to repeat this exercise with different tapes or practice in a more casual way in other contexts. You can practice as you read novels, as you watch television, or during otherwise boring meetings.

VI. Recognizing Nonverbal Symbols

Bandler and Grinder were extremely impressed with Erickson's ability to read nonverbal cues. They and their colleagues devised many exercises to give people practice noticing the association of particular visual, auditory, or kinesthetic expressions with particular subjects or states.* This exercise is our own variation. To do it, you need a factual interview that's at least 20 minutes long.

---

*See *Frogs Into Princes* (Bandler & Grinder, 1979) for exercises of this type.

1. Tune into an interview on television.
2. Pick one person to focus on.
3. Each time that person answers a question affirmatively, note his or her facial expression, muscle tone, posture, breathing rate, coloration, etc.
4. Do the same each time the person answers a question negatively.
5. When you think you can tell the difference between the two sets of nonverbal symbols, check yourself by predicting whether an answer will be positive or negative before the person has a chance to answer verbally.
6. When your predictions are consistently accurate, pick more subtle distinctions to observe the nonverbal symbols of. For example, notice nonverbal symbols for the subject of the person's spouse or the person's work.
7. Now, turn the sound all the way down and then, when you notice the symbols for the subject you have picked, turn the sound up to check yourself.

This exercise and others like it are very helpful for training yourself to attend to nonverbal aspects of communication. Their limitation is the built-in presupposition of consistency in verbal and nonverbal communication. Because of people's multidimensionality, verbal and nonverbal communications often are not congruent. It is even more useful to recognize nonverbal communication that does not correlate with conscious expression, because the meaning is additive and represents another dimension. The accuracy of an observer's interpretation, however, is difficult to check.

VII. Watching Body Language and Expression*

For those of you who, like us, have frequent videotaping fiascos, here at last is a way to utilize all those tapes with great pictures and awful sound! Do this exercise with a videotape of a therapy session or any human interaction. A television program could also be used, but with it you won't have the luxury of pausing.

---

*Jeffrey Zeig's videotape, "Symbolic Hypnotherapy" is very interesting for its observations of symbolic body language.

1. Turn the sound all the way down on a videotape and watch a single movement of a single person. You don't need to keep watching the same person every time.
2. After each movement, pause and decide what you think the movement might symbolize.
3. After some practice, watch for symbolic body language in tapes while the sound is on and the tape is rolling.

Verbal and nonverbal input may be different and even contradictory, as different dimensions of different people communicate through different channels. The only way to "check" a hypothesis about the meaning of a particular nonverbal symbol is by utilizing it in interaction.

VIII. Making Predictions Based on Minimal Cues

1. Find an intersection that is well used by pedestrians.
2. Sit or stand near a corner where you can observe people as they approach the intersection.
3. Predict which direction they will go at the intersection. Challenge yourself to predict from greater and greater distances.
4. Afterwards, review the cues you used to make the prediction. Are certain cues more reliable than others?

A variation on this exercise can be done in a shop. Predict whether, what, and when people will buy. In either case, you are practicing noticing behaviors that symbolize attitudes or inclinations.

IX. Listening for Metaphoric Communication in Therapy Tapes

1. Play at least five exchanges from a tape of a therapy session, one phrase at a time. After each phrase stop the tape.
2. (a) For client communications ask yourself the following questions: What could this mean in relation to the stated presenting situation? What could this mean in relation to the therapy goals? Could this be a communication from a dimension of the client system that I haven't yet consid-

ered? What could this mean as a communication about my relationship with the client?

(b) For your communications, ask yourself these questions: What beliefs may I be communicating? What could the communication mean in relation to the stated presenting situation? What could this mean in relation to the therapy goals? Is there a metaphoric meaning in this phrase that is in some way relevant to the tasks of therapy? What could this mean as a communication about my relationship with the client?

3. After you have considered the above questions for at least five interchanges, keeping in mind your goal, identify a message that, in terms of the goal, would have been useful to convey metaphorically to the client system. For the same segment of conversation, imagine how you could have kept the content of the conversation the same while using metaphor to convey the goal-related message.

X. Listening for Literal Meanings

One way to realize that a word or phrase is metaphorical is to notice that its *literal* meaning is different from the meaning it has in its present context (Gilligan, 1987).

1. Play a phrase of a therapy tape.
2. Make a picture in your mind of what is *literally* being described in the phrase.
3. Make a note of the phrase if it is being used metaphorically, that is, if the picture you make is different from what is actually happening or what is being described in the session.
4. Go on to the next phrase.

Here's an example:

T: "Hello."   No big metaphor here.
C: "Hello."   Still no metaphor.
T: "What do you want to accom-   I thought we said everything was
plish today?"   metaphor. This is all pretty
                                                    straightforward.

C: "I'm not sure, but I think I
have to do something about my
feelings toward my husband. He's
really a pain in the neck."   Bingo! Write this one down and
go on listening for more.

There are many ways you could utilize the metaphors you discover through this exercise. Probably the simplest use is for pacing.
The client in the example above is more likely to feel in sync with
you if, when talking about something that is bothering you, you
call it a pain in the neck than if you call it a huge hassle.

One of many other options would be to tell a story about a
woman who had a pain in her neck and how she finally managed
to find comfort, thus suggesting a possible type of solution for the
spouse difficulties.

XI. Considering Problems as Metaphors

It is characteristic of Ericksonian approaches that problems are
utilized. The better you are at finding metaphorical significance in
problems, the better you will be able to utilize them. Here's a way
to practice:

1. At the end of a work day, list the problems of each person
   or family that you saw.
2. For each problem, think of as many possibilities of metaphoric meaning as you can and list them. Consider these
   questions: What could this mean in terms of the ways
   family members relate to each other? What could this
   mean in terms of the developmental stage of the individual
   or family? What could the problem mean in relationship to
   the context in which it occurs? What positive value or
   action could this problem stand for? How can the problem
   bearer be a symbol for the entire family?

Sources of Metaphor Outside the Client System

XII. Memories as Metaphors

The experiences that you most often remember from your own
life are a good place to turn when you want to find metaphors.

(And they're much easier to work with than the experiences that you DON'T remember.) You may remember an experience for a number of reasons. Perhaps it was intensely emotional or the source of an important learning. It may have been an experience that had many dimensions and therefore is associated with many other things that can call it to mind. In any of these cases, such a memory is excellent metaphor material.

1. Pick three clients you are currently seeing and an experience from your own life that you frequently remember.
2. One at a time, imagine telling the clients about this experience. Take as much time as you need to vividly imagine that person in front of you, hearing your words and responding to them. You may find that with each client you relate the experience somewhat differently, just as you speak differently to different friends. You may change your voice tone, word choice, emphasis, etc.
4. What meaning might the experience have to each of these three people?

It's in a relationship that the meaning of a metaphor emerges. Therefore, any time a metaphor is shared with a new person, new meanings or shades of meaning emerge.

Memories can also be an excellent inspiration for symbols and ceremonies. You can probably identify at least one symbol in the memory you shared in this exercise.

XIII. Symbols You Surround Yourself With

I(JF) saw a young man briefly in therapy. He moved, having decided to go back to college. I recommended that he continue therapy once he got to college. A month or so after he moved I received a letter mentioning that he had followed through but was not expecting much from his new therapist.

His only explanation was, "She wears silk blouses. How can I tell her anything?" Since I also often wear silk blouses, I found this intriguing.

1. Pick three clients who you think are very different from each other.

2. One at a time, identify with each of these people and encounter yourself and your office from the standpoint of that person. (a) and (b) are two different ways to do this.

   (a) Stand outside of your office and in your mind review the client's posture, expressions, concerns, ways of thinking, etc. Begin to take on these qualities and ways of doing things one at a time. For example, put yourself in a posture typical for the person. Then begin to walk in a fashion similar to the person. Say some things to yourself that the person might say, etc. Only as quickly as you experience yourself in the person's shoes is it time to enter the office and examine it from the eyes of that person. Be aware of what you notice and what it means to you. As you sit (perhaps in the waiting room), you may think about the therapist you are about to see. Consider the importance to you of any of the external qualities of the therapist (dress, hairstyle, etc.). If you haven't done so already, take yourself into the therapy room and imagine as vividly as you can actually working with the therapist, all the while recording your impressions of the office. When you are ready, walk to the office door. As you leave the office, leave the client's identity in the office, so that as you cross the threshold, you take on your own posture, your own thoughts, your own perceptions, and the new knowledge of how a particular client may respond to your office and your person.

   (b) You can do this exercise completely in your mind. Simply allow yourself to begin to identify with the client, feeling how he or she might feel, thinking about what he or she might think about, taking as much time as you need to settle into that way of being. Then, in your mind's eye, you can find yourself in the therapy office, being aware of what you notice there both about the office and the therapist. Take as much time as you need to learn . . . and then let yourself shift back into the experience of being you, finishing this step of the exercise, bringing back only some new awareness of how a particular person may view the symbols you surround yourself with.

3. Repeat with the other clients.

XIV. Ceremonies in the Culture

The customs, festivals, holidays, and routines of daily life abound with ceremonies. Whether they are held in common by your larger culture, your local community, or some culture you have only visited or read about, already-existing ceremonies can serve as the raw material for the construction of psychotherapeutic ceremonies. *

1. Identify a cultural ceremony. (Hint: any activity that regularly occurs in connection with a particular context is probably a ceremony. To be sure, check for symbolic meaning.) Singing the National Anthem at the beginning of a sporting event is an example.
2. Identify what is being symbolized in the ceremony—one thing the National Anthem at a sporting event symbolizes is our participation in a national unity and identity even as we compete in different team identities.
3. Identify a therapeutic context where the symbolism of the identified ceremony would be useful and consider how a similar ceremony could be utilized in that context. For instance, you could suggest that a family that is concerned about constant arguments write a family song. Family members could then be instructed to continue arguing as they have been, but before each argument all participants would join in singing the family song.

XV. Personal and Familial Ceremonies

On cold mornings, when everyone else was still in bed, my(JF) father always loudly sang the words to the old advertising jingle, "It's Cream of Wheat weather, I repeat, so guard your family with hot Cream of Wheat!" That was the ceremony that alerted the rest of the family to a temperature drop. It also paired the cold weather with comfort and humor. For the singer, it probably also symbolized a desire for someone to get up and join him for breakfast!

*See *Rituals in Psychotherapy* by Onno van der Hart (1983) for an extensive exploration of this idea.

Every family, as well as each individual in any family, has unique ceremonies that could inspire therapeutic ceremonies.

This exercise is a repeat of the previous one, except that it is based on personal and family ceremonies.

1. Identify a personal or familial ceremony. You may want to consider some of the following: What customs have evolved in your family for the different holidays? What do you do on special occasions that are not holidays? Do a review of times of day. What kinds of things happen as the day starts, at breakfast, etc. (Meals often involve ceremony.) What happens on different days and in different seasons? Imagine that you are someone else spending a month inside your home. Review that month in your mind to notice ceremonies that occur in the household. For each possible activity, ask yourself if it qualifies as a ceremony.
2. Do steps 2 and 3 from the previous exercise, Ceremonies in the Culture.

For example:

1. My personal ceremony is jogging along the lake shore at sunrise.
2. It symbolizes beginning each day in rhythm with the world.
3. This symbolism would be useful for someone who feels isolated and alienated from the world. Such a person could be asked to begin the day outside at sunrise. Running would not be essential. The sunrise might further symbolize a new beginning.

Multiple Meanings

The following three exercises are designed to help increase your awareness of the multiplicity of meanings that can be ascribed to almost anything. The more you perceive this sort of multidimensionality, and the more you use your ongoing experience as a training ground, the more natural the use of metaphor in psychotherapy will become for you.

XVI. Words as Symbols

Most words have more than one meaning, as a glance in any dictionary will show. Erickson said:

> Now, every word in any language has usually a lot of different meanings. Now, the word "run" has about 142 meanings. . . . The government can run. A run of luck in cards. The girl can run. A run of fish. A run in a lady's stocking. A road runs uphill and downhill, and still stands still. A hundred and forty-two meanings for one word. (Zeig, 1980, p.78)

When we use a word in one way consciously, we tend to unconsciously evoke other meanings.* That is, any particular use of a word has associations to other possible uses of that word. If we begin to listen to the words that come up in therapy and for each ask ourselves, "What else could this word stand for?", we can discover some very useful possibilities.

For instance, when we use the same sound to stand for several different things, especially if those different uses are close together in time, it tends to create an atmosphere of ambiguity. This ambiguous atmosphere can be utilized as an indirect way of saying, "We are working in metaphor here; it's important that you search for the metaphorical meanings of my communications." In this sort of atmosphere, people often find meanings that you wouldn't consciously think of suggesting to them.

At a workshop in Rockford, Illinois, we read this children's story out loud:

The Wishing Well

A mouse once found a wishing well. "Now all of my wishes can come true!" she cried. She threw a penny into the well and made a wish.

"Ouch!" said the wishing well.

The next day the mouse came back to the well. She threw a penny into the well and made a wish.

"Ouch!" said the well.

---

*For a full discussion of this topic, see *The Structure of Magic I*. (Bandler & Grinder, 1975).

The next day the mouse came back again. She threw a penny into the well. "I wish this well would not say ouch," she said.

"Ouch!" said the well. "That hurts!"

"What shall I do?" cried the mouse. "My wishes will never ever come true this way!"

The mouse ran home. She took the pillow from her bed. "This may help," said the mouse, and she ran back to the well. The mouse threw the pillow into the well. Then she threw a penny into the well and made a wish.

"Ah. That feels much better!" said the well.

"Good!" said the mouse. "Now I can start wishing."

After that day the mouse made many wishes by the well. And every one of them came true. (Lobel, 1972)

Penny Shaw was a participant at the workshop where we read this story out loud. She happened to be having some health problems at the time. She was delighted with this story and heard it as a very personal metaphor about her and her wellness.

The following exercise was inspired by Kay Thompson, who has people do similar things in her workshops on the language of hypnosis.

1. Pick a word from the following list:

light	well	rose
fire	sweet	right
see	no	run

2. Write your chosen word in the middle of a blank piece of paper, along with a notation of what specific meaning it tends to have for you. For instance, if you pick LIGHT you might write:

   LIGHT
   (not heavy)

Figure 7.

3. Find as many other possible meanings as you can for the chosen word and write them on the page so that they branch out from the original meaning (what we show in Figure 8 is not an exhaustive diagram; it's just enough to give you an idea of how to proceed):

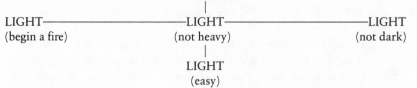

Figure 8.

4. Find any words that sound like your chosen word but are spelled differently, and include them with as many of their possible meanings as you know in the diagram. We could add LITE, as in lite beer, to our diagram in this step.

5. Find any longer words that contain your chosen word or one of the words that sounds like it, and add them to the diagram; as in Figure 9.

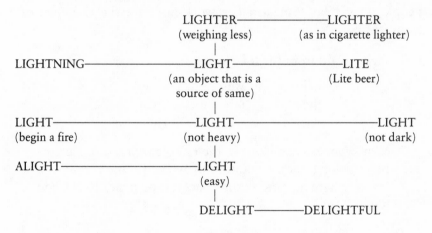

Figure 9.

6. Write out at least one way you could use one word and/or meaning from your diagram as a metaphor for another word or meaning.

For an unhappy person who talks about how everything seems heavy, you could talk about "the light at the end of the tunnel" or having a light workload on a certain day or you might describe watching a butterfly alight on a flower.

The diagrams generated by this exercise can be inspirational in a variety of ways when working with metaphor. When you tire of playing with the words on our list, you can begin to listen for other intriguing words and do this exercise with them.

XVII. Metaphoric Meaning in Mundane Experiences

A nice thing about working metaphorically is that almost any of life's occurrences can serve as the medium through which to conduct a piece of therapy. In the following exercise you practice finding multiple meanings in a commonplace experience. We learned an exercise similar to this one from Stephen Gilligan.

1. Pick an *ordinary life experience*, such as going to the grocery store or visiting at a friend's house. Imagine that you are sitting with a particular client and tell him or her the story of the experience.
2. Imagine that you want to elicit the resource of enthusiasm in the person with whom you are talking. Retell the story that you told in step 1, this time telling it so as to *focus on the theme of enthusiasm* in ways that might begin to lead the person to feel more enthusiastic.
3. Now imagine that the person is castigating him- or herself for being too reluctant in a particular situation. Retell your story from step 1. to *pace the feeling of reluctance and frame it positively.*
4. This time tell your original story to *emphasize the idea "you have more choices than you realize"* for your imaginary client.
5. Tell the story one more time, this time using it to *suggest the idea "it would probably be enjoyable for you to spend more time connecting with other people."*

Here is an abbreviated step-by-step example of how this exercise might go:

Step 1. (Basic story) "Yesterday afternoon I went to the grocery store. I like to go in the early afternoon, because it's less crowded then, but yesterday it was about 5:30 before I got there, and the store was very crowded. I bumped into my old friend Hannah and had a nice talk with her, but I didn't enjoy standing in the long checkout line."

Step 2. (Enthusiasm) "Yesterday afternoon I felt lazy, so I put off going to the grocery store 'til the last minute. The thing that finally got me to go was when I remembered the brownies I made last month. It was a new recipe, and they were the best I've ever had. I began to taste them in my mind, and the more I tasted them, the more I just *had* to have them. I got so involved in wanting to make them that I almost forgot the shopping list as I left the house. When I got to the store I went straight for the baking chocolate. I picked up the other things on my list as I went from the eggs to the butter to the flour to the sugar to the nuts. I really wanted to make those brownies! On my way to the checkout counter, it was a really unexpected pleasure to suddenly encounter my old friend Hannah, whom I hadn't seen for months. We only had a short visit in all that crowd, but we made a date for lunch tomorrow, and all through the long checkout line I was anticipating what a good time we'll have (and occasionally giving my brownies a mental taste). I really want to catch up on what's been happening in her life; I can hardly wait! I think I'll try to save her a few of my brownies."

Step 3. (Pace and reframe reluctance) "You know how it is when you really don't want to do something? Well, that's the way it was with me and grocery shopping. Yesterday I put it off and put it off. Even as I dragged myself to the car, I felt like hanging back. When I got to the store, sure enough, it was crowded and hectic. I couldn't see a thing as I fought my way down the aisles. But then I had a nice surprise! I ran into my old friend Hannah, who I hadn't seen for months. If I'd gone earlier, I would have missed her."

Step 4. (You have a lot more choice than you realize.) "Yesterday I knew I had to go to the grocery store. I usually go at 12:30 or so, but I didn't really feel like it then, so I said to myself 'I don't have to go now, I could go at 1:00 or 1:30.' It wasn't until 1:30 arrived that I realized that I really could put it off until 2:30 or even 3:00, and at 3:00 it dawned on me that I could go at 3:15, 3:45, 4:00, 4:15, or 4:30 just as well. At 4:30 I had the further realization that I could put the whole thing off 'til the next day, but I actually ended up choosing to go at 5:30, and I had an enjoyable shopping trip."

Step 5. (You would probably find it enjoyable to spend more time connecting with others.) "Yesterday I was having so much fun at home that I had a hard time getting myself to go grocery shopping. I've been working a lot, and my cat was obviously glad that I was home. He misses me when I have to be gone, so I stayed home most of the afternoon. I brushed him thoroughly and got out a new catnip-filled mouse from the drawer where I'd been saving it. We both sat in the window and basked in the sunshine together. About 5:30, I finally did go to the store. It was very crowded by then, but in all that crowd I bumped into my old friend Hannah. That made me realize how much I've been concentrating on my work and excluding other pleasures. Hannah said she'd really missed me. We made a date for lunch and I'm looking forward to it."

Feel free to substitute other purposes for the four we have suggested. The idea with this exercise is that any story can be used for many purposes—to suggest an idea, elicit a resource, reframe, etc. The more purposes you practice, the better.

XVIII. Using One Object to Symbolize Different Things

With the following exercise you take a potential metaphor and shape its meaning for a number of purposes.

1. Pick an object that arouses no strong feelings or ideas in you.
2. Find a way of describing that object so that it becomes a symbol for a therapeutically useful idea.
3. Find a way of describing the same object so that it becomes a symbol for a particular emotion or physiological state.
4. Decide what would be the opposite emotion or state to the one used in step 3, and describe the object so that it becomes a symbol for this new emotion or state.

Here's an example of how one full repetition of this exercise might go:

Step 1. (Pick an object.) How about one of those clothespins that is made of two pieces of wood held together by a metal spring?

Step 2. (Describe it as a symbol for an idea.) Let's use the idea "sitting still can be useful": "Even in this modern age of miraculously moving machines like tumble dryers, nothing works as well as the old silvery, weathered, wooden clothespin that grasps our line through sun and rain and change of season. It's dependably there to hold wet wash, and won't wander off even if it's forgotten for weeks at a time."

Step 3. (Describe the object as a symbol for an emotion or physiological state.) Let's do *calmness*: "You might picture in your mind an old weathered wooden clothespin hanging in the sun, gently swaying in the breeze. That clothespin has nothing on its mind, it's not going anywhere. No matter what goes on around it, it just hangs there swaying in the warmth of the sun."

Step 4. (Describe the object so that it becomes a symbol for an emotion or state opposite to the one chosen in step 3.) Let's do *disturbed*: "There's this one clothespin on our line that has some missing hunks and jagged splintery edges. The metal piece doesn't hold it together very well, and it scrapes and jars when you try to get it in place."

As you can see, you will need to alter how you describe the object in order to have it symbolize different things. It may at first challenge your ingenuity to find descriptions that let it symbolize opposite emotions or states. You can comfort yourself with the knowledge that this is exactly the sort of challenge that will help you to grow in your facility at using metaphor.

Metaphors for Particular Clients or Particular Presenting Situations

Most of the exercises so far have dealt with metaphor in a rather general way. The following five exercises will develop your ability to design specific metaphors for selected goals with particular people.

XIX. Matching Pictures

One way to find a metaphor that's useful in a particular clinical situation is by searching your stored experience for pictures that in some way match your way of picturing the current situation.

1. Identify a particular client system and a specific situation typical for that system.

2. Create a mental portrait of the client system that through physical posture, facial expression, interpersonal distance, etc., symbolizes the system in the chosen situation. For instance, a shy and confused young adult might be pictured sitting where she sits in therapy with legs crossed, hands clutched in her lap, and shoulders and head curled inward. Her face might look worried and a little sad.

3. Ask yourself, "What other pictures does this picture remind me of?" and begin to search through the images that this question generates.

4. When you have found a picture that fits (such a picture for the client described in step 2 might be one of a mouse cringing in a corner), ask yourself, "Is there some way I can utilize this image?" The mouse image might remind you of the belief that elephants are afraid of mice, of Tom and Jerry cartoons, or of a particular situation in which you've encountered a live mouse. Each of these trains of thought could lead to a different intervention.

5. Use the answer to the above question to design a symbol, story or ceremony and decide how you would go about offering it to the client. A very simple way to offer the symbol of the mouse as something that big, powerful things (elephants) respect would be to ask straight out, "Do you think it's really true that elephants are afraid of mice?" Be ready to utilize the response.

XX. Body Posture as the Inspiration for Metaphors

Specific postures of clients can serve as the inspiration for therapeutic metaphors.

1. Pick a client with whom you feel less than maximally resourceful.

2. Ask that person to describe what seems to be stopping him or her from achieving his or her goals and carefully note the predominant posture that he or she assumes in answering your question.

3. Ask that same person what he or she imagines it would be like to have achieved his or her goals. Again note the pre-

dominant posture the person assumes in answering your question.

4. After the session, take on the posture that the person used in describing his or her difficulty. You might want to write out a description of the posture immediately after the session that can be used as a guide for taking on the posture later.

5. When you are in the posture that represents the person's difficulty, ask yourself, "In what situation or context might I assume this posture?" Although clients usually remain seated in therapy, you can find a context in which you are standing or moving with the same sort of posture.

6. Assume the solution posture. Ask yourself, "In the context discovered in step 5, what would have to happen for me to move from the original posture to this posture?" For example, you may discover that the original posture is one that you assume when caught in the rain. You would then ask yourself, "If I were caught in the rain, what would have to happen for me to move to the solution posture?" The answer may be that you would have to notice something more important so that you forgot about the rain, or you would decide to dance in the rain, or you might find shelter.

7. Use your answer as material for a story or ceremony that might help your client move closer to his or her goal. You might tell a story about being caught in the rain and finding shelter or devise a ceremony involving a commitment from the person to go out and dance in the rain whenever it rains in the next month.

8. Imagine, in as detailed a way as you can, actually using the metaphor with the person. If your metaphor is a ceremony, you may need also to imagine a frame for suggesting it. Predict how the person would respond to the metaphor.

XXI. Using Feelings to Find Metaphors

1. Pick a particular client in a particular situation.
2. Let yourself experience how you would feel if you were that person in that situation.
3. Allow the feeling to remind you of a time and context when you felt that way.

4. Translate that life experience into a story, symbol, or ceremony.
5. Imagine using the metaphor with the person.
6. Identify how this might be a useful metaphor for the person.

XXII. Borrowing Ceremonies from Friends and Family

1. Identify a client you are currently seeing and a situation
that client wants to resolve in therapy.
2. Identify how people you know or have heard about have
resolved a similar situation or taken a step toward its solution.
3. As specifically as you can, write out the steps involved.
You might want to backtrack. What steps laid the groundwork for the solution? (Some solutions defy specific written formulation, usually because of lack of information.
For this exercise find some that can be specified.)
4. Make whatever adjustments are necessary to make the
steps you listed above into a ceremony that could be assigned to the client.

For example:
Step 1. (Identify client and situation.) Larry has come to therapy
shortly after the woman he lived with for eight years ended their
relationship. He feels very alone and isolated.
Step 2. (Identify how other people have resolved the situation.)
In general, people resolve this kind of situation by grieving and
getting involved with some new people and new things. There is a
choice here—to identify how other people have grieved or how
other people have gotten involved or both. Let's choose getting
involved.

Our friend Yvonne moved to a new city where she had only a
few acquaintances. She quickly evolved the routine of having a
dinner party every Tuesday night. During the week, whenever she
met anyone, as long as they seemed nurturing, she invited them to
her next Tuesday night dinner party. Tuesday she never felt like
having a party, but there was no choice, people were coming. She
honed the menu to the sharpest edge of simplicity: quiche, green

grapes, brie, and blender chocolate mousse. On New Year's Eve she was invited to two different parties, but chose to stay home and work on a quilt. Two friends joined her. Soon thereafter she gave the quilt to Charlie, to whom she is now married.

When our friend Frank moved back to St. Louis, he had been away for several years and there were very few of his old friends still around. He set up an arrangement with a friend he met at work. It turned out so well that they're still doing it. Every Sunday night they meet for dinner at a particular restaurant. If either of them is with other people as the appointed time approaches, they bring them along. They alternate who treats.

Step 3. (Identify the steps involved.) Yvonne: (a) Decide to have a party every Tuesday night. (b) Notice when meeting people whether or not they are "nurturing." (c) Invite those who pass the nurturing test to the next party. (d) Prepare for the party. Frank: (a) Identify one good friend. (b) Arrange details with the friend for a weekly dinner meeting at restaurant—where, who pays, how to bring guests, etc. (c) Show up at the appointed time. Have dinner and the possibility of meeting new people to look forward to.

Step 4. (Devise a ceremony that could be assigned to the client.) Either of the above could be used as a ceremony in its present form. For Yvonne's ceremony, your client may have criteria other than "nurturing." For Larry, Frank's solution would probably work better, because he would have to do less on his own initiative. He also does have one or two friends who might be interested in making this kind of arrangement.

After some practice with this exercise you may want to widen its scope to include solutions that you can't describe in steps but that may serve as the inspiration for a ceremony.

XXIII. Metaphors from Your Past Learnings

1. At the end of a day's work, think back over the clients whom you saw that day and identify the family or individual by whom you feel most challenged.
2. Identify a learning that would help your chosen client system move toward its goal.

3. Ask yourself how you learned what you identified in the previous step, and let this question lead you back to an experience in which you had such a learning.
4. What most clearly and completely symbolizes the experience for you? Identify this symbol and remember it.
5. Would the symbol be meaningful apart from the experience? With the proper frame, would it elicit the learning? If not, would it be possible through addition or change to develop a symbol whose use could be meaningful in eliciting the learning?
6. Write out the story of the experience and edit it so that you think it might hold the attention of your chosen client as you told it.
7. Ask yourself, if the client had your experience or a similar one, would the system learn or take a step in learning the lesson you have identified as useful?
8. If the answer is yes, what ceremony could you suggest that might facilitate a similar experience?

Using Metaphor in Different Contexts

XXIV. Trusting and Extending the Use of Your Natural Talents

You may be a master in metaphor in some context other than therapy. If you have a friend or associate who would agree to switch on a tape recorder at times when you are talking, particularly in casual social contexts, you may discover some hidden metaphoric abilities.

1. Have a friend or colleague tape you in several social interactions, each at least 15 minutes long. Ideally, these should be recorded candidly.
2. Play them back listening for metaphors that you spontaneously used.
3. If you find that you do use symbols, stories, or ceremonies, identify what state or states you are in when you naturalistically use metaphor.

4. Create a symbol that can evoke for you the resources you use as a metaphor maker. For example, a metaphor you hear yourself using on the tape may serve as a symbol for your abilities. You may want to relive the moment of using the metaphor in your mind and use the feelings or posture you find yourself in as a symbol. Alternatively, you may want to go back to the first exercise in this chapter and create a cluster of metaphors that evoke the needed resources in you.

5. Once you have a symbol, imagine yourself doing therapy and use the symbol. For example, if you picked a particular posture, you could begin by imagining a particular family sitting in front of you. As you shift into the symbolic posture, allow the imaginary therapy session to begin, so that you begin to interact with the family members. As the session progresses, you can practice shifting in and out of the posture.

6. Assess how well the symbol worked for you.

7. You may want to repeat the practice, imagining other clients or incorporating other symbols.

With a number of practices, therapy may become a context where you automatically use your metaphoric abilities.

XXV. Using Symbols to Shape Your Own Learning

1. At the beginning of each week, identify the skill, attitude, or belief that you would most like to incorporate into your way of working.

   For example, you might pick the belief that each client has the resources needed to live a full and meaningful life.

2. Find a symbol for that skill, attitude, or belief.

   For the belief stated in step 1, you might pick the dwarfs' gem mine from *Snow White and the Seven Dwarfs*.

3. Place the symbol (or a symbol of the symbol) in a prominent place, so that you'll see it as you work.

   Staying with our *Snow White* example, you could find a picture of the dwarfs working in their mine or you could construct a tableau with miniature figures of the dwarfs grouped around a picture of a mine entrance or a cluster of quartz crystals. Whatever representation you chose, you could place it so that it was within your general field of view when you were doing psychotherapy. Then, after each session or at the end of each day, you could assess how effective the symbol had been in helping you incorporate the belief.

XXVI. Making Storytelling a Part of Your Daily Life

This exercise and the one that follows it invite you to use stories and symbols for enrichment of your own daily life. They are self-explanatory, so we have not included examples.

1. Before work each day tell yourself a story. Feel free to tell whatever comes to mind, whether it be an elaboration of a passing thought, what happened the night before, or a story about telling stories.
2. Take a few minutes to congratulate yourself for the things that were good about that particular story.

XXVII. Ceremonies for Yourself

1. At the end of a day, identify what you did that you are most pleased about.
2. Ask yourself how you could celebrate what you did.
3. Perform the celebration as a ceremony.
4. At the end of another day identify what you did that you would most like to change.
5. Ask yourself what ceremony could help you learn from or create future change in this area.
6. Perform the ceremony.

Summary

As my piano teacher used to say: "Practice, practice, practice, practice, and you'll be surprised how easy it will get to be!"

5

STRATEGIES FOR DEVELOPING AND UTILIZING SYMBOLS

LANE HIMSELF LIT A cigarette as the train pulled in. Then, like so many people, who, perhaps, ought to be issued only a very probational pass to meet trains, he tried to empty his face of all expression that might quite simply, perhaps even beautifully, reveal how he felt about the arriving person.

Franny was among the first of the girls to get off the train, from a car at the far, northern end of the platform. Lane spotted her immediately, and despite whatever it was he was trying to do with his face, his arm that shot up into the air was the whole truth. Franny saw it, and him, and waved extravagantly back. (Salinger, 1955, p.7)

Anything can be a symbol. One time I(JF) was going to collect mail with my friend Frank. He said that going to check the mail was always exciting for him because he was waiting for Uncle Freenorb to die and leave him a modest fortune. That reminded me of the year I dreamed of winning the lottery, without ever buying a ticket. When I mentioned Uncle Freenorb some years later, Frank had no memory of him at all, but for me he had become a symbol of an unlikely windfall.

My mental associations to Uncle Freenorb include lottery tickets and the humor of human dreams. So when I catch myself waiting for Uncle Freenorb to die, I'm indulgent of my humanness and I also know that if I really want something to happen, I had better get on it myself.

A thing can become a symbol simply by being used to stand for another thing. If it is not as memorable as Uncle Freenorb, repetition will assure its function as a symbol.

For example, if a client is vacillating between two alternatives, every time the therapist mentions one of them, she could make a gesture with her right hand. Each time she mentions the other, she could make a gesture with her left hand. After several repetitions, when she says "this one," making a gesture with her right hand, the client will generally know which one she is talking about. The client will then often begin to utilize the symbols himself, pointing toward where the therapist made each gesture to indicate the alternative he is discussing.

Some symbols, such as the hand gestures mentioned above, are place markers or cues. No new experience or meaning has to accompany the use of such symbols, but they can be very useful in helping clients access and stabilize particular experiences.

The primary strategy for using a symbol as a cue is to pair a chosen symbol with the thing that it is to cue. Depending on the particular person, if this pairing is done often enough, with enough intensity, over a long enough duration, or in an environment sufficiently free of distractions, the person will come to associate the two things with each other. Such a symbolic association allows one thing to be used as a cue for the other.

Instead of choosing a symbol like a hand gesture, a therapist can notice the function of something already there and elevate it to the level of symbol by focusing attention on it. For instance, asking a client who claims to be unable to make decisions, "Who picked which clothes you would put on this morning?" highlights choosing the day's outfit as a symbol of the ability to make decisions.

Often it's not necessary to elevate something to the level of symbol. People already have lots of personal symbols. Noticing and utilizing such symbols is also effective.

Heather stated that her gracefulness is only apparent when she plays the flute. Asking her what "the flute-playing Heather" would do in a tense social situation would be one way to utilize her own symbol.

Symbols like the hand gestures that we use as cues don't necessarily have rich or varied meaning. Other symbols, like Heather's playing the flute, include associations and meaning beyond what is strictly being symbolized. For example, asking what "the flute-playing Heather" would do in a particularly tense social situation is very different from asking Heather what she would be doing in that same situation if she were being graceful.

The symbol of the flute-playing Heather includes music, so that there is a rhythm and a background to harmonize with in being graceful. Feelings of lightness and joy are part of the flute-playing Heather. She also has a history of being part of a group and a belief that practice brings results. These extra meanings are probably not coded in the word "graceful," but they *are* coded in the symbol of "the flute-playing Heather," and they could be very helpful in a tense social situation.

In training other therapists, we sometimes give them practice exercises in which they have the opportunity to work towards personal changes. In describing what they would like to be different, participants often recount the same memory in several different exercises. Particular memories come to serve as symbols, while others are rarely thought of. These symbolic memories stand out and are often associated with intense feelings.

An important way we use symbols in psychotherapy is to facilitate a re-sorting of experience in which people can discover neglected memories that will support growth in new directions. Therapists can help these memories become symbols by using them repetitively and by helping clients associate them with intense feelings or important ideas.

Martha viewed life pessimistically and stopped herself from doing things in her own behalf because she believed that they ultimately would make no difference, since things never did work out for her. She recounted several past experiences to support her ideas. At the end of a session, I(JF) suggested that before our next session she write accounts of two experiences in which she initially thought that things were hopeless but they got better in the end.

Even though Martha thought that she had no such memories, I assured her that she did, and she agreed to search for them. She came to the next session with two written accounts. We worked during that session to describe, relive, and validate those two memories so that they could become symbols that things eventually get better for Martha, even when they seem hopeless.

Instead of developing or noticing symbols themselves, therapists can ask clients to find or create them. This can be as simple as asking a person to give a name to a complex series of interactions so that everyone involved can refer to it with a single word. It can also be a lengthy ceremony, such as asking a woman to examine all of the gifts that her husband has ever given her and to decide which one most lets her know that her husband experiences her in a way that she wants to be experienced by him, but might not have realized he did, had it not been for that gift.

Different symbols require different strategies for their development. For this reason, we are offering detailed strategies for developing several types of symbols, which we have grouped according to the therapeutic processes for which they are used.

Symbols for Accessing and Utilizing Resources

When symbols are properly developed and chosen, they can be used to access or stabilize resources. This is important because having resources present in a stable fashion makes utilizing them easier and more predictable.

The first step in finding a symbol for accessing and utilizing a resource is to identify the resource that would be useful. Often, if you inquire closely enough, you will find that the resource is already being used some of the time.

Asking, "What is different when you are not experiencing this problem?" and then following up with more questions until the answer is specific often yields information about resources already available in the system. Or the appropriate resource can be identified by asking, "What do you need in order to achieve the goal (or to take a step towards it)?" The answer is the resource. *

At other times, a therapist may identify a resource that she thinks would help a client reach a goal and ask the client if he

---

*If a client answers in the negative, the resource can be identified by making it positive (i.e., Therapist: What do you need to achieve the goal? Client: If I stopped feeling X. Therapist: If you stopped feeling X what would you be feeling? Client: The resource). If the answer a client gives is another person being there, this answer can also be transformed into a resource by asking the client, "If the person were there, how would you or your experience be different?" The answer is the resource. If the client doesn't know what resource would be helpful, the therapist can ask, "Who in your experience has or could achieve the goal?" When a person is identified the therapist can ask, "What about him makes it possible for him to reach the goal? The answer is the resource.

agrees: "If you were to wake up tomorrow with complete confidence in your professional abilities, would you then be able to achieve your goal?" (The resource here is *confidence* within a particular context.)

When a symbol is used to access and utilize a particular resource, it must actually *elicit* the resource in the client, not just remind the client of its existence.

In the movie, "The Wizard of Oz," the wizard declared that back in Kansas where he came from, men with no more brains than the scarecrow were regarded as great thinkers, but they did have one thing that the scarecrow didn't have — a diploma.

When the wizard presented the scarecrow with a diploma, the scarecrow began spouting mathematical formulas. The diploma was a symbol for a brain. When the wizard utilized the symbol, the scarecrow experienced himself as having a brain and showed it behaviorally. If the scarecrow had only thought, "Lots of people without brains have diplomas," or had continued to proclaim his inability to make decisions while clutching the diploma tightly in his hand, it would not have been an effective symbol. The test is always in how well the potential symbol works for the client system.

For a symbol to function appropriately in accessing a resource, either it must already be experientially linked to the resource or the therapist must establish an experiential link between it and the resource. Either of these factors can assure a successful symbol.

The following are six strategies we use in developing symbols for accessing and utilizing resources. In each, either a pre-existing experiential link is found and utilized or a new experiential link is established between a chosen symbol and a needed resource.

— Utilize people's experiences and memories to find symbols of resources.
— Access the resource and pair it with a cue that then becomes a symbol for it.
— Presuppose that the person has the resource and help him or her develop a symbol for it.
— Through a re-sorting process, co-create new meanings for memories. The memories can then become symbols of a resource.

—Engage people in experiences that call for the resource. Once the resource is accessed, use some aspect of the experience as a symbol for the resource.
—Co-create an experience of the resource in imagination. Then use some aspect of the experience as a symbol for the resource.

In the first three strategies, we presuppose that people have experienced the resource at some other time but do not experience it now in the problem context. The last three strategies listed presuppose that, whether people have experienced the resource or not, they have the capability to do so.

Utilize People's Experiences and Memories

A person's experiences and memories are excellent sources of and symbols for that person's resources. Simply listening to what clients spontaneously talk about and the different emotional qualities that go with different subjects will go a long way in letting the therapist know what symbols for resources are already there, although they may not be labeled as such.

In recent years we have begun to encourage people in the initial sessions to talk in detail about the ideas they are excited about, the activities they are involved in, and the contexts in which they are confident. Besides making therapy sessions much more enjoyable and positive, encouraging talk about areas other than problems yields clues to the resources clients can use in the situation about which they are consulting a therapist.

For example, one couple was stuck, undecided about whether to get married. Hal thought of himself as a very indecisive guy who could never make up his mind. Leslie was becoming uncomfortable and unsure of the relationship as Hal's agonizing went on.

One thing we knew about Hal was that he had a sailboat and was very involved in sailing and racing. We began asking him about the decisions involved in sailing, particularly when he raced. He described the excitement and glory of making quick decisions, doing what felt right, and knowing that there were risks, acting anyway. His boat was pitched over in one race, dumping the crew in a very cold lake, but they all survived and went on to sail more together.

We asked, "How would *Captain Hal* progress with this relationship?"

Hal chuckled, blushed, winked at Leslie, and said, "How about a weekend away, kid?"

By calling Hal "Captain Hal" we could consistently help him be in touch with aspects of himself that were more adventurous, less involved in continual worrying about possible negative consequences, and more decisive. These aspects served him well in balancing his understandable caution about taking the big plunge.

In searching for an experience or memory that could symbolize a needed resource, consider everything that person has talked about. Think about whether the resource has been evident in your presence. You can ask about concrete symbols like rings and often-worn colors that may have important meaning and associations. Consider contexts that you know are part of a person's life and whether they might call for the resource in question.

Clients, of course, can and should be consulted in the search for symbolic memories. A family can be asked, for example, "When have you as a family pulled together in working towards a common goal?" They may identify either a time in the past or a context that occurs currently but apart from the problem context.

If a person can't immediately find a time when the resource was experienced, she can be assisted by saying something like, "I know that you have not usually experienced yourself as a self-confident person, but I bet there was a moment you can look back on where you can say, 'The person in that memory at that moment is self-confident,' even if that feeling lasted only a moment."

If a person is very used to perceiving herself as someone without the resource, it may be helpful to name some possibilities: "Maybe when you were with a particular relative as a child, or at the first birthday party you can remember, perhaps in a particular class in school, or maybe a team you were on?" The possibilities the therapist suggests may not be right on the mark, but they will lead clients to explore some general areas and associations from which they can discover events in which they did experience the resource.

Similar questions can be asked about current contexts: "Often-times couples who report they have trouble communicating make themselves very well understood during a fight. Is that true for you?" or "Everyone relaxes somewhere. Is it with a pet? a long bath? a particular friend? a good book? . . . "

Many times, in the process of identifying resources, people actually experience them. In order to pick a memory that exemplifies peacefulness, a person may reexperience the memory vividly enough to feel the feelings of peacefulness in it. Couples recalling how they met and their early courtship often take on the glow of the beginning stages of love and look at their partners with new eyes.

When clients identify memories without showing that they are experiencing resources, therapists can encourage experiential in-volvement. This can be direct encouragement, such as, "You might allow yourself to reexperience that memory, stepping inside and seeing what you saw then, hearing what you heard then, and let-ting yourself feel what you felt then, and whenever you're ready you can bring the relevant part back with you." The facilitation could also be more indirect. For example, you might engage a client to talk more about the memory and ask particularly about his feelings in it.

Memories and past experiences, then, can provide symbols for use both in accessing resources and in offering validation that people already have the resources that they need. The whole mem-ory or experience itself can be used as a symbol, but frequently some particular piece of the memory, such as the way a person looked to himself, comes to serve as the symbol. The distinction between these two possibilities can blur. The important thing is to have some symbolic way of referring to the memory or experience so that a client feels the resource.

Once this is accomplished, the next task is to use the symbol in the context in which the resource is needed. This can be accom-plished in many different ways. The simplest is asking something like, "How would the you in that past memory be handling this situation?" Alternatively, the therapist can suggest that a client vividly and intensely review the memory and apply the learnings in the present situation. Sometimes it is useful to develop and utilize a concrete physical symbol for past experiences of a resource.

For example, Karen had the experience of being lost late at night, driving alone, in a storm, about an hour's drive away from home. She eventually knocked on a door, sobbing, and the people who lived there called one of her relatives who came and got her. When she came to see me(JF) five years later, she had never again been that far away from home or driven anywhere unfamiliar alone. She thought of herself as a phobic person.

I learned in the course of the first interview that Karen is a nurse. In asking her about her job, I began searching for a set of resources to counter her self-description. I discovered that as a nurse she is comforting, firm, and competent. She told me a number of stories about helping people who were scared, immobilized, and facing disaster. It seemed clear to me that these work experiences held a valuable resource for Karen.

I asked Karen to bring her nursing uniform to the next session. We then used the uniform as a symbol of all her experiences as a nurse in preparing for a drive an hour away. As Karen began to talk about her fears, I suggested that she look at the uniform, imagine the nurse in it, and hear her advice. Immediately her breathing slowed and became more regular and her body relaxed. Throughout the session, whenever she became worried about the planned drive, we repeated this procedure. Near the end of the session I asked Karen if she would rather be accompanied on her drive by an internal image of the nurse or by the uniform. She chose both symbols, and surprised herself by completing the drive with ease.

Access the Resource and Pair It With a Cue

The basic strategy in using a symbol as a cue is to pair something with the thing that it is to cue. Depending on the particular person, if this pairing is done often enough, with enough intensity, over a long enough duration, or in an environment sufficiently free of distractions, the person will come to associate the two things with each other. Such a symbolic association allows one thing to be used as a cue for the other. Bandler and Grinder (1979) call this process *anchoring* and call the cue an anchor.

Alfred had a tendency to get so excitedly involved in heady matters that he forgot about his body altogether. He came to therapy wanting to do something about his lonely, isolated way of living. I(GC) hypothesized that Alfred's mile-a-minute intellectual soliloquies made other people want to avoid him, so I taught him intentionally to slow his breath rate, talk from his diaphragm rather than his throat, and maintain a closer association with his body.

As Alfred began to develop competence at purposefully entering the new state, I began to pair the emergence of the state with what I hoped would become a symbol for the state. I would hold my breath, and just as Alfred really began to slow down and settle in to his body, I would let out a long sigh. (This, by the way, was a very congruent response for me; I really *felt* like giving a sigh of relief at those moments.) I timed the sigh to coincide with Alfred's exhalation.

Soon the sigh was established as a cue for the state. Any time Alfred began to get really wound up during a session, I would take a deep breath, hold it, and sigh just as Alfred began an exhalation. Once the symbol was established, Alfred never failed to respond to it by moving into a more centered and less intellectualized state. Over time, he learned to maintain the state entirely on his own.

Another choice is for a person to be in charge of using the cue herself when it is needed.

A number of years ago I(JF) was working with Mary, who wanted to be more calm when she had to intervene in unexpected situations. She had recently begun a new job teaching music in a school where people seemed to thrive on conflict. It was very different than the highly structured teaching situation she had just left.

I asked Mary to choose a context in which she was calm. She did, and then she identified a particular experience in which she was very calm. This experience did not involve an unexpected situation or any need for Mary to intervene. I said something like, "In your mind's eye review that situation, seeing it and hearing it as clearly as you can. Then pull the image around you or step into it so that, instead of watching yourself in that memory, you are reexperiencing it, seeing what you saw then, hearing what you heard then, and feeling what you felt then . . . and that feeling can build. . . . When you really feel it strongly, squeeze your hands together. Then take as long as you like to enjoy that feeling of calmness before coming back here." I somewhat arbitrarily chose the hand-squeeze as a cue that could become a symbol for the resource of calmness that Mary could use herself whenever she needed it.

A few moments later we reinforced the cue. I suggested that Mary squeeze her hands together as she had before, and allow the feelings of calmness to sweep over her. Next, she replayed some emergency situations in her mind, squeezing her hands together as she reexperienced those times with a feeling of calmness. We repeated this procedure with a made-up experience that could happen in the future. Knowing that calmness was just a hand squeeze away, Mary left the session feeling better equipped to handle her new job.

That evening, Mary's teen-age daughter, Joan, received a call telling her that a classmate had broken a leg and Joan was needed to fill her classmate's part in a play. The first performance was only three days away. Joan was understandably frantic and a little overwhelmed.

Mary said, "Squeeze your hands together." Joan looked at her like she was crazy. Mary repeated, "Squeeze your hands together and feel the calm." Joan did. Then Mary said, "Okay, now keep your hands together, feel calm, and plan what you'll need to do to get ready." Joan began this process. Whenever Joan began to wail, "Mom . . . !" Mary replied, "Squeeze your hands together."

Joan ended up handling the situation like a trooper!

After Mary had accessed a state of calmness, I picked squeezing her hands together as a symbol and paired it with her reexperienced memories of calmness. Through repetition of the pairing, the hand squeeze became a cue for the calmness. I could have picked a particular body posture, pinching an ear lobe, making a humming sound, or any other such thing; properly paired and repeated, each could have worked as well.

Mary repeated a similar process with Joan by repeatedly interrupting her emotional state and instructing her to be calm while she squeezed her hands together.

Presuppose a Resource and Find a Symbol for It

After being divorced, Nina felt that somehow she had lost herself as well as her husband. She had difficulty making decisions and felt uncertain about even small, unimportant things. There was something in the way she turned to anyone around her for an opinion, rather than trusting her own, that gave me(JF) the idea that the wisdom and knowledge that she was only seeing in others was inside her, but lost.

I suggested that she have a friend take a number of candid photographs of her. She plastered these photographs all around her apartment, and although at first she felt pulled to continue consulting others, whenever she felt confused or in need of someone's opinion, she consulted the woman in the photographs. She found many answers there. The idea that she could trust her own wisdom and knowledge began to make sense to her, and the pictures were symbols that helped it make sense.

My conviction that Nina would find what she needed in images of herself, combined with her willingness to consult those images, gave the photographs symbolic significance. The conviction of the therapist that a client does indeed have the needed resource is central to the effectiveness of this strategy.

There are a variety of ways to help a person develop a symbol for a needed resource. One possibility is to give examples of such symbols for a particular resource and then ask the person what his symbols are.

In a masterful presentation at the First International Congress on Ericksonian Approaches to Hypnosis and Psychotherapy, David Gordon told a series of entertaining stories about his favorite scars, hitching up his pants leg to show one, and describing in detail how he acquired each of them.

I(GC) lost track of what he was saying for a while as I went off into a reverie about the scar on the palm of my right hand. I could remember the particular game of tag I was playing with Ernie Powell, Hi Pauley, and David Fletcher. I could smell the wet, dank aroma of the playground dirt on that early spring day in third grade. I was especially fascinated by the way the sunlight gave a gemlike quality to the green shard from a Coke bottle that I was falling toward in super slow motion. Then there was the surprise that it didn't hurt at all as my palm contacted it, and the wonder of seeing all those red and white and pink muscles and tendons and things inside the cut as I walked to the school nurse's office. . . .

When I next became conscious of David, he was asking the audience what their favorite scar was, and I certainly knew mine. Almost every one of the thousand people in the room also raised their hands to report that they had a favorite scar. His next question was a shocker. He asked, "How many of you knew you had a favorite scar before you came to this talk?" Hardly anyone raised a hand.

In telling about his own experiences with "favorite scars," David had helped each of us see our scars as symbols of something positive—in my case I found a symbol that could bring the fascination of childhood perception into my adult life.

Similarly, clients are much more likely to respond with their symbols for security or assertiveness or joy if therapists first talk about their own or those of other people.

Another way to help people develop symbols for resources is to encourage an internal search for fitting symbols. Hypnosis, guided imagery, and simply suggesting that a person go inside and allow an image or sound to develop are all possible approaches. Helping people develop representations of who and how they will be after they have solved their problems can be very useful. They can then use such representations as symbols to access motivation in making choices that will lead to their becoming the person in the representation.

Therapists can also suggest ceremonies to help clients discover a symbol. For example, a therapist could ask a client to take a walk of not more than a half hour and on that walk to be looking for and wondering how a symbol of peacefulness would present itself. Again, the therapist's congruent expectation of success is important in making this method work.

Once a symbol is identified, one must continue to use it or its meaning may fade.

In a session we supervised, when a woman searched inside to find a symbol of dissociation and objectivity, she found the image of a bird soaring through the sky. At difficult points in the session, when the woman began to identify herself too closely with the problem, the therapist asked her to see that bird soaring through the sky in her mind's eye—to just be with that bird for a moment, and then to consider the dilemma again. Each time, the woman came back to her search for a solution with the resources of objectivity and renewed energy. Each time the woman used the symbol, she reinforced its meaning.

Co-create New Meaning for Memories

Following Bateson, we think of people as thinking in stories and remembering their personal histories as stories. There is an interaction between people's ideas about themselves and the stories they remember. The stories and the ideas coevolve, with each selecting for a shape that supports the other. In other words, people tend to use memories as evidence to confirm what they already believe. Conversely, their beliefs influence what they remember.

Certain kinds of questions and tasks can be helpful in re-sorting memories so that different stories emerge and different meanings are found in familiar memories. These memories, then, can become stories that support the resource, or some aspect of a memory can become a symbol for the resource. In situations where actual experiences are scarce, these same techniques can be used to create *hypothetical* experiences, which can then symbolize needed resources.

Questions provide a wonderful format for inviting people to examine their experience in new ways.* All questions contain presuppositions. The question "What experience exemplifies your determination to excel in your field?" presupposes that the listener is determined to excel in her field, that she has experiences that exemplify this, that she has a field, etc. In order to answer the question, the person also adopts the presuppositions. Simply basing questions on the belief that people already have the resources they need may be enough to help them find examples of those resources.

However, when a person's self-description does not spontaneously include a resource, it may work better to build the presupposition of the resource in smaller steps. For example, in

---

*Our work with using questions in this way is grounded in the important contributions and developments of Michael White (1988a, 1988b; White & Epston, 1990), the Milan associates (Selvini Palazzoli, Boscolo, Cecchin, & Prata, 1980; Penn, 1982; Tomm, 1985), and Karl Tomm (1987a, 1987b, 1988).

presupposing an experience of confidence, the following line of questioning might be more successful than any single question.

"At what time in your life would you have been most confident that you could have accomplished this?" (This presupposes that the person has experienced the resource and establishes a general range of time during which the resource was available.)

"What experience was most important in supporting that belief in yourself?" (This encourages the selection of a particular experience from the general range of time. This particular experience can then serve as a symbol of the resource.)

"What does that experience tell you about yourself?" (This invites conscious awareness of the resource's availability.)

"How is that knowledge important in beginning this accomplishment?" (This invites the person to use the newly-reclaimed confidence in the present.)

Sometimes it is useful to begin more indirectly in introducing awareness of old experiences of a needed resource.

"Who in the family is most hopeful that you will succeed?" (This invites awareness that people are hopeful.)

"Who next?" (This suggests that more than one person has hope.)

"What do you think they see in you that you might not recognize in yourself that makes them hopeful about your success?" (This invites the person to step into the other people's shoes and view himself from their perspectives.)

"What experience have you had with them that lets you know that they see you this way?" (Now that the ground has been carefully prepared, this invites the person to identify an experience of the needed resource.)

"What experience of you may they be thinking of that makes them hopeful?" (This invites awareness of the symbolic experience from another perspective, thus increasing its vividness.)

In answering either of the above sets of questions, a person identifies an experience of a resourceful state. Once this experience is elicited, it can symbolize the resource, although it may not have done so before. Through the answering of the questions, a person begins to tell himself a different story.

In order to pick a memory that is relevant to the resource presupposed in a question, a person must search for memories charged with the resource. This search is easier to do experientially than cognitively. It therefore invites experience of the resource rather than thoughts about it. Certain kinds of questions heighten this process.

Comparative questions can facilitate a person's experiencing the resource a number of times. For example, the questions, "Which of your children made you laugh most? . . . Who next? . . . Then who?" will tend to elicit a separate round of laughter and mirthful stories for each of the person's children.

Hypothetical questions, such as the following, can also be used. "If you were to experience yourself now in the way you did at that time in the past, would there be any unforseen changes in your life?" (This question would be quite difficult to answer without stepping into an experience of the resource in a present context.)

Another way, already hinted at above, to facilitate the re-sorting process so that memories can take on new symbolic meanings, is to set up experience of them from someone else's perspective. Family or group sessions are ideal for this purpose. One member's description of an event is often a surprise to another member, but becomes part of the memory of the event. I(JF) had a surprising experience of the usefulness of this method recently.

Rhonda, a woman I was seeing individually, brought April, her supervisor from work, to a session because she was having difficulties getting along with people at work and was not trusting her own perceptions. She therefore thought that April might be helpful in the session. I was asking a variety of questions about what Rhonda wanted. When I asked her, "Who will be the first to notice when you have made the changes you are seeking?" April answered, "I've already noticed some of those things." She began to describe examples of times Rhonda had used resources that, before hearing this answer, Rhonda didn't realize she had. April, also, was pleasantly surprised to hear her own testimony of the extent to which Rhonda had already changed. Their new awareness of times Rhonda had exhibited resources let those times become symbols of the resources.

Another method we use to co-create new meaning for memories as symbols of resources is ceremony. Ceremonies used for this purpose generally involve exploration to find a memory that contains evidence of the resource. For example, spouses who believe that they have done nothing but fight throughout their relationship may find it useful to look through their photograph album together and reminisce. A person who believes that she has always been depressed may profit from sitting in each room in her house, one at a time, only leaving a room when she has a memory of being excited and energetic in that room, even if it was only briefly and long ago.

Once memories are re-sorted as examples of resources, they can be utilized as symbols of those resources and used to link resources to the contexts in which they are needed. Questions such as, "Now that you recognize this about your family, what do you expect to be different?" and "How could a person with a past like yours handle this present situation?" begin to link the resource with the context in which it is needed. Frequently, the work in the session carries over into other contexts in unpredictable ways. Asking questions to help families and individuals share the changes in subsequent sessions helps validate the changes.

Engage People in Experiences of a Resource

In some of these strategies, we have suggested using people's past experiences as sources of particular resources. In this strategy, we suggest using present experiences for the same purpose. Once the needed resource has been identified, a therapist's task here is to notice when a client is already using the resource or to think of a process in which she can engage the client to elicit the resource.

Families who come to see us complaining of communication problems sometimes communicate elegantly about that very problem. Individuals worried about their lack of confidence have talked in our office with confidence and poise. The things that people do and say in the office are a source of symbols for important resources. To find and use these symbols, therapists must attend to all therapeutic interaction with the added question, "How is the client already showing a needed resource?" * When something is

---

*See Eve Lipchik's (1988) article on interviewing with a constructive ear for a thorough description of one way of attending for answers to this question.

found, it can be pointed out and utilized as a symbol of a resource.

Therapists can also invite clients into situations where they are likely to use a resource. This can be done in the office.

For example, I(JF) asked a husband and wife, who had been in great conflict and had lost the habit of listening to each other, to share with each other, one at a time, an important secret. They accepted my invitation with fear and solemnity. They attended to each other with an intensity that had only been present during violent interactions before.

The secrets became symbols of their ability to really listen to each other. This ability carried over into the rest of the session. During subsequent sessions, it could easily be re-accessed when needed by asking if they would like to share secrets again. They told me about a time at home when they decided on their own to tell secrets to change the mood between them. "Exchanging secrets" became a lasting symbol of their newfound ability to listen to each other. It was central in their creating the relationship they wanted to have.

We also use ceremonies outside of the session to create new experiences that can become symbols of a resource.

Manny and Liza thought that it was time for them to have children, but they weren't sure that they would be good parents. Liza had especially strong reservations because she had been abused and neglected as a child. She wanted to be certain that she wouldn't treat children the way she had been treated. She had kept herself apart from children as an adult because she feared she might unwittingly harm them in some way.

We suggested that they seek out opportunities to babysit together. When they reported on each babysitting experience, we treated it as a ceremony that contained symbolic information about their abilities as parents. Their cumulative success as babysitters became a symbol of their parenting skills, and it wasn't long before they decided that they were "good enough" to have children of their own.

For more discussion and examples of using ceremonies to develop a resource (that can then be used as a symbol for that resource) see Chapter 7.

Co-create an Experience of the Resource in Imagination

Experience in imagination can be just as meaningful to people as actual experience. It is one more area where symbols of resources can be developed. Experience in imagination can be elicited by developing hypothetical or future representations and by asking hypothetical and future-oriented questions.

Most people who think of themselves as not having a particular resource will respond by using that very resource when they are asked to act "as if" they have it. We have seen this work repeatedly, and it continues to delight us. One formula we have used to facilitate this "as if" process is an odd day, even day ritual,* in which families or individuals are asked to continue their current behavior on odd days, to behave as if they have the resource on even days, and to act spontaneously on Sundays.

We find this kind of ceremony more effective than simply asking people to behave as if they have the resource all the time. When trying on the resource is offered in this frame, people tend to regard it as an experiment in which they can learn and compare two different ways of being. When they return for the next session, they have more refined ideas about either what stops them from using the resource or what its limits are. In many cases people just go ahead and utilize the resource and are only surprised at their ability to do so when we ask about it at the next session. In that session, the therapist can validate their achievement, begin to use some aspect of the experience as a symbol that they have the resource, and use the symbol to build the use of the resource into the future.

To form a hypothetical question to bring forth a resource, therapists can ask themselves, "What circumstance would call for this resource?"

Parents feeling disconnected as a couple could be asked, "If one of your children had been born with a serious illness, do you think you would have pulled together to face the crisis? . . . And how do you think you would have functioned as a team?" To answer, the couple must experience the situation in imagination. That experience can be utilized symbolically the same way that memories can be utilized as symbols of resources. For example, after the parents

---

*See Chapter 7 for a more complete discussion of this type of ritual.

describe how they would have functioned as a team, this imagined resourceful behavior can be linked to the present as a symbol by the question, "Once you had that intense, prolonged experience of pulling together as a team, how do you think it would affect other aspects of your relationship? . . . What would be different in the areas where you are currently dissatisfied?"

Once the experience is elicited in imagination and described, it becomes a shared symbol of resourceful behavior that is possible in the system. It can be used as the groundwork for more descriptions of resourceful behavior in other contexts.

Future-oriented questions function in much the same way. The question, "After this situation is resolved what will your family be doing differently?" elicits representations of the future that can be symbolic of resources. The question can be followed up by asking, "When are you already doing (whatever behavior they have identified)?" or "From the position of having solved the problem and looking back, what might you realize about yourselves and your possibilities that would most help you in the present situation?" Both of these questions utilize the answer to the first question as symbolic of resourceful behavior and serve to extend that resource into the present.

Questions are one way of eliciting hypothetical experience. Acting "as if" is another. There are countless ways to develop representations in imagination; symbols of resources are limited only by the bounds of imagination.

Robert Dilts (1988) has developed a system of working with people in which he asks them to imagine a "time line" on the ground that represents their whole life: past to the left, present in front of them, and future to the right. When they step onto the line they are to associate with the time represented by that segment of the line. When they step off the line they are to dissociate so that they can talk about things that happened.

As a person steps into the future (toward his goal), sometimes he experiences himself as being held back by a feeling. When this happens, he can walk back into his past until he discovers the time that he "first" had that feeling. He then stands in the shoes of each of the people in that experience, including himself, and discovers what resource each of those people needed in order for him to have had a more positive experience.

Once a needed resource is identified, clients use the time line to

go into a time in their lives in which they experienced that particular resource. The spot on the time line associated with an experience becomes a symbol for the resource experienced there. The
symbol makes it easy to access the resource and bring it to the
person who needed it. Once this procedure is complete with all the
major characters in an experience, people find it easy to change
beliefs that they formed during that experience. This usually
makes it possible for them to walk unimpeded into their future.

I(JF) was working in this way with Sarah, who had been repeatedly sexually abused as a child. We had already done a great deal
of work, and this session was only a small segment of her therapy.

At one point in the session, Sarah was standing in her mother's
shoes and had identified "clarity" and "courage" as resources that
would have enabled her mother to protect Sarah. I asked Sarah to
find an experience on her time line in which she had experienced
clarity and courage. To my great surprise, Sarah walked into her
future!

I repeated the instructions and she said, "Yeah. When we've
finished this work I'll have clarity and courage." As she stood there
in her "future," she was obviously feeling clear and courageous. So,
as I recovered from my surprise, I asked her to bring that future
experience of clarity and courage into her mother's experience in
the past so that she could discover what her mother would do
when she had it. Sarah accepted my invitation, and the procedure
worked just as it would have if she had accessed the resource from
an actual memory. The symbol of a spot on her future time line
allowed Sarah to experience a resource that she thought was not
available to her in the present.

Symbols to Suggest Ideas

After repeated sexual abuse by her grandfather, Robin, an 11-
year-old, was taken out of her home by court order. She had told
her mother what was going on and her mother had ignored the
situation for years.

Robin was placed in a series of foster homes. In each placement
she acted up and got kicked out. The social service staff hypothe-

sized that she misbehaved out of a sense of loyalty to her "real" home and family, whom she desperately wanted to rejoin.

She was eventually placed in residential treatment. Her mother and grandfather accepted her calls to them every couple of weeks, but they never visited. They didn't initiate phone calls. In spite of the distance they kept, Robin often talked about how wonderful her "real" family and home were. She was completely opposed to considering another foster placement.

One day when Robin was on a field trip, her bus passed the house where she had lived with her mother and grandfather. It was obviously empty, the windows were boarded, and there was a "for sale" sign propped in the front yard.

She was severely distressed and would hardly talk for weeks. When she finally did talk about her experience, she said that the minute she saw the boarded-up house and the "for sale" sign, she knew that her family really didn't care and there really wasn't anywhere for her to go back to. For the first time, she agreed to a foster placement, and for the first time the foster placement was successful.

The boarded-up house and the "for sale" sign were not planned, but they worked as undeniable symbols to suggest to Robin the ideas that her family didn't care and that, if she wanted a family who would care, she needed to look elsewhere. The symbols were more effective in communicating these ideas than all the years of abuse and all the years of well-meaning advice put together.

Once they have an idea in mind, therapists can use the following strategies to find appropriate symbols for the idea:

- Through a re-sorting process, co-create new meanings for memories. The memories can then become symbols of the idea.
- Engage people in experiences that suggest the idea or provide evidence of its validity. The experiences then become symbols of the idea.
- Co-create experiences in imagination that can serve as symbols for the idea.
- Utilize something from the current context as a symbol of the idea.

For any particular case, some of the strategies may be more fruitful than others. Obviously, there is a great deal of overlap between these strategies and those for finding symbols to access resources. This makes sense, since ideas and resources co-evolve within a system. Because we have described analogous strategies in the previous section, here we give less description and focus more on example.

Co-create New Meanings for Memories

In the section on co-creating new meaning for memories so that memories can become symbols of resources, we described the co-evolution of people's ideas about themselves and the stories of experiences they remember. This process does not apply just to self-image; rather, there is an interaction between people's ideas in general and the stories of experiences they remember. People form their ideas through generalizing from the experiences they have, and the ideas that they have influence the experiences that they remember. The memories of these experiences then become symbols of the ideas they have adopted.

This natural process can be adopted for therapeutic use by guiding clients in calling up memories to serve as symbols of ideas. The memories have always been there, but they can stand for something new. They can take on a different meaning by the way they are selected and emphasized in therapy.

In using this strategy a therapist must first consider what kinds of experience might be evidence of a particular idea and in what contexts the particular client might have had those kinds of experience. Then she can help the individual or family access the relevant memories so that they become symbols of a chosen idea.

For example, to co-create a symbol to suggest the idea "learning can be fun" to a child who has always hated school, the therapist can ask the child to name things that he enjoys doing or is good at. Then she can ask him to describe his memories of learning each of these skills.

Generally, when people like to do something, they enjoyed learning it. Such experiences may never have been thought of as learning before. They may have been thought of as "experimenting" or "copying" or "fooling around." Once they have been labeled as such, though, they become symbols of enjoyable learning.

The therapist can continue to refer to the symbols so that the idea becomes linked with the context where it is needed: "For someone who knows every ball player on every team, learning the capitals of each state should be a snap."

This same idea can be used in a more indirect fashion. The therapist can describe pleasurable learning experiences in general ways so that the child fills in his own memories.

For example, the therapist might say: "I don't know which board game you most enjoyed learning. Some people read right through the rules before beginning. Others plunge in and only consult the rules when they don't know what to do. Some people rely on descriptions from friends who already know how to play. Others prefer to watch a game or two and let the game sink in that way before actually playing. It doesn't seem to matter how they learn. People find their own ways. And when you play that game you probably don't even realize there was a time you knew nothing about it, and now you know enough to teach it to someone else."

She could then continue describing other contexts in which she knows that the child has learned something enjoyable. The memories that emerge during these descriptions give different meaning to the concept *learning* and can become symbols for the idea that learning can be fun.

Another way to access memories that can support new ideas is through family meetings or discussions. These can take place in therapy sessions, or an individual client can be coached on approaching family members. Other people with common experiences may have readier access to memories that could support the new idea. They may also provide different perceptions for memories that currently symbolize an idea that conflicts with the one the therapist wants to suggest.

Miranda was a competent, efficient businesswoman. She came to therapy at the age of 40 because, although she had had many relationships with men, she experienced them as convenient or businesslike, certainly not intimate. She was disturbed because the men seemed to become much more involved than she did and when she ended relationships they seemed to feel real grief. She felt that she was not congruent or real and wondered if she could have more life outside of work.

As I(JF) assisted Miranda in becoming more associated to her feelings in social situations, she became terrified and quickly dissociated. It became clear that when she let herself know it, she was convinced that she wasn't attractive or lovable. The experiences of friendships and romantic relationships did not count for her because she had never allowed herself to be "real." What did count were a series of memories of her father being in bad moods and punishing her "out of nowhere." She was sure that neither of her two brothers had the same effect on their father.

Miranda's father had died eight years before. She had never discussed him or her perceptions of how she was treated with either her brothers or her mother. I encouraged her to do so to find out if they had different or similar perceptions and to discover what meaning they had made of those experiences.

Since Miranda's family was scattered across the country, she arranged the conversations in a series of visits. Her family did agree that she had been severely punished without reason. They unanimously explained this as a result of her father's alcoholism, a label which had never occurred to Miranda. One brother told her that her being the scapegoat made room for his childhood, and he always loved and appreciated her for taking the punishment for them all. He felt guilty for not doing anything about it, but had seen Miranda as superhuman. The other brother preferred not to talk about it beyond calling their father an alcoholic and their childhood crazy.

Miranda's mother took some coaxing, but eventually poured out her grief at not being able to protect her precious, beautiful daughter from her husband, who grew increasingly irrational with time.

Through this series of difficult and time-consuming talks, Miranda's memories changed meaning. She began to feel great sorrow for the little girl who was her, as well as appreciation. Seeing herself as a child through the eyes of her brother and mother allowed her to see herself as lovable, rather than as the cause for her father's fury. With that accomplished, Miranda had access to other memories that symbolized her lovableness. Some memories of being appreciated and loved as a child spontaneously came to her. She found more through talking about the good times with her mother and brother during phone conversations.

With these new symbols in place, she slowly allowed herself to enjoy social situations and to really let other people get to know her.

Engage People in Experiences that Suggest the Idea

To arrive at relevant experiences that can become symbols for an idea, we ask ourselves, "What experience could the person have that would give him the idea?" or "What experience would show the person that this idea is valid?"

Sometimes people offer this information spontaneously. Listening for experiences that people believe would make a difference or have made a difference in the past is a good place to begin.

For example, one family came to therapy because the mother found a note that her 11-year-old daughter wrote to herself, talking about suicide. In talking to the daughter, I(JF) believed that this was not a serious consideration, but a romantic musing and a way to express sadness. The parents thought the same thing but did not trust their judgment about such a serious issue. "If a professional would tell us that we handled it right and we know our own daughter, well, we could think that we're good parents again. It's hard to think that when you find a note like this," said the father.

When I said, "I think you handled this just right. No one knows your daughter as well as you," the parents relaxed and showed a renewed sense of competence. I thought it was important to suggest the idea that they could be good parents even though their daughter wrote a frightening note. They essentially instructed me on how to suggest that idea to them. My "professional opinion" was a viable symbol for the idea.

Of course, clients don't always volunteer their symbols for the ideas that we want to communicate. However, we can always ask. A simple example is a couple in which each partner feels unloved even though both consistently and congruently declare their love. If a therapist wants to find a symbol to suggest the idea that each member is indeed loved, she can ask each what the other would be doing if in fact the other loved them.

The answers would describe behavior that was symbolic of being loved for each partner.

In other instances people don't know what would symbolize a particular idea or a therapist judges that an idea could be communicated more powerfully if a person encountered the symbol by surprise—as Robin did—rather than having a part in its development. In these situations the therapist can ask, "What experience could the person have that would give him the idea?" inside her own head and find the answer there.

Once she finds a symbol, the therapist needs to develop a strategy to present it to the client. One way to do this is to suggest that the client do an assignment in which he "discovers" the symbol. The surprise involved can increase the symbol's impact.

Sandy came to therapy to lose weight. Since her husband had died a number of years before, she had only been involved with one man. That relationship began when she was 50 pounds lighter. She gained weight during the course of the relationship. In her perception, as she gained more weight she was treated more poorly, until finally the relationship ended in humiliation for her.

Sandy continued to gain weight and stayed socially isolated for two years before coming to therapy. At the time she began therapy she wanted to lose weight so she could have a relationship with a man. However, she also resented men for not wanting her just the way she was. Therefore, she would lose a little bit of weight, a man would be friendly to her, she would be angry that he wasn't friendly before, and she would defiantly gain the weight back.

Another way of looking at what happened was that when Sandy began to feel successful in losing weight, she had a more positive attitude and became more outgoing. As soon as someone responded by smiling or talking back, she thought, "All men care about is weight!" ignoring any possibility that the response was brought on by her more outgoing behavior.

In order to break this cycle, I(JF) gave Sandy the assignment of going to B.L.U.E.S., a great Chicago blues bar, on a particular night. I knew that the performer that night was Big Time Sarah, a very sexy and very fat blues singer. Sarah always has everyone leaning forward, hanging on her every word, with half of the men in the room flirting with her and buying her drinks or bringing her flowers.

Big Time Sarah became an undeniable symbol to Sandy for the idea that it is possible to be fat and sexy at the same time, that men are turned on not only by slender, leggy, bathing-suit-ad types.

This was not the end of the therapy, but it did change things. Sandy now had two goals: to get involved in a relationship and to lose weight for herself. She began to do things to meet men and could approach the weight issue without being weighed down by her old belief that she was undesirable.

Use Experiences in Imagination to Suggest Ideas

Experiences of hypothetical events can be used in the same way as memories or current experiences. Once a therapist has identified the sort of experiences that might serve as a symbol for the idea, if he thinks that they would be difficult to arrange or access in a client's actual personal history, he can work with the client to create experiences in imagination.

The question to ask here is, "What internal experience would suggest and symbolize the idea?"

We supervised a therapist working with a man who believed he was unable to speak in groups of more than three people. In describing his inability to speak when a teacher asked the class members to introduce themselves, Terry said, "If only I could see people smiling at me, instead of looking at vacant faces, maybe I could believe that they were interested in what I had to say."

In listening for Terry's metaphors, the therapist could have noticed that Terry told her his symbol for the idea that people are interested in what he has to say. If the therapist decided to utilize this symbol, the next question would be, "How?"

In the context of group therapy, the actual experience could have been provided. Since Terry was being seen individually, providing the experience in imagination would be easier. For example, the therapist could ask Terry to identify people who are interested in what he has to say and who smile or have smiled at him. She could then use the images of these people smiling as a symbol for the idea.

The therapist could suggest that Terry imagine he is speaking and seeing these people smiling at him. With repetition, this symbol could begin to appear automatically in Terry's mind any time he faced a group. Eventually, Terry would probably not be aware of the symbol but would have incorporated the idea and its associated resources.

In using this kind of strategy it is important to watch for cues that convey clients' internal experience. When the strategy is working, they will be showing signs of increasingly positive feelings. If clear cues of positive experience are not evident, it is important to ask what's going on inside and to make any necessary adjustments.

Another strategy is to consider what context or set of circumstances would be likely to evoke experiences in particular clients that could suggest and symbolize the idea. Rather than suggesting that a person have a particular internal experience, the therapist can ask hypothetical questions about the context or set of circumstances. In answering the questions, the person experiences the context in imagination.

For example, Yvette seemed to collapse and withdraw when she had experiences that were more than mildly unpleasant. After a poor work evaluation she stopped going to work and lost her job. After a burglary she stopped seeing friends for such a long time that she had few friends left when she felt like socializing again.

I(JF) wanted to suggest the idea that Yvette could experience adversity and continue to function at the same time. I knew that Yvette had a seven-year-old daughter, Sandra, of whom she was fiercely protective, so I described a number of hypothetical circumstances in which Sandra was in trouble, and asked Yvette to describe what she would do.

For example, I asked Yvette, "If you and Sandra were driving out in the country at night and had a minor car accident, leaving Sandra in pain, perhaps with a broken bone, and no one was in sight, what would you do?" Yvette described the actions she would take in this and other hypothetical examples. In these imagined experiences, she created symbolic pictures of herself as a person who could act in the face of adversity and unpleasantness.

The job may have been done at this point. To be sure that the idea generalized to include Yvette's taking care of herself, I suggested that, in many ways, we are our own children, and at the same time our own companions, protectors, and teachers. When I asked her, she readily agreed that, in fact, we teach our children to care for themselves through the examples we set.

Since Yvette was such a good parent, she saw how this should extend to how she behaved as a parent to herself. At this point, I repeated all the things Yvette knew she would do for Sandra as things she would do for herself.

She became very involved in what I was saying, probably making a second set of symbolic pictures in her mind: pictures in which she acted in her own behalf in the face of adversity and unpleasantness.

The imagined experiences became symbols of the idea that Yvette could experience adversity and continue to function. They allowed Yvette to change her image of herself. She began to act in accord with the new symbols; each time she did, she generated a new experience — no longer imagined — of herself as a strong woman.

Use Something from the Current Context as a Symbol

This strategy for finding symbols to suggest ideas is both the simplest and the most difficult to specify because it can take so many different forms. It involves running *everything* — what clients say, what clients do, anything in the environment, everything — through the question/filter, "Can this be utilized as a symbol of the idea?" And if so, "How?"

When using this filter, many client communications seem to be metaphoric messages. Therapists can use some of these metaphors as symbols to suggest therapeutic ideas.

Melinda came to therapy reluctantly, persuaded by her only friend. Although she held a job, she seemed frightened of people and was very isolated and withdrawn. As I(JF) got to know her, I also discovered that she was a talented artist and a fascinating woman. I wondered if the isolation protected Melinda from possible hurt and also from revealing a self she didn't feel very good about.

I began looking for ways to suggest to Melinda that she was a beautiful person.

One evening, as Melinda was leaving the office, I asked her what her plans for the weekend were. She answered that she had made new shelves for a closet the weekend before, and just couldn't stand the clash of the new wooden shelves and the ugly old linoleum floor. So she had pried up the linoleum and found another layer of linoleum, and beneath that another. It was very interesting to her to notice the different patterns and colors on each layer of dirty, pitted linoleum, and she kept pulling them up until she finally reached a filthy, but strong, solid oak floor. It took all weekend to get the linoleum up, but she had been thinking about the floor ever since, and this weekend she intended to sand and polish it. She thought it would be beautiful.

This immediately struck me as a metaphoric communication from Melinda about how she was perceiving herself (probably beautiful, but hard to get to, under lots of damaged patterns) and also about how she was working hard at revealing herself. It may have been a message to me saying, "Stick in there; there really is something inside worth getting to."

I saw my opportunity to suggest two ideas: (1) Yes, you are beautiful inside, and there's even more there than you think. (2) You're worth working to get to.

I utilized the symbols in Melinda's story to suggest these ideas. I said something like this, "Wow! If the closet floor is that nice, I wonder what's under the linoleum in rooms where it was meant to be seen? It must be incredible. Some houses skimp on places not for public view, but yours must be high quality throughout. You know, it's a lot of work uncovering a floor like that, and it's really worth it."

This talk in a nonmetaphorical sense was nonsense. Closet floors are pretty much the same as the rest of the floor. It is unlikely that the other rooms were covered in linoleum. It was indicative of the metaphorical appropriateness of the communication that Melinda nodded and seemed to seriously consider what I said, rather than asking, "What are you talking about?"

When talking in this fashion, it is important to communicate nonverbally through eye contact and voice tone that the message is meaningful and important. People are then encouraged to search for meaning rather than dismiss the words as small talk. It is not important that they understand the idea at a conscious level.

A similar process can be utilized even when clients do not offer communication that seems to be metaphoric. In other words, something that occurs in therapy or something that a person says, although it does not necessarily contain a metaphoric message, can be utilized to send a metaphoric message.

For example, a family was referred to us because Jack, the youngest child, was misbehaving in school. On the telephone, Kimberly, the mother, told me(JF) that she had had problems with each of her five children at one time or another, but the others had seemed to straighten out.

At an initial family session, as Kimberly was signing a videotape release form, I noticed her long nails, which looked, from across the room, very well cared for. I commented on them, as a way to begin talking and building rapport. Kimberly thanked me and commented that one had cracked. I said, "Well, it's time to start growing it back, good and strong. You know how to do that, I can tell from the other nails. And that nail knows how to do well, too. I think it'll straighten out pretty quickly. It has all those other nails around it to support it."

Kimberly grinned, looked over at Jack, and said, "Yeah, I think so too."

I used Kimberly's problem nail as a symbol for Jack so that I could suggest the idea that he would do fine. He had done fine before, he had a family to support him, and he could do fine again. It would be only natural. It is likely that as Kimberly noticed her nail in the days ahead she would remember that communication about Jack and perhaps find ways that it was already coming true.

Another possibility is to look around and utilize whatever happens to be in the office or to bring concrete symbols to the office for particular client systems. The therapist then can refer to a symbol directly, use it in an interaction, or just let it sit there in the field of perception.

Erickson liked to hurl a real-looking foam rubber rock at students and say, "Don't take anything for granite!"

Symbols to Reframe

"The Confirmation Suit," by Brendan Behan (1981) tells the story of a 12-year-old boy in Ireland getting ready for his confirmation. A family friend and neighbor, Miss McCann, who makes habits for the dead, offers to make his suit as a special gift. Although he dreads what her idea of fashion for a 12-year-old may be, the decision is out of his hands and the suit is made amidst much fuss and many fittings.

The pants are all right but the shirt has tiny lapels and huge buttons. When the boy first sees it, he is horrified and begs his mother for anything else to wear. He then hits on the plan to simply leave on his overcoat throughout the confirmation, which he does, although it is beastly hot.

On Sunday mornings afterwards, the boy puts on his suit and pops into Miss McCann's for a minute, before taking it off and going out. He and his mother fight about this every Sunday, and one Sunday she loses her temper, announces she is going to tell Miss McCann about the deception, and runs out of the room. When the boy goes next door to see her a few minutes later, Miss McCann is bent over sobbing.

The next winter Miss McCann dies. At the funeral the boy leaves his overcoat in the carriage, although it is a cold and rainy day, and walks behind her coffin in his suit, thinking this was the least he could do.

There are two basic ways that symbols can be used in reframing. One is to consider a situation or some aspect of it as a symbol standing for whatever meaning a person makes of the situation. We can reframe the situation, then, by emphasizing a different meaning for the symbol. The other way is to find a symbol of a different perceptual position and use the symbol to help people perceive their situation from that position.

To experience the difference in these two strategies, consider a card we received with a picture of Earth taken from Apollo 17 on the front. The prominent land mass shown was Africa. The words " . . . and on Earth, Peace and Good Will toward all" were printed around the picture like a frame.

Using the first strategy, the globe can be considered as a symbol of humankind. For North Americans, showing Africa as the prominent land mass points out a different aspect of the familiar symbol, and the new aspect allows us to perceive deeper meaning in the word "all."

Using the second strategy, the camera's position in outer space can be taken as a symbol of a new perceptual position, one not usually available to humans. When people occupy that position, they may have a new perspective on what's included in the notion of peace and good will for all.

The question to consider in deciding which strategy to use is which works best in the given context. We give examples of both strategies along with questions that therapists can ask themselves in using the strategies.

Discover What a Situation Can Symbolize Other Than What It Now Symbolizes

Since each situation is different, it is difficult to describe a specific strategy to use in finding new meanings for a situation. However, the following questions can be helpful in answering the central question, "What can the situation symbolize other than what it now symbolizes for the client system?" We present them along with highly condensed examples, meant to clarify the questions.

How could the situation be a symbol for a solution or part of a solution? Pain is something that symbolizes sickness, suffering, and death for many people. However, it is also a signal that lets us know that our bodily integrity has been compromised. When we focus on its function as a signal, pain can be seen as part of the solution to a broken leg or an ulcer. Many other unpleasant ideas and emotions can be seen to serve useful functions when we look at how they lead toward solutions.

What positive intentions or motivations underlie and could be symbolized by the situation?

A woman complained bitterly about how her husband didn't care about being with the family and was always working. For the wife, her husband's "always" working was a symbol that he didn't care about the family. I(GC) wondered about the positive motivation for the working and asked the husband, "Is it true that you care so much about your family's well-being that you're willing to sacrifice your free time and personal life to insure their financial security?"

When the wife saw her husband's gratefulness at being understood in this way, the previously negative symbol took on a new meaning, and she was able to entertain the idea that he did care about her. This shift created a base for their negotiating a lifestyle to suit them as a couple.

What useful function does the presenting situation have in the system, and how could the situation be seen as a symbol of that function? A way to hypothesize about this is to consider what would happen to the system if the presenting situation were resolved.

A mother brought her eight-year-old son to therapy because at school he talked out in class, was dramatically silly, fearful, and unhappy, and disobeyed the teacher. These behaviors resulted in the child frequently being sent home and the mother often going to the school for meetings as well as to a host of specialists. The child's behavior symbolized craziness to the mother.

In the first session, we learned that the behaviors began after the parents divorced, and that as part of the divorce settlement, the son's older sister went to live with the father. We saw that the problematic behaviors kept the mother and son closely involved with each other, so we wondered whether the boy was a very good son who was making sure that his mother felt she had a meaningful role by trying to keep her as busy as three people had before.

The behaviors that had symbolized craziness now could symbolize "keeping Mother busy." To prove that she was a good mother, and to show her son that she could stay busy without his help, the mother began to spend more time with friends and to interview for a job.

What are the useful results of the problematic situation? How can some aspect of the situation become a symbol of these results? Some people are glad to have herpes because, since they contracted it, they have only had sexual partners who have been interested in serious relationships. A magazine article by a woman in this position, entitled "St. Herpes" (Mills, 1985), describes herpes as a symbol of a guardian of the new phase in her life, a phase characterized by more selective and committed relationships.

Are there any contexts in which the situation could symbolize something positive? This is our "Rudolf the Red-Nosed Reindeer" question.

A father complained that his disrespectful teenage daughter always found something wrong with what he said and often defiantly refused to follow directions. I(JF) said, "You must be glad to have so much evidence that your kid will never give in to peer pressure. Was it you who taught her so well to stand up for what she believes in?"

The behavior that had symbolized disrespect was used to symbolize the daughter's ability to stand up for what she believed.

If process rather than content is considered, what, other than a problem, can the situation symbolize?

A man came to therapy because he didn't know what he wanted to do for a career. He had had a succession of different jobs, none of which he particularly enjoyed, and had now been unemployed for several months. His unemployment, in his eyes, meant that he was a bum.

I(JF) said that it seemed to me that both the unemployment and the series of jobs symbolized the process of exploring and eliminating options, including the option of being unemployed, and that this process was very important in deciding on a career. The new meaning for the old symbol allowed the man to feel better about himself. He was able to start exploring and eliminating options other than chronic unemployment.

What useful meaning can be found by breaking the problematic situation down into smaller chunks? In considering the question, "What can this situation symbolize other than a problem?" it can be useful to break the situation down into smaller components. New meanings might be apparent that are not as obvious when considering the whole situation.

For example, Carrie came to therapy in a state of confusion. She thought she was falling in love with a man she had been out with twice. She believed that she was a lesbian because she had only had sex with other women. She felt totally unprepared for what was happening to her.

She said that she wanted to give this relationship a chance, but with years of lesbian experience, she did not think this was possible.

I(GC) told Carrie that I didn't know whether she was straight or gay or even how absolute those distinctions were, but I did know from what she had told me that she was a woman who had thoroughly enjoyed the experience of falling in love. She had numerous satisfying romantic relationships. She had had intimate conversations, companionship, and sexual experiences. She knew how to negotiate, stand up for herself, and share with someone else. From everything I knew, these were symbols that indicated that a person had all that it took to do well in a love relationship. She had a tremendous amount of preparation for the relationship that she was now entering.

In this reframe, by focusing on the individual experiences making up the situation, I was able to show that each was a symbol of Carrie's readiness for any love relationship, and therefore for a new, heterosexual, experience.

What useful perspective can be found by viewing the problematic situation in a more global way? The inverse of the previous tactic is to take the data to a higher level of abstraction. In the previous case the data then could have been considered not as years of lesbian experience but as years of experience with people. In this way Carrie could have focused on falling in love with a particular person (and she had had the experience before of falling in love with people), not a person of a particular sex.

Sometimes it is useful to first create a symbol for the problematic situation. Then a reframe can be built around the symbol. The same strategies and questions apply when this second level of symbol is added.

For example, in a workshop demonstration, Virginia Satir began by asking each family member in sequence around the circle what he or she hoped to get by being there. The teenage son scowled throughout this questioning and remained silent when Satir spoke to him.

She asked if he had ever played poker, and he answered with a nod. She told him that in poker it was perfectly fine and in fact wise at times to pass, adding that a pass on one round did not necessarily mean that someone would pass on the next. With this comment she enlarged the time perspective and reframed his silence as just one move (perhaps wise) in many that would happen over time.

He was then free to talk later in the session without feeling he was "breaking down" or changing his stance. Satir accomplished this by offering a pass in poker as a symbol for the teenager's silence. She then was able to cash in on another aspect of passing in poker, that it has no bearing on later moves (Satir, 1982).

In all of the examples given up to this point, the therapists directly suggested the new meanings. Therapists can also facilitate clients' discovering reframes for themselves. The simplest way to do this is to ask clients the kinds of questions listed above and promote their discovery of other meanings their situations could symbolize. This works best when therapists keep in mind that the intention in using reframes is to introduce multiple meanings into the system so that clients experience themselves as having more possibilities. It is not important that people trade in one frame for another. Instead, we can co-create multiple perspectives, insuring that people be in positions of choice.

For example, Lila came to therapy at the age of 30 because she was dissatisfied with many aspects of her life. She was single and wanted to be married. She felt that she was overly dependent on her parents and sister. She was unhappy with her nursing job and felt that her supervisor had unreasonable expectations. She was overweight and had had a history of gaining and losing weight. One of the resources that she felt would help her in several of these areas was assertiveness.

Lila came to a session directly from work. She was very upset because she thought she probably jeopardized her job by telling her supervisor she would not take another patient. She already had two more patients than the other nurses at her station and she refused to take another. Now, "on top of everything else," she thought she would probably lose her job.

I(JF) said to Lila, "Your job may be in jeopardy. I don't know. But for just a minute let's think about this differently. If you look at the process of what you did, not think about the content of your job, but just look at the actions you took, what can you see in yourself? What did you do?"

She answered, "I guess I was assertive!"

We validated her assertiveness and also talked more about her worries about job security. She now saw her actions as symbolizing two things instead of one.

Another way that people can effect reframes for themselves is through tasks in which they examine symbolic experiences to find different meanings.

For example, if a man considers himself to be incompetent and this self-concept prevents him from doing things in his own behalf, he can be asked to draw up a list of experiences that are evidence of his incompetence.

Perhaps he will list a variety of experiences in which he made mistakes, didn't take opportunities, or saw other people performing better than he did. Whatever he has found, each experience on his list is a symbol of what he calls incompetence.

He can then be asked to take each memory and write out any positive thing that occurred because of the behavior he had in that experience. His therapist may want to demonstrate with one of the memories, by asking some questions and pointing out some positive results, to get him started. In this manner, each example of incompetence can become a symbol of something positive about the man.

Find a Symbol for a Different Perceptual Position

In using the second strategy for reframing the basic question is, "What could symbolize a new way of thinking about, organizing, or looking at this information?"

Possible new perceptual positions include the following:

— a different time frame (past, present, future, seconds, hours, years, slow, fast)
— a different person (seeing through someone else's eyes)
— a different cultural perspective
— a different aspect of the client's experience
— an expert in some relevant field

Without necessarily thinking about it this way, therapists and therapy teams work as symbols of new perceptual positions all of the time. Whether a therapist symbolizes an objective position, an accepting one, an optimistic one, an empathic one, or even the perspective of an all-knowing guru is determined by the interaction of how he presents himself and the expectations of a client.

Much of the power of a developmental reframe (e.g., a therapist defining a teenager's angry words and constant disagreement with his parents not as craziness, but as a normal stage kids go through in differentiating from their parents) is due to a client's acceptance of a therapist as a symbol of authority. Similarly, when Jay Haley advises a trainee to tell a woman that the problems she came in for are not therapy problems but "artist problems," and as such they don't require therapy, this reframe is accepted because it is given by people who symbolize expertise in therapy. The same conclusions drawn by a well-meaning friend or relative might be ignored.

A team can be used to heighten the power of the symbol. During sessions in which we invite families or individuals to listen to the team reflect about what they have heard in a session, people are often impressed with how many people care. If team members represent a variety of ideas, that are either shared in this way or through the therapist, a number of symbols for a number of perceptual positions is offered at one time.

A dramatic way for a therapist to become a symbol of a perceptual position is to take on a symbolic role.

Our friend, Patrick Sweeney, in his work in a residential center for "wayward lads" in Dublin, had the idea of having "Madame Wong" make weekly visits to the center for individual meetings with each of the boys. *

Madame Wong was a fortune teller, and therefore represented the future. She was played by a staff person, who each Thursday wore distinctive clothes, makeup, and a wig. She entered the building a different way on Thursdays so that the boys only saw her in a particular room looking a particular way. The room had special candies and decorations on Thursdays.

Madame Wong did not talk to the boys about problems and goals, as other experts did. She predicted their future, particularly their immediate future, and gave them advice as any fortune teller might. She also sometimes gave out symbols to remind the boys of her messages. For example, Madame Wong predicted that one boy was about to embark on a new path. She gave him a new pair of socks to help him be sure footed in going this new direction.

For each boy, Madame Wong came to symbolize a future orientation. This was a totally new perceptual position for many of the boys. As she became a part of their conceptual world, they began to be able to see things that they hadn't seen before. They could see that present actions had future consequences. They began to reframe options in terms of long-range significance.

Milton Erickson also sometimes took on a symbolic role for the purpose of reframing a problem. In one case he accomplished his goal without ever directly meeting the client.

The parents of a six-year-old who was stealing consulted him. Erickson's intervention consisted of writing a series of letters to the child that were from her six-year-old-growing-up fairy.

Erickson's description of himself as the fairy included the fact that he was covered with eyes and ears, so that the child was metaphorically told that she was being observed. He was paying attention to make sure the child learned everything a six-year-old needs to learn to be ready to become a seven-year-old. (Rosen, 1982)

*The staff of the hostel, Patrick Sweeney, Colette Richardson, Ann Richardson, Dierdre Shanahan, and John Hannon, told us this story when we were consulting there.

By setting himself up as a symbol of expertise on how a six-year-old grows up, Erickson represented a perceptual position from which stealing could be understood as something to be set aside by the time a child reaches seven. The problem was thus reframed as a type of growing pain rather than a criminal flaw.

There are other ways to utilize a symbol of a different perceptual position for reframing. By far the most common is for the therapist to describe the symbol and the way things look from the symbolized viewpoint. Describing another person with a different way of experiencing things can set that person up as a symbol of a particular perceptual position. Stories and references to other clients and stories about the ways things are done in other cultures are two possible ways to introduce other people and their perceptions. For example, a child who thinks her parents impose too many rules may see her situation differently after hearing stories of a relatively unsupervised child, left alone days at a time, on her own to get together meals, launder her clothes, and take care of basic needs. Another possibility is to suggest reading material that is written from a very different viewpoint.

Sometimes a therapist can utilize a different aspect of a client as a symbol for a different perceptual position. Cloé Madanes (1985) has developed a method for doing this in which she identifies a different role the client has in a different context and utilizes it as a symbol of a resourceful perceptual position. When a person looks at her problem from that role, it is automatically reframed.

For example, in working with a couple, Madanes might ask the wife who works as a business manager to write a memo outlining her policy for employees who have a certain problem. Madanes would choose a problem that was isomorphic to the couple's problem, but place it in the context of business. A similar task would be given to the husband, tailored to his line of work.

Once new frames are added, people have new maps and more choices.

Symbols to Facilitate New Patterns of Thought, Feeling, and Behavior

The strategies we use to develop symbols for facilitating new patterns of thought, feeling, and behavior are the same as those already described under other categories. Perhaps most commonly we identify a resource that would make a positive difference in an unsatisfactory pattern. We then utilize the strategies described in the section on resources to develop a symbol, and find a way to use that symbol in the pattern so that the resource is incorporated. For examples, see the cases of Rebecca and her family (pp. 72–74) and Ronald (pp. 78–82) in Chapter 3. We give two different examples here to give a sense of the wide variety of forms using symbols to facilitate new patterns can take.

Our friend Jennifer Andrews told us about a case in which she used a symbol to interrupt and work towards shaping a new pattern.

Jennifer found Sally very difficult to work with because she so frequently changed the subject, going off on very tangential connections. After a couple of sessions of Jennifer's consistently interrupting and asking Sally to fill in connections, Jennifer devised a plan. Throughout the remainder of therapy, Jennifer put paper and a magic marker on a small table. When Sally brought up a subject Jennifer drew a tree trunk. If she began to veer off the main subject Jennifer drew a limb. If Sally didn't go back to the main topic, she would say, "You're getting out on a limb." If Sally continued, Jennifer would draw a branch off the limb and then a leaf falling from the tree. Jennifer would announce, "You're off the tree now, Sally." Then it would be up to Sally to go back to the subject or to define a new "trunk" that she really wanted to stay with. Sally found the symbol of the tree very helpful in monitoring her own communication skills and developing new patterns of talking with others.

The second example is of a woman I(JF) worked with who had severe pain and discomfort both before and at the beginning of her menstrual period. Her physician believed that Ruth's symptoms were caused by either too much estrogen or not enough progesterone. Taking supplemental progesterone did not work, because Ruth had a toxic reaction to it. When she came to see me she was taking many kinds of medication and still experiencing incapacitating pain.

First, I taught Ruth self-hypnosis for pain control. She was able to use it with some success. We continued to validate and extend her pain-control skills. In one session I suggested that Ruth find a symbol for a healthy and painless menstrual cycle. The image of a peace rose came to her. She had a garden of yellow and pink peace roses in her backyard. She thought they were an apt symbol for the peace she would feel when this situation was resolved. I was struck with the idea that the two colors of the rose could represent the two unbalanced hormones.

In consultation with Gene and his medical books, we devised a plan. Our first step was to make a 29-day calendar to match Ruth's cycle. In preparation for this, I borrowed Ruth's record of daily symptoms that she kept for medical consultations. The calendar that we made lays out the stages of the life cycle of a peace rose.

1 First petals dropping	2	3	4	5 All petals dropped
	More petals dropping --------------------->			
6	7	8	9	10
Petals fertilizing earth		Prune plant	New stalk grows	
11	12	13	14	15 Bud begins to open (yellow)
	Bud developing -->			
16	17	18	19	20
	Rose slowly opening --->			
		(yellow with pink tips)		
21	22	23	24	25
	Rose slowly opening --->			
			(with more pink)	
26	27	28	29	xxxxxxxxxx xxxxxxxxxx xxxxxxxxxx xxxxxxxxxx
Rose slowly opening ---> Bud fully open (pink center)				
(3 rows petals open but center closed)				

Figure 10.

In our planning the yellow stood for estrogen and the pink for progesterone. We attempted to match a normal hormonal cycle in the amount of pink and yellow visible on any particular day of the cycle.

I gave the calendar to Ruth, explained our thinking about it, and suggested that every morning, using self-hypnosis, she focus on the image for that day of her cycle.

At the very least, these daily self-hypnosis sessions symbolized Ruth's ability to communicate with herself at a deep level. We were delighted, as was she, that much more happened. Within three months she was off all medication and having virtually pain-free periods.

Summary

All communication involves the use of symbols. While all therapists — frequently without thinking about it — make use of symbols all the time, practice with developing and using symbols can make therapists more creative and effective.

There are many ways that we use symbols in psychotherapy. In this chapter we have given an overview of several important uses: to access and utilize resources, to suggest ideas, to reframe, and to facilitate new patterns of thought, feeling, and behavior. For each use, we have suggested specific strategies for developing and using such symbols.

Exercises I, II, III, IV, VI, XIII, and XVIII in Chapter 4 deal specifically with finding and using symbols. If you haven't tried them already you may want to experiment with some or all of them now.

6

---·‹⚬⚭⚬›·---

STRATEGIES FOR
FINDING STORIES

THERE ARE A NUMBER of strategies in the literature for creating therapeutic stories (Gordon, 1978; Dolan, 1985; Lankton & Lankton, 1986). Having practiced them and used them rigorously for years, we noticed that we also spontaneously tell stories, often in the same sessions, without much planning at all. These stories are usually recountings of things that have actually happened. We find that these unplanned stories seem to be as effective as ones we have agonized over, that they are much easier for us to "come upon," and that they leave us free to attend to what is happening in a moment-to-moment way between us and clients. Since we haven't spent time before the session planning them, we are also much less invested in stories of this type. When nonverbal feedback indicates they aren't fitting for a person, we can let them go.

Aware of the risks of turning spontaneous natural processes into formal, conscious strategies, we have spent some time exploring our thought processes in finding relevant stories. Here we offer our ideas about these thought processes to you. We encourage you to use them as guidelines only if they help you discover the stories that are already within you waiting to be told.

At a very general level we have four basic purposes in telling stories:

1. to pace people's models of the world and current situations,
2. to access emotional states or attitudes,
3. to suggest ideas, and
4. to embed suggestions.

Our purpose in telling a story is not to completely resolve clients' presenting situations. We have much smaller ideas in mind that we hope can contribute to a resolution. Occasionally, families or individuals do find complete solutions in interaction with a story we've told. More often they experience a shift in feeling, a new way to perceive their situation, or new ideas about what to do in a particular context.

Even though we have specific purposes in telling a story, the meaning of the story evolves in the telling and in clients' understanding of it. Also, given the multidimensional nature of metaphor, there are always different aspects of a story, each with different possible meanings. We may use the same story, emphasizing different aspects, for very different purposes.

We have a different group of thought processes for each of the four kinds of goals. In this chapter we describe each group of thought processes. With some reluctance, we have also decided to include examples of various stories that we developed using these thought processes. Be warned, though, that the thought processes and stories can never tell the whole story. It is in the joining of client, therapist, and thought process that useful therapeutic stories emerge. The therapist and the thought process alone may develop interesting stories, but these will not necessarily be relevant to a client. What is missing in the printed examples is any sense of the nature of the rapport, the feel of the relationship, the experiential tone of the client-therapist mind. Also, while our stories work well for us, your own stories will probably work better for you.

Although a therapist can use these strategies ahead of time in thinking about and planning for a client, as Erickson was fond of teaching, each client is a new person each time you meet. So, although you may want to practice developing stories with these strategies outside of therapy sessions, they are best used in the actual client-therapist context.

The successful application of these strategies requires two things: (1)enough joining between client and therapist for a working therapeutic mind to emerge, and (2)a certain degree of clarity about a particular purpose within that mind. As you will see, each story is found by having a rather specific purpose in mind — suggesting an idea, accessing a resource, etc. We believe that if you have clear moment-to-moment goals and cultivate a good therapeutic relationship, the right stories tend to find you at the right moments.

To give you a flavor of how we actually use them in a therapy session, we have included two transcripts. We have annotated both transcripts with the thought processes that led to each story, so that you can see how these strategies can work within a session. The second transcript shows how stories can be used in hypnotic work.

In the first section, below, we describe the context and internal thought processes for arriving at a single story in detail. We'll let that example stand as a metaphor for the thought processes that we used, but don't describe in detail, for the other examples in the chapter.

Stories to Pace People's Models of the World and Current Situations

When we are aware of wanting to use a story for pacing, we ask ourselves, "Who or what is this like?" or "What does this remind me of?" These questions can be asked in relation to what people have described, their emotional quality, their facial expressions, posture, or voice tone, the way they are interacting with each other during the session, or anything else that stands out for a therapist.

An image, a memory, a description, or something of this kind will usually emerge in response to one of the questions. The therapist can then develop this fragment into a story that communicates understanding or acceptance and helps develop rapport.

For example, a family was referred by the school because Jeffrey, a second grader who had previously done quite well, was becoming withdrawn and uncommunicative. He had stopped doing any of his school work. The school had had several conferences with the parents, and Jeffrey was being seen by the school social worker, but the situation was deteriorating. During the last conference, the school recommended family therapy and cautioned the parents that if Jeffrey's performance did not improve soon, he would need to repeat second grade.

The first thing that Elaine, the mother, said was, "I think I should tell you that I don't want to be here. I don't believe in this. I think people should solve their own problems. I grew up on a farm. We always worked hard. We expected to. It was part of life. When something was wrong, we just worked harder. We didn't call in anyone else. It was our farm. If it was just up to me, we would just work harder, not come to talk to someone else about this."

I(JF) responded, "I used to work at a residential treatment facility for kids. I thought it was a really special place. The staff worked hard, and we loved the kids. No one watched the clock. If there was something going on that needed to be taken care of, we would take care of it, which often meant staying late, and always meant working hard. And I mean everybody, not just the therapists—the house parents, the teachers, everybody.

"One thing that really rankled me and was hard to get used to was staffings. Every Wednesday afternoon we staffed three kids. We had a consulting psychiatrist who was there every Wednesday. In the morning he spent an hour each with the three kids. Then in the afternoon, we would spend an hour staffing each kid. The houseparent would talk about how the kid was doing socially and with his household responsibilities, the teacher would talk about how the kid was doing in school, and the therapist would talk about how the kid was doing in therapy. If a kid wanted to, he could come and say how he thought he was doing. We all spent lots and lots of time with the kid and really knew him. But then the psychiatrist, who had spent one hour with him, would tell us all what to do! I knew that no degree was more important than knowing a kid."

Elaine sighed, seemed to relax, and said, "It's nothing personal. And as long as we're here, let's see what can be done."

During Elaine's initial comments, when I became aware of wanting to establish rapport, I asked myself, "What does this remind me of?" A memory emerged—my sitting at a staffing, hearing a consultant give what to me seemed like directives, and feeling resentful. There were many things I could have said in making this single image into a story. In sitting with this family, having the image in mind, and wanting to establish rapport, I felt a little uneasy because I had been a student in the memory. However, I had also had similar experiences as a staff member. I decided to tell the story as a staff member, because I wanted to communicate that I saw the parents in a prominent role with their child, not a subordinate one. As I looked at Elaine I found myself emphasizing the hard work the staff did because she talked about working hard. I was also aware that Jeffrey was listening, which reminded me of the option of children speaking at their own staffings. That seemed to fit with the message I wanted to establish, so I included it.

If we are keeping our purpose and the people present in mind, we can make many of these decisions as we tell a story. It can be helpful in this regard to listen to the story in your mind through the ears of your clients.

If the memory that initially emerges in response to internal questioning seems inappropriate, we let it go and ask ourselves a different question or the same question again.

Stories to Access Emotional States and Attitudes

We use a cluster of questions in finding stories to access emotional states and attitudes. Any of the questions may lead to an experience, which we can then develop into a relevant story. We ask ourselves these questions during a therapy session as we become aware that we would like to bring forth a particular emotional state or attitude in a client:

— What does the state or attitude remind me of? How can I elaborate within this realm to evoke the state?
— When have I experienced the state or attitude?
— When has someone else experienced the state or attitude?
— When could someone experience the state or attitude?

There is no sequence to the questions, and we certainly do not use all of the questions in finding material for a particular story.

Instead, when we want to access a specific emotional state, we consider a question, only going on to another if nothing emerges, until some material does emerge. It may be a memory of an event, something that someone else told us, or something imagined.

We take what has emerged and, keeping in mind the state we would like to bring forth, tell it as a story to the client. If the material seems off the mark, we let it go and ask ourselves one of the other questions.

The following are stories that we developed in asking ourselves these questions in the therapist-client context. We tell them here, as examples, in the same words used in the original contexts, along with the questions that helped unlock the material.

When Have I Experienced the State or Attitude?

I(JF) developed the following story to elicit a sense of feeling appreciated. The question, "When have I experienced being appreciated?" led to the story.

A number of years ago we invited some of our closest friends from around the country to come do what we called a hypnosis retreat with us. There were five of us, Charlie and Yvonne and Maxine and Gene and me. And we had all these workshops going on at the same time. It was at kind of a resorty place, and we had some workshops outside, some in cabins, in different places. And we each had one or two periods of time when we weren't working, and the rest of the time we were.

My friend Maxine decided to come to my workshop on using self-hypnosis in your daily life. I got lost finding the cabin my workshop was going to be in, and I walked in out of breath and feeling apologetic. And all I saw was Maxine sitting in the front row with a wonderful smile lighting her face. And I felt the tightness sweep out of my body when I saw that smile. She sat there in the front row, beaming at me the entire time, as if everything I did was a delight, but not a surprise. She seemed to completely expect it. It was such an interesting thing having her in the front row. Everybody else looked different. I don't know if her feeling spread to everybody or it was my perception, but everything changed.

Teaching that workshop was one of the easiest things I've ever done. The words seemed to glide between all of us there, effortlessly. And I still put her there, right in the front row, from time to time.

When Could Someone Experience the State or Attitude?

The goal of this next story was to access humility. The actual experience it draws upon was one in which I (JF) felt a wide variety of feelings. I kept thinking, as it was going on, "This is important. You are learning something here." Only in summary, afterwards, did the meaning seem to have a lot to do with humility. Maybe that's why the experience came up for me in response to asking myself, "When could someone experience humility?" I'm not sure that I did experience humility at the time, but I believe I could have, and did after the fact.

The college I went to had a program where you could spend a year in Oxford. And I did. My friend Sherri and I had one floor of a wonderful house on Polstead Road, which is where T. E. Lawrence lived. You can just get a glimpse of the street at the beginning of "Lawrence of Arabia" when he rides by on a motorcycle. At the end of our block there was a pub and across the street from it a bridge onto a footpath called Aristotle Lane. And the lane led into the port meadow that the Thames flowed through.

That was the year of the movie, "Butch Cassidy and the Sundance Kid," and Mrs. Watkins, whose house it was, was a big fan of that movie, so many mornings we'd wake up to "Raindrops Keep Falling on my Head" being played over and over and over again. Or else we'd hear calling back and forth, "Jonathan!" "Mummy!" "Louisa!" "Mummy!" "James!" "Mummy!" "John!" (that was Mr. Watkins). Mrs. Watkins would come sweeping into our rooms, throw open the curtains, hand us our mail and tell us to get up.

It was quite a different relationship from one you'd usually have with a landlady here. Mrs. Watkins lent me clothes, I joined her and Mr. Watkins in front of the telley sometimes in the evening, we'd share ale from the pub, and at times we were mutual confidantes.

Louisa was the baby, so she was around the most of the Watkins children. And she was allowed free reign of our flat. She loved Smarties, which are like our M&Ms, and I thought she was the sweetest thing that ever lived. I attended her third birthday party.

That was in 1970 to '71.

When I left I thought about England all the time, I thought about the Watkins and other friends I had made, and being a child myself, I did absolutely nothing to stay in touch with anyone.

So when Gene and I were traveling in Europe, we knew that we would go to Oxford and I kept putting it off, sometimes saving it the way you would the best chocolates, but sometimes just wanting to keep it the way it was already in my mind.

But we went. We stopped at the tourist office to read the list of bed and breakfasts, and there it was—J. Watkins, 19 Polstead Rd. They were using their house as a bed and breakfast, instead of doing long-term rental. The phone was busy so we just walked over there. And as we approached, Mr. Watkins walked down the driveway looking exactly the same as he had 16 years before!

We stayed there for a week, looking out the same windows, walking up the same stairs that I had 16 years before. The houses you could see from the windows were the same, but they looked different. It took a while to realize the difference was that the trees had grown a lot in those 16 years. Louisa was about as old as I had been when I lived there, and she was off traveling in South America. I was about the age Mrs. Watkins had been. And instead of staying home, she now went off to work each morning. Mr. Watkins had stopped running the post office. He ran the bed and breakfast now. James, who was the oldest child but just a little boy then, now talked politics and had his own business. I took a picture of his red truck that said, "James Watkins, Construction," across it.

I wanted to walk every street, eat in every restaurant, walk past every friend's house that I had left behind, and we did, just about.

I'm embarrassed to admit that somehow I was surprised that it had all kept growing and changing and thriving without me. But it had.

When Has Someone Else Experienced the State or Attitude?

This story was told by Mary Ellen Hynes, in a training program in which we were teaching this material. It answered the question, "When has someone else experienced an attitude of persistence?"

A Spanish teacher, Señor Ruiz, told me this many years ago.

Señor Ruiz was a Cuban exile, and over the course of the weeks of his class he told us a lot about his life. He was born rich, very rich, in Cuba. They were aristocrats, and they had a villa, and cars, and motorcycles, and jewelry, and many fine things. He was well-educated, and he grew up with all the luxury that a person of his class in that place had—in pre-Castro Cuba.

In the early sixties, when Castro came to power, the aristocracy was systematically stripped of everything they had, and eventually Señor Ruiz's family was approached in this way. What they did was to come to Señor Ruiz's house and to make an inventory of every single belonging they had, from their cars down to every last piece of jewelry. And then they kept them in suspense for a couple of weeks. . . . And then they came and told Señor Ruiz that he had 24 hours to leave the country.

He was told what he could take with him. He could take one small suitcase full of clothes and the equivalent of about 200 dollars in American money, and no jewelry whatsoever. They searched him thoroughly, and of course his belongings, at the airport, to make sure that he took nothing else with him. He was even forced to leave behind the chain his parents had given to him when he was baptized as a baby—a little tiny gold chain with a gold cross on it that he had worn all his life. He had to leave it behind.

He came to Miami with nothing, except the clothes on his back and that little suitcase. And because he was a very bright, gifted person who also had a lot of contacts, he started making a new life for himself. And he was a pretty spunky guy and adaptive. He adapted.

About two-and-a-half years after he left, he noticed, in a letter from his mother, who was still back in Cuba—they had not made her leave—that there were two or three tiny, little links of the baptismal chain. His mother had somehow kept this chain behind when everything else was appropriated. She sent three links of the chain in a letter.

It took her seven years, but eventually every link of the chain was with Señor Ruiz. So he kept them all in a little box, and when he had accumulated the entire chain again, he took it to a jeweler and asked if it could be reassembled. And the jeweler said, "Why would you want to do that?"

So Señor Ruiz explained how the necklace had come to be disassembled in this way. When the jeweler heard the story, he reassembled the chain for free, and now it's back on Señor Ruiz's neck.

What Does the State or Attitude Remind Me of?

The next story was used to access calmness. I(JF) developed it from the answer to the question, "What does calmness remind me of?"

The other day I was sitting at my computer typing out a plan for a workshop. We had just moved two weeks before. As I was sitting there I realized that where we used to have our computer was very different from where it is now. We used to have our computer on a little table that exactly fit an alcove of a window. Sometimes when I would get frustrated working on the computer I would look out through the window of our apartment.

And we were living on a street in St. Louis that was all Victorian houses. They were big, glorious Victorian houses, painted in grays and pinks and blues and greens. And it was usually very still and very quiet during the daytime when I'd be working at the computer. There was usually very little movement on the street at all, and I'd look at those houses and I'd think about how old they were, how long they'd been there, wondering about the generations of people who had lived in them, and just begin to notice the stillness, and then begin to notice that I didn't know how much time had passed, but that I could feel a real slowing down. And when I'd look back at my computer, things were quite different for me.

And when I was typing out the workshop notes, just the other day, I realized that just in thinking about that, even though our computer is on a desk now that faces a wall, that I had that street with me.

General Considerations in Accessing States with Stories

In accessing states, we want clients to have emotional experiences, not intellectual understanding, so it is important to make material into stories that people can identify with rather than summaries that simply report feelings. We use stories to suggest states indirectly by describing contextual cues relevant to the experience of those states. This can be accomplished by examining the material that emerges as a result of one of the questions for the contextual cues suggesting the particular state. Then the story can be developed emphasizing those cues. We believe this type of story is more effective if the desired state is never named directly. Not directly labeling the state usually results in the teller's providing a more thorough description of relevant cues.

Generally, if a character in the story is experiencing the state or attitude, that character's internal thoughts and sensations during the experience are the relevant contextual cues. In imagining experiencing these things, the listener will usually feel the associated feelings, and also have his own associations that have to do with similar cues and similar feelings. For example, someone listening to the story of Maxine at the workshop might imagine leading a workshop and seeing a friend in the front row beaming at him and feeling very appreciated, and also remember a wonderful talk with a smiling friend, a teacher who smiled when she taught, and other past scenes. All of these become part of the experience for the listener.

The story of Señor Ruiz did not describe internal and external cues in the same way. The situation described there is so dramatic and extreme that listeners putting themselves in the situation have a universal response.

It is also important to use voice tone and tempo that are consistent with the state or attitude. These serve as indirect suggestions to access the state.

Also, it is helpful to contrast the state with something else in the story. This contrast both heightens the state and allows the opportunity to lead to it from a state that may be closer to the client's experience as the story begins.

The test of the effectiveness of a therapeutic story is always in the listener's response. If the goal is to access a state of pleasure, and during the story the listener is frowning and becoming agitated, the therapist needs to change how the story is being told or find a different story altogether.

Stories to Suggest Ideas

The thought processes we use in finding stories to suggest ideas are similar to the ones we described for finding stories to access emotional states and attitudes. Again, we can represent the process as a cluster of questions that we ask ourselves, one at a time, in no particular order, until something emerges that we can tell as a story. We begin asking ourselves these questions during a therapy session as we become aware that we would like to tell a story to suggest a particular idea:

— What illustrates this idea?
— What does the idea remind me of? How can I elaborate within that realm to suggest the idea?
— How do I know this idea is valid? What is convincing evidence to me that it is so?
— What would be evidence of the idea's usefulness to the person or family?

— How did I learn this?
— How has someone else learned this or how could someone else learn this?
— What will or could happen if the person or family does not learn or believe the idea? What does that remind me of?

These questions are of two different types. The questions, "What illustrates this idea?" and "What does the idea remind me of?" will yield stories that illustrate ideas. Stories of this kind may serve simply to remind someone of something she already knows or to present a possibility in an interesting way.

The other questions will yield stories that demonstrate or prove the importance or validity of an idea, rather than simply illustrating it. For this kind of story we want a person to have a vicarious experience that results in having the idea. The client's confrontation with believable data, convincingly framed to mean something or to undeniably represent a possibility, is usually what is important. The questions are aimed at accessing such data from the therapist's pool of experience.

Most of the questions elicit data that represent the idea in a positive way. The question, "What will or could happen if the person or family does not learn or believe the idea?" will access negative consequences, which for some people are much more compelling than positive experiences.

With these stories, in contrast to stories to access states, it may not be important for a listener to identify with a particular character or to feel what that character feels. If stories to access states or attitudes can be thought of as invitations to enter particular emotional experiences, stories to suggest ideas can be thought of as presentations of information and possibilities that can affect people's thinking.

These stories do not necessarily *logically* follow from the questions; rather, the questions serve to stimulate experiences that are relevant in some way. We then take the experience that we access with a question, look at the people in front of us, and develop the experience into a story that seems relevant to them and to what they are there for at that moment in time.

We developed the following stories in asking ourselves the above questions in the therapist-client context. We offer them to illustrate what the questions can stimulate.

What Does the Idea Remind Me of?

I(GC) used this story to suggest the idea, "You can be afraid without being immobilized by the fear." The following questions helped me find the story: "What does the idea that you can be afraid without being immobilized by the fear remind me of? How can I elaborate within that realm to suggest the idea?"

When I was in my psychiatric residency, my best friend was my fellow resident, Mohan. One of the interesting things about Mohan was his name. He was from India, and Mohan was his only name — it means "beautiful" — and he got irritated with Americans demanding that he have two names, so he took the name of the village he grew up in, Sivanandam, and told people that his name was Sivanandam Mohan, Dr. S. Mohan.

Mohan was something of a mystic, and during our second year of psychiatric residency he was reading a whole lot of Krishnamurti. I don't know if you've ever heard of Krishnamurti, but he was a guy who was raised from a very early age to be the head of the Theosophy Society, which at the turn of the century was a very influential movement of British intellectual people who were very taken with Indian mysticism. They had done this sort of blend of European religion and Indian religious ideas that they called Theosophy.

Somehow someone had decided that this kid, Krishnamurti, was very blessed, was very wise, sort of like the Maharaj Ji during the sixties. But at the age of 21 or so, he rebelled and said, "I don't want to be the head of anybody's religion." And he went into retreat for a long time.

But he ended up the leader of a movement anyway. It just wasn't Theosophy. Part of his whole thing was that nobody could be a leader of anybody's movement, but a lot of people liked to come and hear him talk about that.

So I started reading this book about Krishnamurti that Mohan gave me, and it was transcripts of a bunch of his talks. Part of what he was saying all the way through this one talk was, "If you are not understanding what I'm saying as I say it, don't listen any further. Each thing that I'm saying builds on the next, so only listen until you become full. Only listen as long as you are understanding, because everything that I'm saying builds on the next."

And I got to a place where he was saying, "What's important is to see the thing that is fear, and not name it." And I was with him right up to that point . . . but somehow that seemed real important, " . . . to see the thing that is fear, and not name it."

I tried to read the next sentence; I couldn't get to the next sentence . . . "To see the thing that is fear, and not name it . . . "

I felt like I was failing Mohan, because somehow I wasn't quite understanding it. It was compelling, and I couldn't quite understand it, and it's stuck in my head ever since.

I think at times I'm beginning to understand some of the things that he meant when he said " . . . to see the thing that is fear and not name it," although I've never picked up the book and finished the rest of that talk.

How Did I Learn This?

I(JF) wanted to suggest the idea, "Don't create limitations where there are none." The question I asked myself was, "How did I learn not to create limitations where there are none?"A literal answer to that question is that I still have a way to go in that area. However, two different experiences came up for me that both have to do with the idea. We often use a number of stories for the same purpose and feel that stories are often more effective if you use more than one. The following is just one of the stories that I told to suggest the idea.

My worst birthday was my thirtieth. I planned for it, really, to be bad, weeks in advance. It was just that there were a number of things I thought I would have done by then that I hadn't. In fact, I was nowhere near close to my plans for myself and somehow the number 30 seemed like a deadline for a lot of things.

The night of my birthday I stayed home and had a long cry. And the next day I went to work pretty dragged down. I was doing some consulting for nursing homes at that time and that's where I went the morning after my birthday.

Part of my job was periodically to talk to the residents in the nursing home and make sure that they were adjusting well or inquire about any difficulties they were having. And that morning I had just finished talking to a woman and was walking out of her room, when another woman in a wheelchair reached out a long gnarled arm to me and proclaimed, "Yesterday was my birthday."

"Mine too," I told her.

She had sparkling black eyes in a soft, weathered face. And she began to tell me all the changes she'd seen in her lifetime. "And yesterday I turned 90," she said.

I told her that I had turned 30.

She smiled a big smile, nodded her head, and said, "Ah! Thirty years old . . . a young woman. You have your whole life before you!"

What Could Happen if the Person or Family Does Not Believe the Idea?

To suggest the idea, "Sometimes you need information to be able to accomplish what you want," I(GC) used this story. The questions I asked myself were, "What will or could happen if the family does not learn or believe that you sometimes need information to accomplish what you want? What does that remind me of?"

One Christmas, we bought our niece Emily a toy that we really liked. It was a soft plastic bear filled with bubble soap. When you unscrewed the bear's hat and squeezed his tummy, a soap-filled circle of plastic would rise from his head. If you then blew at the circle, you could fill the air with bubbles. We had great fun playing with the one we bought for ourselves.

After Christmas, we got a note from Emily thanking us for the nice bubble bath. We gave her the right stuff (she already had a fine pair of lungs), but didn't tell her to first unscrew the hat, then squeeze the bear's tummy, then blow, then release the tummy so the ring would go back down for more soap, then squeeze again so it would rise, etc. Consequently she missed a lot of fun, but she sure was clean.

How Has Someone Else Learned the Idea?

I(JF) wanted to suggest the idea, "Take one step at a time." The material emerged from the question, "How has someone else learned to take one step at a time?"

My brother stayed with me one summer about eight years ago, and neither of us is known for our neatness. I was living in a little apartment at that time and Stevie was camped out on the sofa bed in the living room. There really wasn't room for his stuff and my stuff in that little apartment and, as I said, neither of us is known for our neatness.

One day I came home from work with just a couple of hours until a study group would be meeting at my apartment. Stevie had met some people on the beach and they had spent the afternoon jamming in my apartment, and eating, and hanging out, and having a good time in general, which seems frequently to include making a mess.

And the place really was a mess. I sat down on that unmade sofa bed, in the middle of dirty plates, scattered records, my own piles of papers, and assorted heaps of stuff, and thought about turning off the lights, locking the doors, and pretending no one was home when people showed up for the study group later that night.

Instead I got mad at Stevie who said, "I'll tell you what we'll do. My father taught me how you clean house."

Now I had never noticed either my father or my brother doing much house cleaning, so this whole thing really surprised me. But what he said was, "It's the same as with anything else. You decide what to do and you do only that and you think about only that until you finish doing it. Then you decide on the next thing and you do only that until it's finished. So I'm going to pick up records. You gather dishes. Don't think about anything else until they're all picked up. Then we'll decide what's next."

So we did. And the place was neat for my study group, which I didn't think was possible.

What Illustrates This Idea?

I(GC) wanted to suggest the ideas, "You can maintain a sense of connection with your family and still be different from them," and "You can explore connections with family members, one at a time, slowly." The question, "What illustrates this idea?" yielded the memories that make up this story.

My father hated to water-ski, but he loved to drive the boat. He took great pleasure in teaching other people how to water-ski, and he was a great water-skiing teacher—having never done it at all in his life. He was also a great water-skiing boat driver. He had a sense of connection, whether one, or two—we even had a boat for a while that was powerful enough to pull four water-skiers at the same time. He had a sense of how fast you can take a turn without getting those people all tangled up with each other in a way that was scary.

What Would Be Evidence to the Person or Family That This Is a Valid Idea?

I(GC) used this story to suggest the idea, "Something that you may perceive as a fault in yourself may seem wonderful to someone else." The question that led me to the story was, "What would be evidence to the person that this is a valid idea?"

A wonderful thing about going to conferences is you get to see all these old friends and colleagues. And one of the first things that Jim did when we bumped into him was to pull out his wallet and say, "I've got a picture of my kid." And he showed us this picture of his daughter, who looks like a kid off the front of a cereal box—in the nicest way, the kind of kid you would pick to represent "kid." She's got these freckles and blond hair and this wonderful gap right here between her teeth. And I said, "She's got just the right space between her teeth and just the right freckles." He said, "I know. Last year she knew that that was a wonderful gap, and this year she's a little self-conscious about it. She's not so sure it's a good thing." But I knew that gap was a wonderful thing when I saw it in that picture.

What Is Convincing Evidence of This Idea?

The idea I(JF) wanted to suggest was, "Time is subjective; the same time period can be experienced as long or short." The questions that helped me find the story were, "How do I know this idea is valid? What is convincing evidence that time is subjective?"

I have this incredible dentist. Her name is Ilene Greenblatt, and she is wonderful. First of all, she is delightful to talk with. She always has some project or something exciting to tell you about. And second of all, she doesn't hurt. She also really enjoys looking at and sort of complimenting her own work. She likes to look and say, "Oh, that is such a beautiful gold filling!" She acts like you have a piece of jewelry in your mouth.

And so this really interesting thing has happened for me. I used to spend incredible amounts of time putting off going to the dentist and really worrying about it. I was particularly worried about it because I had braces for 11 years, which created this gum problem at a very young age. It's unusual to have this problem until your mid-forties, but I had it in my twenties, so it's real important that I get my teeth checked. But I would always put off getting my teeth checked for very long periods of time, and worry about it, and then find myself in a dentist's office, spending interminable amounts of time, in a moment or two, worrying about the pain.

And so when I met Ilene it was a totally different experience of being able to spend a few minutes in a half hour, having a wonderful time in her office, in the same amount of time that I used to spend hours in a few minutes before.

It's so funny to me to think about pleasure with a dentist!

Stories with Embedded Suggestions

Richard Wagner is generally credited with the development of the *leitmotiv*, a short musical phrase which represents and recurs with a given character, situation, or emotion. He used this device in many of his operas. The repetition and interplay of the leitmotivs for various characters, moods, and contexts give an added layer of richness to his work.

The strategies for storytelling that we have discussed so far have emphasized ideas about the general shape, content, and mood of therapeutic stories. You might say we have been focusing on the lyrics, the tempo, and the key of our little "operas." Embedded suggestions allow us to add a new dimension to stories.

An embedded suggestion has a form similar to a leitmotiv, although it may function in a more subtle manner. It is a stimulus that bears no necessary direct relationship to the story within which it is embedded. In good storytelling, as in good music, the embedded theme must fit with the overall structure in some aesthetically pleasing way, but there is no need for a precise or logical relationship between the two.

Stories may be used simply and purely as a neutral ground within which to embed suggestions that are figural for individuals or families. The suggestions may be of any kind—to access a particular state or attitude, to entertain a certain idea, or to try out a new behavior.

Such suggestions are inserted within the story, often repetitively, sometimes as something that a character in the story says. The effectiveness of these suggestions can be enhanced by using a different voice tone and setting suggestions off from the rest of the story by brief pauses. Although these cues may seem very obvious to a therapist who is new at using them, they are rarely noticed by listeners. In fact, this is a very naturalistic approach. People often mark out important parts of their communication without realizing it.

The following story is one that I(JF) adopted after hearing our friend, Christie Turner, tell her version of it. The suggestion I offer is to experience security. I embed the suggestion by repeatedly saying the word "security" throughout the story.

One of the big disappointments of my life was that I didn't go to Woodstock. I kept being reminded of it a few years later when I was living in England. The movie "Woodstock" came out in England while I was living there and people kept coming up to me and saying, "Were you at Woodstock?" Or they would come up to me and say, "I saw you in the movie 'Woodstock.'" I'd say, "I wasn't there." They thought all Americans of that time looked and walked alike.

Anyway, when there are big festivals like that, one of the big problems is that there can be violence, things can erupt, lots of people camping out, constricted together.

There were all these preparations going on: all this land was being cleared off, all these tents were being put up, all this stuff was going on. And the local police kept going around and saying, "Who is going to be in charge of *security?*"

The people getting Woodstock together kept saying, "We've got someone in charge of *security.* Don't worry about it. It's not going to be a problem. We've got someone for *security.*"

And day after day as the preparations were going on the local police kept asking, "Who is going to be in charge of security?"

The answer was that the person in charge of security was Wavy Gravy and he had everything all worked out. But he didn't show up until the day that the concert was going to start. And when he did show up the local police couldn't believe it. They were expecting this force of people and instead a group of hippies showed up, led by Wavy Gravy. They called themselves the Please Force.

And what they did was they walked through the crowds and let themselves feel how people were doing. If he felt that someone was in*secure*, Wavy Gravy sat down next to that person and just hung out with him until he felt *secure.*

And you know, there was no *security* problem at Woodstock. In the history of rock festivals, the violence, stealing, all those kinds of problems that people would expect to be there, really weren't there. You could *feel really secure* at Woodstock. And a couple of babies were born.

I have used variations of this story several times to access a state of security and to suggest the idea that security can have a number of meanings. Having these goals in mind, I have found this story at different times by using the thought processes already described for accessing states and suggesting ideas. In the telling it seems additive to mark out the word "security" each time I use it.

Several other stories that we've given under "stories to suggest ideas" also include embedded suggestions: e.g., " . . . see the thing that is fear, and not name it," and "You decide what to do and you do only that and you think about only that until you finish doing it. Then you decide on the next thing and you do only that until it's finished."

In working with clients, we find that having goals in mind creates opportunities for embedding suggestions, and that frequently, as we tell a story for one purpose, we find ourselves marking out instructions that we hadn't consciously realized were there, either for another purpose or to underline the original purpose. In other words, when we find a story using one of the strategies we have already described, we find ourselves marking out "leitmotivs" that we hadn't consciously selected. Sometimes the suggestions are already there, such as the words in the Krishnamurti book. At other times, we may be telling a story to suggest a particular idea and notice as we are talking that we can also embed suggestions to access a particular state. (See the hypnotherapy demonstration transcript at the end of this chapter for an example of embedding "peace" throughout while talking about other things.)

This strategy rests on much practice outside of therapy sessions in picking a message to embed and then finding ways to embed it. With this kind of practice, embedding suggestions in the course of a story becomes second nature.

Summary

In this chapter, we have offered an overview of our favorite strategies for finding and using stories in psychotherapy. These strategies usually result in relatively unplanned and informal stories that are based in the teller's personal experience. With practice, they are relatively easy to use during therapy sessions.

We have discussed four basic purposes for telling stories:

1. to pace people's models of the world and current situations,
2. to access emotional states or attitudes,
3. to suggest ideas, and
4. to embed suggestions.

We have offered strategies for discovering stories for each purpose and have given brief examples of stories found with each strategy. What is missing in the printed examples thus far is any sense of the experiential tone of the client-therapist mind in which the stories emerged. To give you a flavor of how we actually use stories in a therapy session, we have appended the two psychotherapy transcripts that immediately follow this summary. We hope that they give some feel for the type of relationship within which we find and utilize stories. Both transcripts are annotated with the thought processes that led to each story told.

If you desire exercises to practice specific storytelling skills, you might turn to exercises XII, XVII, XVIII, XX, XXI, and XXVI in Chapter 4.

Annotated Transcript I: A Therapy Session

This session was a single interview with a woman who does not live in our area. When she was in town visiting a friend, Carol requested a consultation about difficulties she was having with her son.

The transcript begins several minutes into the session. Carol has said that her son is not motivated to learn to read in school and that she has a feeling that she needs to be more flexible in dealing with that.

Carol: . . . This is something that is real important to me, so if there is any chance that I can get any kind of wisdom or whatever in looking at it, I'm excited about that . . . and I realize that I need to bring in another, I'm thinking that I need to get another, somebody to help me access something buried in me.

Jill: So, if everything went just how you'd like it here, what will be different for you when we're done?

Carol: My guess is that there will have been some kind of a shift for me in my being able to see the choices, of being able to do something differently that I'm not able to do now, and I think that's going to come from some kind of a shift that I'm going to have to make. And I don't know what that is.

Jill: Okay, but you do know that it's buried in you.

Carol: Yeah, yeah. I'm real sure about that.

Jill: (*I had two ideas in mind here. One was to pace her model of the world, particularly the notion of something being buried, and I somehow also wanted to pace and include the other part of the system, her son, who was not present. Keeping in mind "buried" and "son," I asked myself, "What does this remind me of?" Here's the answer I found.*) As a child I liked to read about buried treasure, but I never actually dug up any. But I did do a lot of digging in my back yard that had to do with a turtle. A turtle that died, and burying him and finding out about different states of (laughter) decomposition with my next-door neighbor. It was a lot of fun. . . . How old is your son?

Carol: 11.

Jill: He's 11. And why are you wanting to work with this now?

Carol: It's been obvious since second grade that he hasn't made much of an effort. I believe that he's very intelligent, and so a part of my belief was that when he found something that interested him he would make a shift to start getting the skills. And lately I feel that belief may be an error, because I've had occasion to meet adults recently who are operating at almost a level of incompetence because, like, their strategies were never developed. . . .

Jill: So one of the things that is happening is that you had this idea it just had to do with finding something he wanted to do and he'd do it?

Carol: Yeah.

Jill: And now you've seen some things that have led you to believe he might find some things he'd really like to do, and not be able to do them?

Carol: Um hmm.

Jill: And how does that change things for you?

Carol: It changes things because I realize the belief I had is likely missing something, but I don't know quite, even though I've seen that, I don't know how to deal with it any differently. I don't know how to approach him. And I don't want to give him messages like, "You're not okay the way you are. You have to learn how to read because that's what I want from you." Because that's not it. I know that. But I'm, if he came back to me, like, if he heard that, that would be real upsetting to me. Because if I had the impression I was trying to tell him, "I want this for you because it will be better for you in the future," and him coming back to me that that's not what he heard, I don't know what I'd do. . . .

Jill: Well, what's more important to you, that somehow you're heard the way that you want to be? If you believe that your support and what you want to say is being heard by your son, and he doesn't learn to read, will that be okay with you?

Carol: I'm sorry. I think because it's real important, I'm not getting it. You're saying it, but it's not going in.

Jill: Well, let's take a minute. . . . Okay, so it's possible that somebody can say something to somebody and it doesn't go in because it's really important?

Carol: Um hmm . . . yeah. . . . In fact my experience has been if it's real important there's a real good chance that it won't— the first time at least.

Jill: Yeah, yeah. Do you think that could happen with your son?

Carol: Oh yeah, yeah, absolutely.

Jill: So, in this particular circumstance, how will you know if you're a good mother?

Carol: For me I think it would be if I can somehow be able to communicate to him that there's a difference between not being able to read and not being a good person. That it's a skill that it would benefit him to have, not me. It wouldn't benefit me if he could read. It would benefit him. And it's part of my job to help him do that. I mean, if I hear stuff like, "Oh, I wish I were good enough the way I am. Oh Mom." If that came up that would be real upsetting.

Jill: (*I wanted to suggest the idea that her son's immediate response may be different from the meaning he makes of her guidance in the long run. I asked myself, "How do I know this idea (the one just stated) is valid? What is convincing evidence to me that it is so?" Here's what I found.*) When I was in high school, we had to pick electives that we were going to take besides the regular subjects. And I always wanted to take art and Spanish. And our parents had to sign our course requests. My father always said I had to take Latin or French and academic subjects, certainly not art or Spanish. They had to be very academic subjects.

You know, as a social worker in the city of Chicago, Spanish would have been really great to have. And in college what I decided I wanted to go into was art criticism.

And I've been through different stages about what my father's rules meant. You know, in high school I was just angry because my friends all took art. Later on, when I got more interested in some of those things, actually interested, I was angry about not getting an earlier start. And only later did it become clearer and clearer what it was that he thought he was trying to provide.

And it's always a hard thing to know whether the intentions that somebody has are more important than the actual effects because you can't know exactly what is going to happen. There are articles all the time about film stars and singers who drop out of school against everybody's protest, and they end up doing great.

Carol: Something tells me that . . . he'd really like it if that happened. I mean, that'd be great. You know, he wouldn't have to worry about what he'd do to earn a living or any of that stuff that's not fun. He could be a professional drummer or whatever.

Jill: Now, how long would it take you to feel like you were a good mother if he didn't worry about any of that, so . . . that gap of time before he became a professional drummer?

Carol: I don't know. I guess I have a belief that's real limited. I mean, the chances of that happening are so slim. I really don't feel like I would be doing what I'm supposed to be doing if I just thought that that might happen.

Jill: Oh I agree, completely. The chances are very slim. But what I'm saying is if it actually did happen would you, . . . how would you feel?

(There's a bit of tape missing at this point.)

Jill: (*I wanted to suggest the idea that helping her child achieve something of long-term significance may be more important than whether he is pleased with her at that moment. I also wanted to access an attitude of commitment. This story answers the questions: "How did I learn this?" and "When have I experienced the state or attitude?"*) I went through a struggle as a young therapist. The terms I thought about it in at that time were being able to confront people. There were things I thought it would be important for me to say, but I was afraid to say them because of how my clients might feel. The thing that made a difference for me was to have an idea of what someone really wanted for themselves, underneath everything. (*I wanted to embed a message here that at some level he really does want to read. I underscored this message by repeating, "They want [whatever it was]."*) I would make it into a concise phrase: "They want (whatever it was)." Then I could repeat that phrase over and over in my mind during the therapy session. "They want (whatever it was). They want (whatever it was)." And that would remind me that something was very important to them, more important than whether they liked me at that moment. So I would go on repeating that phrase to myself until I could go ahead and say whatever will make the difference. (*"Go ahead and say whatever will make the difference" is an embedded suggestion to Carol.*) And it was hard.

The thing that made it a little bit easier was having the experience a couple of times of people being angry, and saying later how helpful it was for them to be able to be angry at me and still hear what they needed to move ahead.

And the question I had to keep asking myself was, "Are you committed enough to sacrifice being liked at that moment?" (*This is an embedded question to Carol.*)

Carol: Um hmm, yeah.

Jill: For me as a therapist, it's the hardest thing.

Carol: Um hmm. I really see what you're saying about keeping in mind what they want from other times. I know one of his real big interests is that he loves to build models of rollercoasters. And that was what he wanted for Christmas, a thing that builds rollercoasters and you take it apart and rebuild them all kinds of ways, and curlicue them and all that kind of stuff. That was the only thing he wanted. (*I was very surprised at this response. I wanted to suggest that underneath it all, her son wants to read or at least he wants the opportunities that reading will bring. The meaning she made of my embedded message was that he wants rollercoasters. This meaning, one I could never have predicted, turns out to be very significant.*) And that's what he does for fun. He gets out papers. Other boys draw race cars. He draws rollercoasters. He likes, you know, seeing how he can put in thrills and chills and all that kind of stuff.

Jill: And he's willing to go through the ups and downs, too?

Carol: Oh yeah, yeah. He loves it. I mean, like he could have had three or four little toys for Christmas. And he knew he was only going to get the one because it cost exactly what we had to spend, and that's what he wanted.

So, in fact I guess I kind of lost sight of the fact that he does have goals for his future, and they're going to include the skill, and I wasn't seeing that. So by broadening the way I look at what I know he wants to do, that may give me the courage to go ahead and pursue it with that goal in mind.

Jill: (*I wanted to suggest the idea that the sole criterion of keeping someone else from feeling bad is not enough to base decisions on. This is another way of coming at the intention I had for the last story, that helping her child achieve something of long-term significance may be more important than whether he is pleased with her at that moment. The questions I asked myself were, "What will or could happen if Carol does not learn or believe the idea? What does that remind me of?"*) It's interesting talking about relationships with parents, because I keep thinking a lot about mine.

I don't know if I remember this story or someone told me this story, but apparently at the age of three I told my father that when I grew up I was going to marry the first man who asked me, because it would probably really hurt his feelings if I didn't. He told me that wasn't a good idea. But that was all he said. (*I wanted to suggest the idea that people have the resources to handle hard feelings. The question was, "How has someone else learned this or how could someone else learn this?"*)

And I remember that years and years and years later I wished he had said more. I was working in a school for kids kicked out of public school and a teacher I was friends with there was having this tremendous struggle about her marriage. She was pretty unhappy after five years of marriage. In fact, she spent a whole year being really unhappy and also, just as much as she was unhappy, she really believed somewhere inside of her, strongly, that her husband would just fall apart without her, that he needed her. She really believed it, and she spent a year struggling with that. And finally she realized that it was her only life.

I fully believe that if she had two lives she would have just given him that one. But since it was her only one, she really "selfishly" decided to go ahead and get out of that marriage. And a really amazing thing happened. Actually, nobody was amazed but her. He did great!

He was so much better off without her, it was amazing. All the kinds of things that she worried about, all the things she thought she was taking care of for him, all the difficulties that she thought she was supporting and making things okay . . . he found a way on his own to go ahead and take care of those things, and he was really happy. Much quicker than she was, as a matter of fact.

It took her a number of years to sort of struggle to a new identity. But he did just fine.

Carol: I like that story because it's . . . I guess I really do believe that the primary energy that I spend was supporting them.

Jill: And I think they need that from you. And I don't think you're the only one with buried treasure.

Carol: That's true.

Jill: So where are we now?

Carol: The point about knowing that he has a broader goal—that I sort of deleted that information. That kind of gave me the courage to take a chance on maybe having him not take it well.

I wasn't willing to take that risk. It would have gone against my "supportive mother" model.

Not only that, now that I see it, I created a family situation where I don't usually have to do that. Because it's uncomfortable for me, I think, I hadn't realized that before, I've created a family situation where confrontation doesn't come up very often. We cooperate a lot.

Jill: That's great.

Carol: Yeah. And when it comes up, I find it . . . it doesn't fit my style.

Jill: It might be an important thing for your kids to have a little experience with that for when they go out and meet other people.

Carol: Oh yeah. True. I'm feeling like a new willingness to be . . . courage keeps coming up, like it's a real courageous thing for me to step out of a model I've been in for so long. When they were babies I supported them on my own . . . and, yeah, in fact, I'm seeing that that behavior served us real well. And I knew that I had a belief that needed to be looked at, but I didn't have any idea that it would really, like, shake my whole way of thinking.

I feel a willingness to try that. Before, it was like fear, and actually *wanting* to manipulate.

Jill: What can you do to support yourself in trying some different things?

Carol: One thing I constantly tell them is that they're in their teenage years, and what they're doing as teenagers is learning, and that this is a learning time for them. And I wasn't including myself in that.

Jill: Life is a learning time.

Carol: Yeah . . . yeah. And my skills in mothering small children—I had years and years to practice those, and now it's time to develop a new skill—but I think for myself, I'm very outgoing really, and developing new skills is something that's real important to me. So if I can keep it as developing a new skill, reminding myself that you won't do it perfectly the first time, and if you don't do it perfectly the first time, you will not be devastated.

Jill: (*I wanted to suggest the idea that some things are worth taking risks for and others are not. I ask myself, "What illus-*

trates this idea?") I'm glad you said that. Because earlier, when you were talking about taking a chance, taking a risk, I was thinking about . . . I was working with somebody who was a trader in the market.

Carol: Yeah.

Jill: And he had in one transaction lost a tremendous amount of money. And the system that he's operating under, he's sort of being supported by — it's a company that hires young traders and pays them a salary to trade for this larger conglomerate. And so he lost all this money in one day, one transaction, a tremendous amount of money. And the person who was his manager was extremely upset, and began talking to him about taking risks.

My client said he didn't understand how this guy who was smoking three packs of cigarettes a day could talk to him about risks, because where was that going to get you in the long run? . . . and that it seemed to him that if you lose a lot of money in a single transaction, at least it was a single one, and you can learn something about next time. So that the next day you could do something different, but the risk of three packs of cigarettes wasn't going to pay off in any way that he knew about in the years to come.

Carol: Um hmm . . .

Jill: So I liked it. So when you talked about risk, I was going, "Hmm . . . do you realize that risks are uncertain?"

Carol: Um hmm.

Jill: And I was glad to find out that you did. And it looks to me that you feel okay about moving ahead.

Carol: Yeah, I do now. I can see that the kids aren't the only ones in this time of the next three or four years who have learning to do, you know, I'm included in that. And I wasn't seeing it before. It's like, "I'm a parent, I learned it already!" (Both laugh.) . . . No-o-o-o-o-o!

All of a sudden now I'm feeling real empathy for fear that they feel of being teenagers and learning new things, and I had missed that, I had forgotten how fearful it feels to take a step past where you are real comfortable . . . um hmm . . . yeah.

Jill: "A step past where you're really comfortable . . . "

Carol: Yeah, that's a scary step to take, especially when you're not really sure where your foot's going to come down.

   We've been through a lot together as a group, and they know I don't do everything perfectly, and yet we're still together as a group and I really trust that we're resourceful enough that if I mess up once, or don't do it well the first time . . .

Jill: Or even the second time!

Carol: . . . or the second time, oh yeah, you're right. And I need to remember that it's just that, and to try, and if it doesn't come out well the first time, the overall goal I still—which I had deleted completely before—and it's real clear to me now.

Jill: Good. And I also think that that kind of support that you've always given is important to get, to keep for yourself, so that you can feel supported in learning something new.

Carol: Yeah, learning experiences. If I remember that this is a learning experience for me, I can cut myself some slack.

Jill: Yeah . . . okay . . . is there anything else that's important right now?

Carol: Um . . . at this point I don't know. I think I'm going to have to roll up my sleeves and get in there and see, and then see what else comes up . . . but right now I'm feeling a strength to go ahead and give it a shot, whereas before it was all . . . hell. As a matter of fact, I found myself wishing that I had another adult whom I could draw on so that I really wouldn't have to see it.

Jill: You do, it's your buried treasure.

Carol: Hmm . . .

Jill: I always think of, "You never have to be alone, because you always have your unconscious mind."

Carol: Yeah, that . . . (laughs) . . . could be . . . I think I can . . . I don't know quite exactly what I'm going to do first, but I feel like I'm in a position where I have the resources now to go ahead and do something, rather than nothing, which is what I was doing before.

Jill: No, you weren't doing nothing. You were creating the support that will allow the hard stuff to be heard.

Annotated Transcript II: A Hypnotherapy Demonstration

This demonstration took place near the end of a five-day residential workshop on Ericksonian approaches to hypnosis and psychotherapy. The form of this session is quite different from that in the first transcript. In that session, the metaphoric work is woven throughout. In this session there is a clearer demarcation between the information gathering and the interventive work.

One way of describing the first session is that information gathering alternates rather seamlessly with interventive metaphors; Carol gives a piece of information in terms of a goal, a difficulty, or an idea and I respond with a story suggesting either a different idea or a state that might be useful in relation to what she has expressed. She then gives another piece of information and I respond with another story. In the following session, the information gathering occurs primarily in the first half of the session and the stories are told in the second half. It is as though I store up all of the information in the first half and respond to it only in the second half. In annotating the stories I refer back to the information from the first half that I utilize or address in any particular story.

Melissa had requested this session privately. She spoke with me briefly about what she hoped to accomplish prior to the demonstration. Some of the information gathering is deleted, but the hypnotic work is included in full. The transcript begins several minutes into the session.

Melissa: Anytime I'm in a new situation where there is some type of learning involved I'm terrified. Even though I can say to myself, "You've had successful experiences," it does not hook up. (*Here I make a mental note that Melissa does have successful experiences. It is just a matter of hooking them up.*) And I would like to be able to be in a classroom, have a new experience like here and not be terrified. I didn't read until I was in the fourth grade. I can remember in kindergarten being very successful; in fact, it was boring. (*This is an example of a resourceful context that I store to utilize later.*) In fact, I dreaded going back to school because it was so dumb. And then we were getting reading books. The teacher ran out of reading books and because I was always five miles ahead of

everybody else, she didn't give me one. And she started explaining what words were and what letters were and it looked
like Chinese to me. I could see no difference between "what,"
"when," "why." I didn't know when a "w" was upside down or
wrongside out or sideways, and I had this tremendous panic
which lasted through the fourth grade. And then in the fourth
grade I was able to read.

Jill: What do you think happened at that time?

Melissa: I don't know. I have no idea. Except that I had a teacher
who was very good and said to me, "This is going to come to
you, and just relax. Before you leave this classroom you will
be able to read." (*This statement seems very significant to me
because we are now in a classroom again and Melissa again
needs a message that she can accomplish her goal. I utilize
this statement in the second half of the session.*) One day I
was following along and all of a sudden I realized I recognized
the words. From that point I read. It was probably sixth grade
before I really caught up. After that I had books stuffed everywhere: in the towels, in the liners of the wastebaskets. Every
room that I worked in I read in. My mother was really neat
about it. She pretended like she didn't know I was sneaking
books all the time. (*This is an interesting metaphor about
secret growth and development. I utilize the concept of secret
growth later in the session.*) I spent years catching up in reading, but the kind of dread in the schoolroom learning situation has never changed.

Jill: So even in the rest of fourth grade and the fifth grade?

Melissa: Every morning I became real hyperactive because I can
remember being so anxious. It was after World War II, so I
would put myself in a straitjacket and I'd say, "Now if you're
going to move you'll get shot," so I could stay still. (*I am
struck by the straitjacket metaphor and hope that Melissa
will free herself of it in this experience.*) And that is how I did
it.

Jill: What experiences of learning have you had that were pleasurable? What if it's nonacademic? A sport?

Melissa: Parenting, anything connected with early learning, sew-
ing, cooking. I am an excellent walker. (*Here are other resourceful contexts that I note for later use.*)

Jill: (Asks some questions about learning to sew and cook, and Melissa maintains that she didn't learn them. She just always knew how to do them.) How did you learn to parent?

Melissa: Umm . . . reading.

Jill: (laughs)

Melissa: (laughs) That's interesting, isn't it? Reading.

Jill: Uh huh. And you enjoy that.

Melissa: Oh yes.

Jill: Now, what do you think is different about that situation than if you were going to learn some new skill, some new academic skill?

Melissa: Parenting was done just with my husband, and I never felt like I was getting a report card. I never felt like I was being judged, which was different from how I felt in class. (*I note that being in a learning situation with her husband is an exception to her usual experience of learning situations. Later I suggest having someone like her husband with her in her mind in learning situations.*) In the classroom I had very angry people because everybody felt I should be able to do it.

Jill: So in this workshop—you mentioned workshop as a place where you also felt terrified—is there an element of getting judged?

Melissa: Sure.

Jill: Who does that?

Melissa: Intellectually I say myself, but there's always comparison. Everybody here works differently, has different techniques. I'm always looking at how do I measure up? What am I doing or not doing? (*Melissa is describing a pattern of comparing herself to others. Later I pace this pattern and suggest other ways to use it that she may want to try instead.*) But to begin with, it's the feeling of not being able to understand a word they're saying. As that changes, my anxiety is reduced.

Jill: So if you compare the experience of being in this workshop to the experience of learning to parent, what would be the difference?

Melissa: I never felt that parenting was performing. (*In the second half of the session I tell a story about someone learning to change performance into teaching with comfort.*)

Jill: Okay, and the performing has to do with making a comparison?

Melissa: (nods)

Jill: So if you were to sign up at one of these learning exchanges where you just got one person who was teaching you how to do hypnotherapy, do you think you could have the kind of experience with this as you did with learning to parent?

Melissa: Probably, but the one difference is that I also learn by doing and I learn by watching and I would cheat myself if I were learning just from one person instead of learning from everybody. Because everybody here is a teacher. (*I like Melissa's notion of everbody being a teacher. I keep in mind the idea of accessing a resourceful state in Melissa by reminding her that she too is a teacher.*)

Jill: What's your expectation of what's going to happen today?

Melissa: That somehow a piece is going to come together for me. (*One of the meanings I hear in this statement is "peace is going to come for me." Another has to do with integration of different pieces of her.*) So I don't have to continually be six years old when I walk into a new experience.

Jill: If you walked in at your age, would that do it? I mean, so that no matter what else happened if you were able to walk in at your age?

Melissa: I think so. (*I believe that people know what they need. When Melissa reveals that this would be an important symbolic experience, I decide to facilitate it. This occurs near the end of the session.*)

Jill: Okay. I can think of a lot of different directions to go, but the one that is always the most interesting or seems like the most essential to me to begin with is wondering what's useful about what you're already doing. And I wonder what it is that you do now to sort of protect yourself or guard against or respond to the terror. . . . Now, I don't know if that is something you can . . .

Melissa: I dissociate. That's definitely what I do.

Jill: How do you do it?

Melissa: Well, when the pain gets real great I just separate from myself, and if like, signing up for this workshop, the only motivation was that I knew I needed it. And the fact that it had to do with working with clients made it legitimate to go through that kind of pain, but I absolutely had no feeling about it. I mean I disconnected. I pretended it wasn't going to happen, until I came back from seeing clients. And then I packed and came. So I mean I didn't entertain. . . . I didn't think about it. I just completely walled it off. (*The metaphor of walling it off is one I utilize later in a story.*)

(In a deleted segment Melissa describes her process of dissociating and how it works for her.)

Jill: Now, what I would like you to do is, back at the time you were really thinking about it [coming to the workshop], checking out things, really thinking about it, I want you to just for a moment, to let yourself not be walled out, but to also know that this means, I'm going to be going through some terror. And to wonder how the terror is useful. I don't want you to really completely have that experience, but just sort of as though you were putting a toe in a swimming pool, to check out the water. Find out something about it, but not commit yourself to being plunged all the way in. (Melissa closes her eyes and goes into herself. Time passes.) Wonder what's useful. Just wonder. (Time passes. Melissa begins to cry.)

Looked like at least a foot to me. I don't think it was just a toe. What was it like? (Melissa has difficulty answering.) Take all the time you want. There is no hurry. Take a deep breath. There's no straitjacket and no hurry. (*I am referring back to Melissa's saying that in the fourth and fifth grades she would mentally put herself into a straitjacket to keep still.*)

Melissa: No, I don't feel a straitjacket.

Jill: What was it like?

Melissa: It is a feeling of like you're being torn to bits. That everything that you think is real is gone.

Jill: I think you've been very, very wise to dissociate. I think you should keep doing that until you have a much better way of handling the situation.

Melissa: What I want are some ways. I don't apologize for dissociating. I mean I know that is good. It keeps me safe and grounded, but I do want other ways to handle it.

Jill: You said that everything you know is true is going to be gone. When have you been able to go into a learning experience without that feeling?

Melissa: Probably until I was six. I know until I was six I had a tremendous amount of confidence. (*Early childhood is a resourceful area that I utilize later in a story.*) I don't think there was anything in the world I didn't think I could do. I had real good nurturing, good parenting, all the little things I needed were there. When I started first grade, not being able to read got translated in everything I did. In this classroom, in this school, with peers. I don't think it changed my family, which is really good. (*I note two things here. One is that her relationship with her family has remained positive—another resource. The second is the unusual use of the word "translated." Later I link "translate" to new, positive associations.*)

Jill: So when you say that if you were to allow yourself to experience being terrified at the beginning of any new learning situation, one of the things that happens is this tremendous fear that the places that you're grounded, the reality you have, is going to be gone.

Melissa: Completely wiped out.

Jill: Your self-image, your beliefs about your relationships, the structure of your world . . .

Melissa: Not completely. With my work, with my peers, and of course that means with my clients and in my teaching, but I'm not terrified that something is going to change in my personal relationship with my husband or my children. That part I always feel pretty safe. (*Again, resourceful relationships. I also discover that Melissa teaches.*)

Jill: That's good.

Melissa: So it's not universal.

Jill: No, it's not universal. Okay, so, if you were going to decide right now what we would proceed to do this afternoon, what would you decide?

Melissa: That I would like to work on some other way of handling that transition as I come into a new learning situation.

Jill: Do you have any idea of what that would be?

Melissa: No. I knew you were going to ask that and I was going to sit here and say, "I have no idea."

Jill: Well, you probably would have done it already if you had an idea. It is real important to me that you get a *piece* of what you want. . . . (*Throughout the following transcript, when I mention "piece," I am offering the embedded suggestion, "peace," by setting it off with pauses and saying it slower and in a softer voice tone than the words surrounding it.*) Because it seems like a really important issue, and I'd like to see it change in a lot of different ways. And I believe that you've demonstrated in many ways that you have everything it takes to be able to really enjoy being in any situation you want to be in. (*"Really enjoy being in any situation you want to be in" is an embedded suggestion.*) And yet, there are so many things, so many possibilities that I was feeling really nervous, with all the information, sort of overwhelmed, flooded, too much. Until I realized something that was very reassuring to me. And that is that I don't have to teach you anything. That you can teach yourself what's important for you to learn. (*Here I am referring back to two things that Melissa said. One is her statement that everyone is a teacher. I want to make sure that the idea includes her in this therapy context. Also, she did mention that she teaches. I want to access the teaching part of her for the work that follows.*)

Melissa: That's good.

Jill: Now that provides a lot of relief for me, but you can also relax, don't worry, because you will learn everything you need to learn before you leave this room. . . . (*The last statement is a paraphrase of what Melissa's fifth grade teacher said. We already know that Melissa links it with her finally learning to read.*) Now I don't know if you want a trance now or a trance later (*Melissa talked about her not reading being translated into various aspects of her life in many ways. Throughout the session I attempt to associate "translate," "translator," and "translation" with various positive meanings.*) because I think that the learning could occur at several different levels. I don't know which are important or when, but I want to establish a kind of a rule, that is that you be the teacher here and that I be a facilitator. So what do you think . . . a trance now . . . a trance later . . . a trance not at all?

Melissa: I think a trance would help.

Jill: Okay. So, you have experienced trances before in the last few days, is that right?

Melissa: Uh huh.

Jill: What was the most helpful for you in terms of going into trance? (Pause) Because everybody's different.

Melissa: I don't think about it. See, I didn't learn it. I just do it.

Jill: You think that there is a distinction?

Melissa: No. I don't know.

Jill: You don't need to think about it now either. If you would prefer to just do it we can bypass this. (*I am referring to a formal hypnotic induction.*)

Melissa: I'd just as soon just do it!

Jill: All right. Now if anything that I say interferes with your just doing it, feel free to ignore me, okay?

Melissa: Okay. That's a deal.

Jill: (*The idea I have in mind is to use learning hypnosis as a metaphor for all learning. I specifically hope to suggest the idea that she knows more about her learning than anyone else could and that she can select what is important and be in charge.*) Because I'm going to talk for awhile. And we have only talked a few times, so I don't know you that well. But you know yourself that well. So if I don't say something that you wish I would say, you can feel free to hear it said. . . . And if I say something that you wish I didn't say, you can pretend that I didn't say it. . . . If I say something that seems really important, you can just keep saying that over and over, because I probably won't say very many important things in a row. . . . I don't think there's any such thing as missing something in a situation like this, because only certain things are important for you and nobody is as good as you in knowing what those important things are. Just as there are a lot of *pieces* to the situation we have been talking about, and you know the next *piece* that is important to put in place, I don't know if your unconscious mind is listening to what I'm saying while your conscious mind is identifying the next *piece* to go in place or your unconscious mind is identifying that *piece* while your conscious mind is listening to what I'm saying. . . . It doesn't really matter which part does what because all the whole of you can create the experience that's important,

without thinking about it, by simply allowing it to occur.
. . . Many times when you begin to enter trance you don't
know just where you're going to go, you don't know just what
you're going to do or what you're going to find that's important. I'd like for you to do something just for you in the trance
that you can keep hidden, if you'd like.

(*I want to pace and acknowledge Melissa's strategy of dissociating and at the same time suggest the idea that even
though she has dissociated in this context she has continued
to grow and develop. I think of utilizing Melissa's metaphor
of a wall to represent dissociation, so I ask myself, "How can
I illustrate the idea of continued growth and development
behind a wall?" I remember a childhood story. It seems particularly fitting because it is about secrets, and secrets have
positive meaning for Melissa. She kept her books secret and
hidden as she was catching up in reading.*)

When I was little, my favorite book was *The Secret Garden*.
I don't know if you read it, but there was a garden, a walled
garden that a little girl who had lost her parents spent some
time in with a little boy who thought that he was very sickly,
although he became healthier every day in the garden. And
there was also a very ruddy boy who knew everything about
planting seeds, making them grow. And so the three spent all
this time in a garden that had been locked for years and years.
No one knew about it for a long time. I never understood just
why that appealed to me so much. I think it was in about the
first grade.

(*I have two things in mind. The first is to pace Melissa's
pattern of comparison and judgment leading to dissociation.
She has described how she compares herself to other people
in learning situations and then dissociates. The second thing I
want to do is access an attitude in which self knowledge is
more important than others' evaluations. I ask myself, "When
have I experienced this attitude?" and remember an experience I had in the first grade.*) One of the things I discovered at
that time was there are a lot of different ways to look at
something. . . . I had a workbook sheet, and it had pictures
of people, and you were supposed to circle sometimes the
right hand, sometimes the left hand, sometimes the right

foot, sometimes the left foot. It was something that seemed pretty easy, just sitting there circling these different places on the body, but some people were pretty uncomfortable about it. And Karen Weinhaus and I both circled the left hand when we were supposed to circle the right hand, and mine was just wrong. The teacher explained to Karen Weinhaus that the person was turned around, that's why she did the wrong hand. And I heard her making that explanation and I wondered why she thought that Karen knew, but didn't understand the difference when somebody is turned around, and she just thought I got it wrong. . . . And so I decided to keep my distance a little bit. Because a teacher can read you wrong, and it's important to know in you a way to read you right, even if you have to keep it a secret. (*"Know in you a way to read you right" is an embedded suggestion.*) There are different levels being on the inside and different memories on different levels.

(*I want to suggest the idea that resources from Melissa's past can be used in her present. She has said that until she was six she didn't think there was anything in the world she couldn't do. She was successful in kindergarten. She had positive experiences of learning to cook, sew, and parent. Early in the session she said that she had successful experiences that didn't hook up. I am interested in hooking them up and I believe that the confidence from her past can be useful now. I ask myself, "How do I know that this idea is valid?" An experience I had with Paul Carter is the answer.*)

A number of years ago I was a demonstration subject in a hypnosis workshop. And the demonstration was supposed to be about hand levitation. I was real interested in hand levitation because I was already teaching hypnosis at that time. And my hands always stayed firmly on my legs, which I saw as a problem because I wanted to be able to do it. I looked around and other people could have their hand lift automatically, have their fingers jerk. My hand stayed firmly on my legs, so I volunteered to be a demonstration subject. (*I am pacing Melissa's practice of comparing herself to others in learning situations.*) I sat at the front of the room. And the hypnotist spoke on and on about childhood, about all the things that children play in the long days before school ever starts . . . jump rope . . . dice . . . bicycles . . . chalk on concrete . . . pick up sticks . . . cards . . . but not really cards yet . . . toys inside of cereal boxes . . . jump ropes . . . balls. . . . (*Although I began with the notion of suggesting an idea, I spend a lot of time here accessing states having to do with play, pleasure, and mastery.*) And I wondered when he'd get to the point. All this talk about playing. After a while there were some words about moving your hand up. And I wasn't sure what really happened because my eyes were closed. Other people said my hand went up. And I still don't know for sure, but I did spend a lot of time thinking about those wonderful feelings of a four-year-old . . . the wonderful experience of the world being all yours . . . the mastery of playing . . . the excitement about outside. . . . And so we had the experience, and when it was over I felt pretty good, nice feeling, comfort. I wasn't so sure about that hand levitation, but the comfort was nice. (*The story up to this point includes indirect suggestions for hand levitation. Utilizing Melissa's pattern of comparison, if she does have a hand levitation and compares herself to me in the story, she is accomplishing more than I did. If she doesn't have a hand levitation, she is doing what I did. Ideas expressed already in the metaphor are "if you don't accomplish something you can request help" and "you can enjoy yourself even when you don't learn what you set out to." I am finding so many opportunities to suggest relevant ideas that I still haven't gotten to "confidence from one's past can be useful in the present," the idea that prompted this whole story.*) And I went back to my room and spent some time with a friend over lunch . . . did a number of things . . . had a long talk . . . and a number of hours later I reached up to touch my glasses, just to adjust them, and I discovered my glasses weren't there. I looked around. No glasses. I looked at my watch and I probably had been without glasses for about three hours. So I went back to where the demonstration was, and my glasses had been sitting there. That was my guess that they must have been there. At that time I always took off my glasses to go into trance, so that nothing will interfere with that trance . . . (*"Nothing will interfere with that trance" is an embedded suggestion.*) And an interesting thing happened. I had never spent that long without glasses. Sometimes after that I could see perfectly. And my eyesight got better . . . and better . . . and better. . . . And I kept getting glasses with milder and milder prescriptions. And I began to understand that my eyes were fine when I was four. (*Here I am finally getting to the idea that prompted this story.*) And I learned something just from reviewing those times that became translated into physiology. And those eyes changed permanently. The same person you were at four knows some things then . . . can't really lose them . . . they're always there. There's a certain *peace* in that awareness.

(*I have the idea of suggesting a new pattern of bringing nurturance and appreciation from other contexts into areas where she is fearful. I am remembering that Melissa did not experience these difficulties with her husband and family and I think that their appreciation of her must be a resource that can be utilized here. I ask myself, "How has someone else learned this?"*)

Now about that time I had a student who had a tremendous amount to share, but whenever he stood in front of the room he was nervous. (*I use the phrase "stood in front of the room" because Melissa conceptualizes learning situations in terms of performance. I want to access and work with that context and state.*) That makes it very difficult to be a teacher. And so we practiced standing in front of the room. He could see out of the corner of the eye a nurturing smile from someone who really believes in you. (*"See out of the corner of the eye a nurturing smile from someone who really believes in you" is an embedded suggestion.*) And so practice standing in front of the room with that nurturing smile, and letting go of some of the sadness with the nurturing. Practice that over and over until you realize, people who love you are always there. Because it's only in one superficial sense that they're one place and you're another. And one thing you can really learn deeply, in a trance, is that space and time can be experienced a lot of different ways. A 40-year-old can have a four-year-old's confidence. You can be one place and have the love there of someone only physically far away. And so you can experience a lot of different things as you walk into a room. Now you've had the experience just a few days ago, one side of experience, preparing to be here, walking into this room here. . . . And I'd like you to do it in a different way, in the comfort of a trance. (*Melissa has said that if she doesn't have to continually be six years old when she walks into a new experience, it will make a big difference.*) I'd like to have you walk into the room knowing full well that you're a teacher and no one can teach you the material but you.

(*I want to suggest the idea that integration of the parts of herself, rather than dissociation, will bring her more peace. I ask myself, "What illustrates this idea?"*)

We were at a conference about a year ago in Brussels. And the conference was in both English and French. And so everybody wore headphones because there were translations. And it was a little disconcerting because sometimes someone would tell a joke and only half the room would laugh. And a little bit later on a more serious note, the rest of the room would start laughing because they just got the translation. And so it took a while to adjust. But one of the things that began to occur was a kind of understanding that could never have happened in just one language . . . a coming together of cultures and beliefs . . . in a way that was very moving. And I do believe that intermingling, that translation, that meeting of the parts, is what ultimately brings *peace*.

(*I want to suggest the idea that instead of trying to do everything, Melissa can do only what seems important to her. In asking myself, "What would be evidence of the idea's usefulness to Melissa?" I remember that she teaches. This experience that Gene and I had teaching seems to flow from the last story and fit.*)

Just a year ago, when we were teaching in Germany, we had to go real slow because people understood the language at different levels. One woman was translating. Other people were trying to understand on their own in a second language. And we learned more from teaching that workshop than any one before because we could get just the essential things . . . really focus on what is important and what is needed. You can choose that . . . you know that . . . you can feel that . . .

So I'd like to have you, in the privacy of your mind, in the comfort of the trance, delight yourself, surprise yourself, by walking into the room knowing completely that you're a teacher and that what there is to learn, only you can teach yourself. And from that position you can look back at a first grader with an incredible amount of courage and determination and appreciate the bravery, appreciate the persistance, notice how much strength she has, and watch all that she went through for all those years. . . . Because in just a little bit, I'm going to ask you to teach her that she really can relax now, (*"Relax now" is an embedded suggestion.*) that she really has moved beyond that point, that she really can let go, (*"Let go" is an embedded suggestion.*) that she really can trust her own abilities . . . that she was read wrong, but she knows how to read right now. And so as you watch her, as a teacher, I'd like for you to decide just how you can teach her that she has a lot of confidence in that four-year-old self, a lot of maturity in that grown up self, and it's time to let go . . . that it's safe to feel . . . that it's okay to know . . . you really can learn. . . . There's a lot of different ways to make comparisons. An important one is to look into your past and to see how far you've come. And it's equally important to realize that when your students compare themselves to you, they know they've got a long way to go, but you can still appreciate them.

And so when you're ready, in your mind's eye, I want you to teach that little girl that it really is okay now . . . that the world is solid . . . that you'll be with her. . . . And translate for her what she needs to know. . . . Comfort her until you know that she feels the *peace*, until you can feel . . . and see . . . and know in your heart . . . that she has some *peace*. . . . And then, hold her in your arms . . . bring her inside, because she's you. And there's some violent energy in that part of you that will be very exciting to use in some new ways. (Long pause)

Just feel that *peace* and energy. Spend as much time in there as you need. You decide as you teach yourself the right sequence, the right timing. . . . You decide, and I'll be waiting out here when the time is right. . . . (Long pause.)

Melissa: I feel terrific. You sounded wonderful out there.

Jill: I did? I think it was probably your translation. So where are we now? Is this a *piece*?

Melissa: I think it's more than a piece because nothing seems very important. (laughs) I don't feel like I have a dangling participle or anything. I'm sure there might be one but I don't feel it. I'm not aware of it.

Jill: Good. So this feels like a good place to stop?

Melissa: Yah.

Jill: Okay.

7

STRATEGIES FOR
DEVELOPING CEREMONIES

CEREMONIES CAN TAKE a great variety of forms. They are useful in many contexts. At the most general level, they serve two purposes—to validate an occurrence and to promote change. *

For example, a husband and wife came to a session saying that they were now pleased with their relationship, having accomplished what they hoped for in therapy. The wife wanted to end therapy. The husband was uneasy with ending and suggested a checkup session a month or two later. Our friend Irene Esler, who was behind the mirror, had the idea that the couple could come back in a month, not for a checkup, but for a celebration of their relationship and of the changes they had made. She suggested that they design whatever sort of celebration they wanted and bring whatever was needed to carry it out (i.e. refreshments, decorations, proclamations). The purpose of this ritual was to recognize and celebrate something that had already happened. It validated changes the couple had already made.

Members of another couple wanted to get married, but both were intensely jealous. During the several years they had dated, they each also had gone out with other people. Now each was

*van der Hart (1983) makes a similar set of distinctions that he calls transition and continuity.

upset about the other's outside involvements over those years. The jealousy most often seized them when one was visiting the other's home and saw what they called "stuff" that reminded him or her of the other relationships. Over the course of several sessions they each gathered up and brought to our office all the stuff—letters, gifts, pictures, and the like—that had to do with other relationships. Then we asked them how they could use the stuff to demonstrate that the old relationships were over.

After considerable thought and discussion they buried the stuff at sunrise in a secluded spot deep in the woods.

In the burial ceremony they let their jealousy die. The sunrise symbolized a new beginning for their relationship. We worked with the couple in designing this ritual to help them change, to help them to let go of the old and begin a new way of relating.

Other ceremonies have aspects of both validation and change.

For example, we worked with a large family in which there had been multiple incest over a number of years. At the time we saw them, most of the children had left home and were living in different parts of the country. All family members did, however, participate in the therapy at some point. The ritual the family designed at the end of therapy was for each family member to go to the natural body of water nearest to him or her at an agreed upon time. At that time each person would take a stone and throw it into the water. This ceremony both symbolized the family's connectedness (they all did the same action at the same time) and validated their appropriate separateness (each member did the ceremony independently, wherever he or she was). The ceremony primarily recognized a new stability the family had achieved. However, each member's hurling away of a weight also symbolized and promoted a healing change.

Ceremonies can occur within therapy sessions, as did the couple's celebration of their relationship in the first example above, or outside of sessions, as did the burying of the "stuff" and the stone-throwing ritual.

In-session rituals have the advantage that a therapist is built in as an audience-participant. News of change automatically spreads beyond the client system. Some people accomplish more with the support and encouragement of a therapist.

The advantage of ceremonies that occur outside of sessions is that they can be carried out in the contexts in which validation or change is most needed. For example, a ritual in which parents agree to try out different parenting roles will probably be more meaningful if carried out over a prolonged period of time in their own home than if constrained by the time-space dimensions of a therapy session. Also, the changes are built into the system that desires them. The rituals symbolize people's autonomy, as they demonstrate that a therapist is not needed for change or validation to occur. Another benefit is redundancy. People experience the ceremony both as they perform it and when they report about it to the therapist.

Each of the ceremonies above was designed to be used a single time. Ceremonies may also be designed to be used repeatedly within a particular context and time frame.

A husband and wife were concerned with their irritability and bickering after only a year of marriage. A major time of friction for them was when they met at home after the end of a work day. More often than not, they were in different moods, had different expectations for the evening, and became irritated, amplifying rather than resolving their differences. Together we developed a ritualized meeting at the end of each work day that involved a hug and a brief exchange about their moods. They did this ceremony on work days for the month between sessions and surprised themselves with a tremendous decrease in irritability and bickering. After the formal time span for the ritual ended, they continued to greet each other, usually with a hug and often with an exchange of information about how each felt, but in a more casual manner. They were no longer doing a ritual; they had incorporated aspects of the ritual into their daily life.

Although the emphasis in ceremonies is on doing something, preparing for the ceremony, thinking about it, and remembering it afterwards all can contribute significantly to the meaning that ceremonies have.

One woman had never forgiven her mother for dying. By her perceptions, in the wake of her mother's death she went from being the daughter of the Brownie leader and room mother, the girl who lived in the favorite home for after school activities, to being an object of pity who lived with a gruff, critical father and never had the right clothes or toys.

In preparation for a ritual, she filled a box with symbols of the disappointments and losses that resulted from her mother's death. At a therapy session she stated that even though the box was not yet completed, some of the symbols were now striking her as humorous and that for the first time she had visited her mother's grave with feelings of sadness, but no pain. She was worried that so much was being resolved in the preparation, she wouldn't have enough feelings left for the ceremony of destroying the box.

For some people, preparation or thinking about a ritual serves the same purpose as actually doing it. For other people, preparation and reflection heighten the symbolic importance and feelings that accompany a ceremony. Both of these factors serve the purpose of extending involvement beyond the actual time of the ceremony. Talking about a ritual after its completion promotes re-experience of it and adds meaning to it.

Wonderful therapeutic ceremonies are described in the literature but there is much less written about how to arrive at those ceremonies.* Consequently, many therapists use the same basic rituals again and again, modeled on ceremonies they have read about or seen other clinicians use. However, while a therapist's favorite kind of ritual may be very useful at one stage of therapy for a particular family or individual, it may be irrelevant at another stage.

We find it useful to design ceremonies through strategies based on the purposes for which the ceremonies will be used. We have developed the following list of strategies for constructing rituals. Each strategy is based on a therapeutic purpose that lends itself to rituals. Each represents a thought avenue for coming up with a ceremony. We don't believe that this is an exhaustive list, but we hope it is a useful one.

1. Assign a ceremony with ambiguous function.
2. Punctuate time to untangle confusion.
3. Celebrate the uncelebrated.
4. Reframe the problem.
5. Metaphorically solve the problem.
6. Disrupt a problematic pattern.
7. Develop a needed resource.

*The two texts that we have found to be most helpful in designing ceremonies are *Rituals in Psychotherapy: Transition and continuity* (van der Hart, 1983) and *Rituals in Families and Family Therapy* (Imber-Black, Roberts, and Whiting, 1988).

8. Prescribe the presenting situation in metaphor.

In the following pages we will familiarize you with each of these strategies one by one. We think that the most important ones are those that seem strange to you. It's nice to recognize old friends on such a list, and it's even nicer to learn and apply a new strategy.

We don't refer to our list when working with people, and seldom when thinking about them, since at this point we tend to design rituals intuitively. However, we learned the patterns that shape our intuition by experimenting with these strategies one at a time. As our list has grown and changed we have occasionally taken a particular family and challenged ourselves to design several ceremonies, one utilizing each of the strategies, only then deciding whether any of them was actually appropriate for the family. It is more efficient and practical to match therapy goals at any particular point in time to one specific strategy.

For each strategy, we give case examples and offer guidelines for co-creating rituals. The strategies are not exclusive of one another. It is quite possible to end up with similar ceremonies even though you start with what seem to be very different strategies. While the results are similar in such cases, the thought processes leading to the results are not. Effective rituals often pursue several strategies at once.

Assign a Ceremony With Ambiguous Function

Sometimes in therapeutic story workshops, we tell a story that doesn't have any obvious moral or theme and ask participants what the story means. When people find several different meanings for the story, that story has worked much like a ceremony with ambiguous function.

People know a great deal about what would be meaningful and useful for them at a particular time, even if they don't know that they know it. This kind of ritual provides a context in which individuals and families can discover something important but unspecified. They are asked to do something specific that is presented as a meaningful task, but just what the meaning is is not apparent, and the meaning is not discussed by the therapist. The expectation is that people will find the meaning and discuss it with the therapist after the task is completed. Stephen and Carol Lankton (1986, p.143), who have done a great deal of work in this area, write, "The task ought to be specific but the purpose behind it ought to be ambiguous."*

Practice with this strategy will help you present all rituals as meaning-laden. We list it first because we believe that the magic of ceremonies is in the depth of meaning that participants find. It is important for therapists to discover that clients can and will find meaning without having meanings imposed on them.

We find that, if therapists convey to their clients that they can find something meaningful in the suggested actions, almost anything can serve as a ceremony. If they are then willing and ready to utilize whatever response people have to the ceremony, the interaction of the client's response and the therapist's response to the client's response can be therapeutic.

Even if people don't follow through and actually carry out the ceremony, they always do *something*. Creative therapists can usually find some way to utilize that something or learn from the information in it.

Designing and setting up an ambiguous function ritual requires three things:

1. Suggest actions and contexts that you deeply believe can be meaningful, even if you don't know how, ones that induce introspection and a sense of mystery, expectation, or awe.
2. Convey that belief congruently and confidently.
3. Employ the utilization principle to help people absorb every last bit of learning from their experiences.

Erickson expected almost everybody who came to see him in his later years to climb Squaw Peak. Leaving the nature of what they would find along the way intentionally ambiguous, he suggested that his visitors treat climbing Squaw Peak as an important ceremony. Although I(GC) first visited Phoenix a year after Erickson

*See Lankton and Lankton (1986), p. 136–152, for a more in-depth discussion of this material.

died, the invitation to the Squaw Peak ceremony was still so alive
that I accepted it.

I started that first trip up Squaw Peak with a group of about ten
people. It was late in the day, and a thunderstorm was brewing in
the distance. As we climbed, the sun got lower and the thunderstorm got closer. We could see lightning forking over the desert.
Some people began to worry that we wouldn't be able to get off the
mountain before dark, and might get lost.

About half-way up, three of our party decided to head back.
The thunderstorm kept coming closer. When we were about 200
yards from the top, the edge of the storm hit, and its first effect was
to turn the dust coating the rocks we were climbing to a thin layer
of slippery mud. Another third of our initial party departed.

For the four of us who kept climbing, a miracle soon happened.
The storm veered so that its center never struck. Our clothes stayed
more dry than wet. And just as we reached the top, the sun came
out from behind the trailing edge of the storm.

Everything that we could see—and we could see a lot from the
top—was freshly washed and dramatically lit. We could now see
colors that hadn't been there before the rain: deep red-browns in the
rock, the whole spectrum of imaginable greens in the desert vegeta-
tion, rainbows refracted in the water drops clinging to cactus spines.

We made it back to the car just at sunset, and all the way down
we walked through a landscape different from the one we had
traversed on the way up.

Remembering that climb now, I think of its lessons in the re-
wards of persistence. In accepting Dr. Erickson's still-lingering invitation, I learned a lot, and Dr. Erickson didn't prescribe the
content of my lessons. I found them for myself and continue to
find them even as I write this sentence.

What Erickson brought to our collaboration was a deep belief
that climbing Squaw Peak could be an important ritual. He conveyed that belief compellingly enough to make me want to do it. So
I went, even though I couldn't share my story with him in the flesh
as a final step in the ceremony. I did, however, have a circle of
friends who helped me reflect on my experience and make it a part
of my internal autobiography.

In a training program, our friend Geof Cheek and I(JF) suggest-ed that each member of the group "go out and let something find him or her." We told the participants that they would know when that something found them and that they would know how it was important. We believed that if people put themselves into the cere-mony they would find something useful.

One woman went into the huge, modern lobby of the hotel where we were meeting and sat down on a sofa. There were a few philodendron plants hanging over a balcony there, and they caught her attention. As she stared at them she discovered that a secret garden, a garden in the middle of a forest, had found her. She was sitting in the lobby, but it wasn't a lobby anymore, it was a forest, and she was having a vivid experience in that forest. It was a religious experience for her.

At one point she looked up and saw a quilt on the opposite wall; the quilt had many different colors. She knew that each color was a different member of her family. A year earlier a sports injury had left her son paralyzed from the waist down. As she looked, she saw the square, the color, that was him. As she focused on that square, she saw other squares fit around it. What eventually "found her" was a message about how her whole family came together through her son's tragedy, and how her larger community supported the coming together.

We could never have predicted that a quilt in a garden in a forest would find her, but we knew that she could find some deep person-al meaning in carrying out the ritual.

Ambiguous function rituals are especially useful with highly motivated clients in contexts of good rapport. Artistically inclined people often do more with this kind of ceremony than they would with a logical and unambiguous suggestion. We find this type of ceremony particularly helpful if we feel stuck or if the therapy seems to be happening in a way that isn't maximizing client in-volvement or creativity.

When we read Erickson's case descriptions, we think that many of the outlandish things he suggested to his clients were softened by the kind of open-endedness that is present in ambiguous function ceremonies. This open-ended attitude brings in a dose of "the random" when therapy begins to feel too purposive or one-dimensional.

Punctuate Time to Untangle Confusion

We once saw some graffiti that said, "Time is Mother Nature's way of keeping everything from happening at once." Systems in crisis often seem to have lost awareness of this bit of common sense. Problems can arise either when conflicting parts of a system act all at the same time or when one part acts all of the time, leaving little or no room for expression of other parts. Rituals that punctuate time to create room for different aspects of a system are very effective in such situations.

We have developed several variations on this kind of ritual, which we learned from the Milan systemic therapy team. According to Luigi Boscolo (personal communication, 1987) the team was guided by Bateson's ideas about the importance of time in recursive systems.

The classic example from the Milan team is the odd days/even days ritual (Selvini Palazzoli, Boscolo, Cecchin, & Prata, 1978). In an odd days/even days ritual, conflicting approaches to a situation are separated in time by suggesting that a family use one approach on Mondays, Wednesdays, and Fridays, and the other on Tuesdays, Thursdays, and Saturdays. They may behave "spontaneously" on Sundays.

Perhaps the most frequently described use of odd days/even days rituals is in families where the mother and father have conflicting ideas about how to behave as parents. When the therapist perceives such conflict, he can suggest that the family practice parenting in a ritualized manner for the next month. Specifically, "Mother's way" can be used on Mondays, Wednesdays, and Fridays, while father observes, and "Father's way" can be used on Tuesdays, Thursdays, and Saturdays while mother observes.

The people involved have to think more clearly about the two different approaches involved before they can even set up an odd days/even days ritual. Even if they never fully perform the ritual, just thinking about the two approaches gives family members heightened experience of the alternative realities involved. When they have separated the patterns, people can compare and contrast them through the process that Bateson called abduction. Through that process they can perceive patterns that were invisible when everything was tangled up in time.

When families actually carry out the ceremony, they have an even richer experience. The child is not in the position of having to respond to mixed messages on the days the ritual is performed. He probably behaves more appropriately. The parents may notice that the child responds better when he is not given conflicting messages. This may motivate the parents to find ways to work consistently together or to agree to have separate spheres of responsibility.

Another situation calling for the use of time to untangle confusion is when a system is dominated by a single response. For example, if someone complains of constant worry, she can be asked to set aside a particular hour each day to spend doing nothing but worrying. If she accepts the suggested ritual, she is to take the full hour and really worry in detail. Any other time a worry enters her mind, she is to firmly put it aside until the appointed hour.

We have used this particular ceremony several times, with the result that clients were able to enjoy aspects of their lives that were going unnoticed. Several people also discovered that they really did not have a full hour's worth of worries, but had to repeat worries to fill up the appointed time. In each case, this was a revelation, as their previous experience was that they worried all day long.

A month after Jan finished a residential drug abuse program, her parents, Ronnie and Hal, initiated family therapy to help her continue her progress. Jan was staying away from drugs, but Ronnie and Hal still worried about her. To them, she seemed indecisive, lazy, and insecure. Although it was her senior year of high school, she wasn't doing anything about choosing a college. She hadn't yet gotten her driver's license. She talked about getting a part-time job, but she never actually applied for one. She wasn't interested in any of her courses, and her grades were as flat as her facial expression.

Ronnie constantly talked to Jan about these problems, sometimes questioning her, sometimes instructing her, and sometimes pleading with her. Hal seemed to keep a bit of a distance from both his wife and daughter, although when asked he said that he agreed with his wife's perception of the problem. The parents said that they were spending a great deal of time at home talking about the problem and that sometimes Hal would join in questioning and instructing Jan. Jan's response to all talk of her problems was to act bored and say that she didn't care and that she didn't need their help. Ronnie's consistent reply was that she wished that were true.

We asked Jan and her parents if they would be willing to do an experiment to find out what Jan still needed her parents' help with and what she could do on her own. When they said yes, we offered them the idea that life would be simpler if everyone could agree on when to and when not to help Jan. We then worked together with them to tailor our general notion to their specific needs.

Jan said that she could decide what she wanted help from her parents with and what she wanted to manage on her own. She thought a once-a-week meeting would suffice to keep everyone informed. Hal and Ronnie were skeptical, but agreed to help Jan in any given week only with things that she specifically asked for help with during a meeting. They picked Sunday nights as the time for a weekly meeting, saying they wanted to use some of the meeting time to discuss Jan's progress. Hal agreed to help Ronnie not help Jan with things she wanted to do by herself.

These weekly ceremonies continued for two months, and they helped separate previously tangled roles.

Jan thrived over the two months. She got a job. She passed the driving test. She decided not to decide about college too quickly. As this was being written, she was leaning toward living at home for another year while attending a junior college.

As the family reported these developments in therapy, Jan began to take a different role in the sessions, talking freely and smiling some. She requested that the meetings continue so she could use them as a time to brag to her parents about what she was accomplishing. They loved the idea.

As Jan began to make more decisions for herself, Ronnie began to calm down and focus more on her relationship with Hal and her own future. Hal seemed to become more relaxed and involved.

Our main hope in co-creating this ceremony with Jan's family was to clarify a confused situation by separating various elements in time. Instead of happening in an interrupted way several times an hour, the negotiations about who should have how much responsibility for Jan's life happened in once-a-week compartments that were uninterrupted. The clear compartmentalization in the ritual meetings was a metaphor for continued compartmentalization as the week went on. Instead of being the constant fabric of their lives, the negotiations became a separate strand of thread, making room for other separate strands, such as Jan's responsibility for herself, the marital relationship, and enjoyment among all three family members.

Many possible kinds of ceremony result from applying the basic idea of punctuating time to untangle confusion. Therapists should consider planning along these lines when they experience difficulty either with conflicting parts that can then be given separate times or with a dominating part that can be given a clear and limited time.

Celebrate the Uncelebrated

Evan Imber-Black (1988) has popularized this title for a very useful kind of therapeutic ceremony. Birthday parties, weddings, bar mitzvahs, funerals, baby showers, anniversary celebrations, graduation ceremonies, and many other cultural rituals are ways of calling attention to certain events in the life of an individual, family, or group. A ceremony or ritual provides a context in which to recognize and reflect on important events or changes in status. The function of this recognition and reflection is to help participants adjust to new roles or stages in their lives. It also provides support from the community while allowing that community an opportunity to adjust its perceptions of the participants.

If there is not a ceremony, or somehow the ceremony does not function appropriately, people may have difficulty making transitions. In such cases, devising a therapeutic ceremony to celebrate the uncelebrated can be very productive.

My(JF) first experience in devising a ceremony of this kind was many years ago when I was leading a therapy group. A woman in the group named Connie shared a realization that many difficulties she was currently having may have been related to her mother's funeral. She was one of five children, and at the funeral it happened that her father and brothers and sister somehow grouped together when she wasn't paying attention, leaving Connie to walk and stand alone. Without the cushioning support of her immediate family, Connie felt that she could not face her grief at her mother's loss. She purposefully turned it off. In going through the funeral alone, she wondered again and again if, now that her mother had died, she would always be alone.

Fifteen years later, at the age of 30, Connie wondered if her social isolation had something to do with that funeral, and if her choice of career as a nurse working with cancer patients had something to do with the fact that her mother had died of cancer. Connie felt that she had never recovered from the loss of her mother.

In the therapy group we re-created the funeral. Connie described the spatial setup, which we re-created as best we could. She gathered group members around her to walk with her and stand with her through the ceremony (which took place largely in her mind). She cried and described her loss, and group members responded to her and supported her.

An immediate and unexpected consequence of the ceremony was that Connie got her long, straight hair cut and styled, which made her look very different. Up until that time, she had worn it in the style she had when her mother died. After the ceremony, she felt "free to change it."

In Connie's case, there was a funeral, but it failed to fulfill its ceremonial function for her. Because she felt she could not face the grief alone, she went through the motions, but not the experience, of the funeral. For her, the adjusting and healing power of the funeral had been lost.

Difficulties can also arise not because ceremonies fail to fulfill their function, but because there has been no ceremony. Our built-in ceremonies usually work well, but there are not built-in ceremonies for some changes in circumstance or status, such as a homosexual marriage or a child's leaving home.

A friend once remarked to me, on opening yet another shower invitation, "Now that I've decided to stay single, I think that someone should throw a party for me. I'm the one who really needs china and silver, since I only have one income to buy it with."

Phil and Fran brought their only son, Mark, age 8, to see us with a long list of concerns. On the telephone, Fran had told us that Mark was adopted, but that he didn't know it. She asked us not to discuss it in front of him.

In the first session Phil and Fran said that Mark didn't have close friends; he was nervous, insecure, and always wanted to be the center of attention; he sucked his thumb; he was afraid of the dark and couldn't stand to be left alone at all. Between the lines— almost without realizing it—they also said that Mark was very intelligent, had a good vocabulary, trusted people easily and shared well with others, but that didn't matter. Any time we began to focus on his assets, they shifted back to their insecurity about his insecurities.

In the second session, we saw Phil and Fran alone so we could discuss their big secret. We asked about their fears of what might happen when Mark found out that he was adopted. We said that, while we couldn't know for sure what went on in their family, we believed that it was very hard to keep secrets really secret. Even if Mark wasn't already aware that he was adopted, he was certainly aware that his parents were hiding something. Then we told them that they had an intelligent and likable son who seemed to be a little insecure. We wondered if he might be catching his insecurity from them.

We asked if they had plans about whether to let Mark in on the secret. They said they had always intended to tell him, but they were waiting for him to be old enough to really understand, and anyway, the time had just never seemed right. In asking them to imagine what might be a right time, we discovered that the eighth anniversary of Mark's adoption was only a few weeks off. With this realization and our encouragement, Fran and Phil started to plan an Adoption Day party, with gifts, decorations, and refreshments.

While Mark was excited about the party, he took the news that he was adopted as if he'd known it all along. He requested that they celebrate it every year.

The Adoption Day party didn't totally resolve the family's problems, but it did make a difference. To our surprise, it seemed that the celebration was more important for Fran and Phil than for Mark. We began to see their list of complaints as a document of formal evidence that they didn't know that they knew how to parent. In keeping Mark's adoption secret and uncelebrated, they were also keeping their change of status to parents unvalidated. After the party, we found that they could accept our positive observations about Mark and join in on them. They also enjoyed recognizing their accomplishments as parents.

Often the event that needs to be celebrated is in some way sad, frightening, or painful for the people involved. In the realm of metaphor, all transitions involve dying as well as birth. Phil and Fran feared that it would hurt Mark to know that he was adopted. Their fear had to die before their new family could really be born. Rituals that successfully celebrate the uncelebrated almost always address the dual nature of a transition—dying and being born, holding on and letting go, or saying goodbye and saying hello.

Reframe the Problem

Jeff was very jealous of the time and passion Louise put into her painting. "It's like an affair," he said. "She never gets that excited about me. In fact, I'm not sure she loves me at all." Both Jeff and Louise agreed that part of the problem was that she loves her work, but he does not love his. But that understanding did not change the way Jeff felt.

Careful questions about Louise's work yielded the information that in her painting she explores her life and her feelings and that subjects in her paintings are recognizable. Jeff had been a frequent model for her over the years. Also, although Louise had sold most of her paintings, she had slides of all of them on file, in chronological order.

I(JF) asked Jeff to perform the following ceremony: He was to review the slides of all of Louise's paintings, searching for those that demonstrate the strength of her love for him in a way that he might never have recognized if he had not looked at the slides.

The ceremony required Jeff to look for Louise's love for him, rather than her love for her work. By finding that love in her paintings, the paintings became symbols of her love. This new perspective on her painting was impossible to reconcile with Jeff's old one (that Louise was having an affair with her work). Now he sees the paintings as a recording of their love affair. He might continue to be jealous of the time and attention Louise puts into her work, but he can no longer see it as a threatening competitor.

In suggesting ceremonies like the one above, we offer people alternative perceptions of their situations. To come up with this type of ceremony, we ask ourselves, "What experience or context would change the client's perception of his situation or of what he now sees as evidence of a problem?"

For instance, you can encourage a person who believes that nobody would love him to go and sit at a busy shopping mall. Suggest that once he has found a good seat, he can study all the couples that walk by. A person can learn a lot by observing the wide variety of people who somehow manage to find mates.

At one of the international congresses on Ericksonian Approaches to hypnosis and psychotherapy, Jeff Zeig described some of the supervision he had received from Milton Erickson. Zeig presented a case to Erickson involving a man who believed that many objects were contaminated. His evidence for the contamination was white powder. If he saw white powder on something, he refused to touch it. This became a problem, as he saw bits of white powder sprinkled in areas that he might normally touch, such as around the television set. He began to rely on family members to turn the television on and off and to deal with other objects he avoided because of their "contamination."

Erickson's supervision consisted of this advice: "Tell him to go to northern Canada."*

The type of thinking Erickson used is the type used in creating ceremonies to reframe problems. He thought of a context in which the client would have a different perception of "white powder."

A second possible strategy for creating a ceremony to reframe a

*For Zeig's written account see Zeig, (1985), p. 67.

person's presenting situation is to think of what perceptual position a person could occupy that would lead to her finding a reframe for herself. Then devise a ceremony that puts her in that perceptual position.

In Chapter 3 (p. 69) we told the story of Laura and Peter. You may remember that we asked each of them to find or make an actual physical symbol for the traits of the other that they found problematic. This was one step of a two-step ceremony.

When they brought in the symbols and described the negative things they stood for, we offered them the second step. We suggested that they carry their symbols with them each day, this time wondering what about them could be valuable. The second step essentially asked them to do their own reframing. Each of them managed to find a way of perceiving their symbol that was positive, and that helped them see each other in a new light.

The strategy we used in Laura and Peter's ceremony can guide you in designing similar rituals for your clients. You can ask clients to develop symbols for a perceived problem. The symbols can then serve as the focal point for ongoing meditation about how they serve some beneficial purpose. In accepting this assignment, people agree to try out a shift from the perceptual position of "problem noticer" to that of "value finder."

Sometimes we devise a similar ritual that can be done without creating symbols for the presenting situation. We simply ask people to experiment with responding to their presenting situation in a specific way. We ask them, when they find themselves involved in it, to wonder how that situation is important or valuable to them or to the larger system they are part of.

Allan came to therapy because he had heart palpitations that were becoming more frequent and frightening to him. Three trips to the emergency room and consultation with a number of physicians revealed no medical problems. I(JF) asked Allan to do the following ceremony, which I presented to him as an experiment, for the next two weeks: Anytime he had heart palpitations he was to adopt a position of thankfulness and wonder how the palpitations were valuable.

At the next session, Allan described a very dramatic and convincing occurrence. On the previous Saturday morning he woke up early, feeling great, and recognizing that he had a whole weekend in front of him with no obligations. He was quite surprised that the thought came to him of paying his bills. But it did, so he took his bills down from a box on top of his bookcase. A moment later he thought, "This is ridiculous. It's Saturday morning. I should be enjoying myself, not paying bills." He picked up the box and as he began to set it back on top of the bookcase, he began to feel heart palpitations. Immediately, he picked the box back up, said, "Okay, okay!" and set it back on the table. Instantly the palpitations stopped. He began to pay the bills. Fifteen minutes later he thought, "Well, at least I could have a beer while I pay these bills." He went into the kitchen, opened the refrigerator door, and as his hand grasped the beer can he began having heart palpitations. "Okay, okay!" he said, left the beer on the refrigerator shelf, closed the refrigerator door, and immediately the palpitations stopped.

"You know," he said to me, "I believe those palpitations are messages." I had to agree with him based on his experience. Soon after this realization, the messages started coming as mere twinges. We ended therapy.

Now, several years later, when the messages come Allan thinks carefully about what he's doing and whether it really is in his best interest. Signals from his heart have guided him in changing his lifestyle dramatically. He has given up smoking, cut down on drinking, quit his job as a business executive to run a bicycle shop, and is amazed at how right the changes feel for him.

We use this type of ceremony when people seem to be in escalating battles with themselves. It is as though an internal part is being ignored and it escalates the battle to get attention. Just as we can suggest a specific time to make room for a part, we can suggest a different perceptual position to make room for a part and to provide a new perspective on its intentions.

Metaphorically Solve the Problem

In an initial session with Eloise, she explained that her cousin, Barry, convinced her to come see me(JF). He told her that seeing me would be unlike any experience she had ever had. She would be doing strange things she didn't understand, and her problems would go away!

Barry had been in therapy with David Gordon. He went to see David because he was really scared of women. He didn't know how to get along with them. When he was around women he felt he had nothing to say. According to Eloise, David had Barry out doing all kinds of things that made no sense. For example, David told Barry to get a stack of dollar bills, 20 one-dollar bills. Then he said to go out in the street and hand them one at a time to women he didn't know. David suggested that, as he handed each woman the dollar, he should ask, "Will you give me change?"

"I don't understand it; Barry doesn't understand it. But he has really changed a lot," said Eloise. "He just went out on the street, got change from women, and now he's not scared anymore."

David's ceremony worked at two levels. On one level it provided a simple structure for practicing conversation with women. On another level he asked for and received "change" 20 different times.

We can't always be as clever as David was in creating ceremonies to solve a problem metaphorically. Certainly not all solutions lend themselves to such elegant puns. We can, however, train ourselves to design ceremonies that metaphorically offer people a solution to their problems. Anytime we notice a possible solution for a problem, we can ask ourselves what series of actions could stand for that solution. If we then set that series of actions in a meaning-laden frame, it can become a ceremony.

If we embed a chosen series of actions in an activity that a person already enjoys, we increase the chance that he or she will do it.

Robert was having trouble letting go of his ex-wife, who had abruptly and unexpectedly left him. He came to therapy because every time he began a new relationship he did something to sabotage it. He explained his behavior by saying that he compared any new woman to his ex-wife and either found she didn't measure up or began to fear she would leave him.

Robert loved playing frontiersman and going on rugged camping trips. I(GC) kept that side of him in mind, but initially offered him an inside-the-house, sit-down task. I suggested that every day for a month he take a sheet of paper and draw lines to divide it into four parts. In the top left quadrant he could write five things that had been really nice about his marriage. In the bottom left portion he could write five things that were not so good about his married life. On the top right he could write five things that were really nice about his present life, and below that he could write five things that were not so good in the present. I asked him to save the sheets of paper for a special event.

I knew that he was planning a camping trip in the Rockies, so I suggested that when he was packing for that trip, he tear off the half of each page that related to his marriage and take it along with him. I went on to suggest that at some point in the trip, when he felt he had carried them around long enough, he could do something definitive with the memories of his past relationship. He could bury them, burn them, give them away, hide them carefully in a cave, or do anything else that felt appropriate, as long as he put them in their place.

One night, camped on a ridge among the stars, Robert carefully burned the half-pages one by one in a campfire.

He got involved in a serious relationship soon after he returned from the trip.

Robert already knew that he needed to get on with his life when he came for therapy. He even knew that a possible way out of his situation was to let go of his attachment to his ex-wife. I don't believe that directly saying "You need to let go of your ex-wife" would have been useful for Robert. However, taking that same simple-minded advice and designing a ceremony that let Robert directly experience it in metaphorical form was very useful.

You can think of the process that Robert went through as either two simple ceremonies or one complex one. In the first simple ceremony he symbolically affirmed that while his life had unpleasant aspects in the present, it was also pleasant at times. On the same sheet of paper he affirmed that his past life had unpleasant as well as pleasant aspects. Each sheet of paper that Robert completed was a multi-textured and substantial symbol of his past and present life.

We used the symbols in a second phase of the ceremony. Tearing each sheet of paper in half, carrying the half of each page that had to do with the past around on his back, and then burning each half-page in a ceremonial fire gave Robert a vivid way to let go of his past relationship.

Ceremonies let people access many strands of lived experience and weave them into a new pattern. The ritual-generation strategy of *metaphorically solving the problem* uses the substance- and texture-generating power of ceremony to transform straightforward advice into multidimensionally meaningful communication.

Disrupt a Problematic Pattern

Lauren experienced her parents as very cold and passively unapproving. The way she handled them was to withdraw and not have much contact. This perpetuated her problems by depriving her of any chance for a real experience of approval from them, and she cared very deeply about the fact that she didn't get approval from them.

One day Lauren brought in a letter from her father that really dripped disappointment and disapproval. The mud was all between the lines, but it was palpably there between every pair of them. I(GC) became uncomfortable just listening to her read.

I said, "Do you like him?"

She replied, "Yes, but he drives me up the wall."

"How do you express that?"

"I haven't written him in years, and as a matter of fact, if the phone rings and I think it's them, I don't pick it up — and this is why, you see."

I wanted to disrupt Lauren's pattern of withdrawing in response to her parents' chilly communications, so I suggested a ritual to her.

I said, "I think it would be interesting if you were to go out and buy a stack of 20 postcards and address them all to your parents, and put them in a prominent place. Then on every weekday for the next month you can write a one-sentence message that begins 'I love you for . . . ' and you can finish it with something from your past that you really genuinely love them for."

She started withdrawing and looking like she couldn't do that, so I said, "And what's going to be fun about this is that you're only going to be able to find such picky little things to love that you're going to know in your mind that you're damning them with faint praise!"

She accepted my rationale and energetically followed through with the ritual. The result, however, was not that she got more assertively angry at her parents or that she began to gloat about the great joke that she had pulled. Instead, she broke the pattern of totally withdrawing every time her parents came around. She now has more choice about how to respond to them and, as often as not, feels warmly when she thinks of them.

Our thoughts in constructing this type of ceremony begin with noticing a problematic pattern. We then ask ourselves, "Given what I know about this person, what is she likely to be willing to do that will disrupt the pattern?" In Lauren's case, I knew that asking her to write a letter or to call her parents on the phone wouldn't work. The pre-addressed postcards seemed to fit her rhythms better and didn't require too much communication too fast.

How the idea for a ceremony is presented can be as important as what is suggested for its content. In Lauren's case, she probably wouldn't have followed through without the "damning with faint praise" rationale.

Another way of looking at how Lauren's pattern-interruption ceremony worked is to focus on how she had to re-search her personal history to do it. In the search she found counter-examples to the behaviors that she remembered most vividly in her parents. As she did this over successive days, she began to rewrite their parts in her life story.

Jenny is a single mother in her late thirties who had been bulimic for a number of years. Together with her twin sister, she began bingeing and vomiting as a teenager. It began as a choice they made to "pig out" and stay slim. She continued the behavior into her marriage. It became more frequent during marital difficulties and after her divorce.

When she came to see me(JF) she was bingeing and purging at

least once a day. She no longer experienced it as a choice. Jenny would discover herself in the refrigerator, shoveling food down her throat, until she felt sick. It was as though someone else were doing it. She then felt compelled to go to the bathroom and throw up, even though she knew that her children knew and that this must be very difficult and confusing for them.

I did some hypnotic work with Jenny and suggested the following ceremony, giving the instructions both when she was in a trance and in a more conscious way: When her hand touched the refrigerator door without her "deciding" to touch it, she was to take a deep breath, go inside herself, and ask, "What do you really want?"

Jenny had stopped bingeing before the next session, and three years later has still not binged again. After the pattern was interrupted, she had many difficulties that she still needed to address, but feeling in control about her eating contributed to her sense of self-worth enormously and helped her be optimistic in dealing with those other issues.

An important part of any pattern is the context in which it occurs. Most ceremonies to disrupt problematic patterns need to take place in the context of the pattern. A few, like Lauren's postcards, can be done outside of the context and will generalize. But most of the time we think of using this type of ceremony to actually interrupt a pattern as it occurs, as in Jenny's case.

Another example of this type of intervention is asking someone who would like to quit smoking to wait 15 minutes after he has the urge to have a cigarette before deciding whether to have it. Both this ceremony and Jenny's leave the person free to continue the presenting behavior but interrupt the sequence that leads to it. Once a sequence is interrupted, people usually have more freedom to exercise choices.

Develop a Needed Resource

Ours is a resource-based therapy. We have already discussed the importance of accessing resources as a therapeutic process (Chapter 3, pp. 52–59) and how to use symbols (Chapter 5, pp. 121–

138) and stories (Chapter 6, pp. 167–173) to access resources. We also use ceremonies to develop more dependable access to resources in contexts where they are needed but not readily available.

The strategy for creating this type of ceremony centers around the following question: "What experience could the client have that would both symbolize and be instrumental in developing the needed resource?"

Darryl's family entered therapy at the suggestion of his school because his grades were dropping and he was getting in trouble there. In an initial session, each member described their concerns.

Michael, the father, said that Darryl did not accept authority. He thought that Darryl felt that no one listened to him and believed he was accused of things he did not do.

Brenda, the mother, was worried that her two sons were always fighting. Her husband thought she should leave them alone.

Billy, the ten-year-old, worried because Darryl threatened to kill himself and to run away. He also held grudges and threatened Billy.

Darryl, who was 14, thought that everyone picked on him, and they should leave him alone.

As the session continued, we were struck by two things. The first was our impression that all the family members were going in different directions. They were rarely all home at the same time, and it was even more rare that they did things together. Darryl played basketball at school, and although his family was proud of this, none of them had ever been to a game. In the session, we heard numerous examples of different members' missing out on information and then misinterpreting things.

The second thing that struck us was a poignant description by Billy of how worried he was because Darryl had stabbed Billy's teddy bear with a butcher knife, and now he didn't even know if the teddy bear was alive anymore.

We suggested the following ceremony: The family could meet together to talk about and decide what they could do to fix the teddy bear. We asked them to pick a time for this meeting in the session. We suggested that Darryl be in charge of making sure that the meeting happened.

We were intrigued with the results of this assignment. When the family returned, they told us that they did not meet at the prescribed time because of some activity that came up for Darryl. Michael had gathered the family together at a different time. They had talked about the teddy bear and decided that it was fine just the way it was. It had a little tear but no one really noticed it. Billy was now sure that it was alive.

Everyone seemed much happier at this session. They reported that they were doing better and that Darryl had received a good report from his school.

Our idea in constructing this ritual was to provide the family with a context in which to develop the resource of working together toward a common goal. We utilized the teddy bear because it was a symbol of comfort that was already in the system. We hoped that a meeting of the whole family around the teddy bear could both symbolize and be instrumental in developing the "working together" resource. We asked Darryl to be in charge of making sure the meeting happened because we wanted to help him take on positions of responsibility.

Because Darryl had stabbed the teddy bear, when the family members decided it was all right the way it was, they symbolically communicated to him that the presenting situation wasn't really so bad. When Michael took on the task of reminding the others about the meeting, he showed his willingness to help Darryl (not just pick on him). The family worked together elegantly, although not in the way we envisioned.

There are many ways to use ritual to develop a needed resource. Remember that in each instance the guiding question is "What experience could the client have that would both symbolize and be instrumental in developing the needed resource."

Here is another example of a resource-developing ritual. It was designed to develop the resource of speaking concisely. Following Erickson's principle of utilization, we looked for something that already interested the client (dreams) and used it to stand for all topics of speech and thought.

Randall could tell me(JF) that he stayed two hours at a job interview and, instead of thinking, "Great, that means he got the job," I would think, "Oh no, I wonder if the interviewer ever got past the first question." The other people I shared an office with at that time dreaded answering the phone because, if it were Randall, it would be so hard to get off. Randall talked a lot, and he went into excruciating detail about everything.

He also took so many notes about personal things that I thought he would have twice as much of a life if he stopped writing about it. He brought reams of papers to me—notes on assignments and illustrated recordings of his dreams.

Randall very much wanted a job, he very much wanted a social life, and he very much wanted to accomplish more than he was accomplishing. I believed that the ability to think and communicate more concisely would be invaluable in all three areas.

We were unsuccessful working to develop this resource with direct approaches. Most of the time Randall was so busy talking that he didn't seem to hear my suggestions, and when he did hear them, he got his feelings hurt and talked even more.

However, Randall did a superb job following homework suggestions. In fact, he usually did far more than I suggested.

I suggested that Randall perform the following ceremony when he came to a session with written descriptions of three dreams. One was 16 pages, the second was 18 pages, and the third was 24 pages. Bringing these descriptions to the session was wholly Randall's idea.

For the ritual, I suggested that between that session and the next Randall write out at least three of his dreams in detail. The next step was to take the full description and condense it into a page, and then to take the page and put it into a paragraph. Then, "so we could really know the essence of his dream," I said he might want to write a single sentence that encapsulated it.

So Randall went to work. He brought in reams of paper. He brought in his first, second, third, and fourth drafts and took great pleasure in reading through each one. He finally got to the one-sentence essence.

It seemed to me that he also became more concise in other contexts, but I wasn't sure until Klaus Boettcher, with whom we shared office space, said, "What's going on with Randall? Now he sits in the waiting room like everyone else instead of pulling me aside for a 45-minute demonstration of a new stretching exercise."

Sometimes, as above, if the problematic context is too threatening, you can offer people the option of practicing the needed resource in a nonthreatening context. You can design a ritual to develop the resource in the safer-feeling context, with the belief that it will generalize. At other times, you might design rituals that invite people to practice a needed resource directly in the problematic context. There are many ways to use rituals to develop needed resources.

Prescribe the Presenting Situation in Metaphor

This strategy calls for taking the presenting situation and feeding it back in metaphor. Sometimes people can reach a different kind of clarity and understanding through encountering their situations in metaphor. Joel Bergman (1985) writes about making the covert overt through this type of ritual. He has developed one ritual of this type utilizing the idea of a "family shrine":

> The ritual, in its most generic form, consists of directing a family or a couple to construct a "shrine" somewhere in their home (or hospital ward, or school). The shrine consists of pictures of family members the therapist thinks still play a critical role in a family's difficulties. This could involve pictures of grandparents, a wedding picture of the parental couple, or pictures of a child who has passed away. Traumatic events which still remain emotionally alive can also be represented (e.g., pictures of an internment or P.O.W. camp).
>
> Instructions are then given for the family (couple) to go to the shrine on a regular basis, light a candle in front of each picture, and talk to the pictures. The instruction of what to say to the pictures will, of course, depend on the family. (Bergman, 1989, p. 50)

How much of the metaphor to prescribe and how much for the clients to evolve varies from one situation to the next. Clients can also be given a structure for which they provide all of the content themselves.

For example, Bart and Lisa separated after 14 years of marriage. They came to therapy to decide whether or not to get back together. They were using therapy to examine who they were now and what was possible for them as a couple. At one point in the therapy Lisa mentioned that the following Saturday was their anniversary; as it was approaching, she was sad about the tremendous waste she would feel if their relationship ended. Bart said that it would probably be best not to go out that night as they had for previous anniversaries, although he was willing to if that was what Lisa wanted.

We agreed with Lisa and Bart that it would not be fitting to go out and celebrate as usual, but suggested that it would be fitting to acknowledge the situation in some way.

We suggested the following ritual as a way of acknowledging their situation: If they accepted our suggestion, they were each to spend some time alone that day with the awareness that it was their anniversary. They were also to exchange gifts, but not spend time together. The gifts would symbolize either something that the giver appreciated in the other that the other might not know the giver appreciated or something the giver thought that the other might find fascinating about the giver.

At the next session, we discovered that they had not done the ritual. They had had a big fight several days before the anniversary, and neither wanted to give the other a present of any kind. Several weeks before, Lisa had arranged a business trip, having negotiated with Bart for him to be with the kids. Bart had scheduled his own business trip at the same time, having forgotten that Lisa was leaving town. When she discovered this a few days before the anniversary, Lisa was outraged and said that it showed that Bart was irresponsible and not committed to their relationship (this had been a major issue throughout therapy). Bart had been willing to change his trip, and was outraged at being called irresponsible. He announced that he was not willing to live with someone who saw him that way.

In a sense, their fight and the events that led up to it symbolized their presenting situation in the way we had hoped the ceremony would. Bart had been the one who had wanted the separation and who was undecided about the marriage. Lisa was in a position of feeling like she had to take care of everything and had never been able to count on him. As they talked about this fight, they began to clarify the areas of their relationship that would need to change if they were to get back together. Lisa wanted Bart to acknowledge all the responsibility she had taken and be willing to divide it differently. Bart wanted Lisa to appreciate his commitment and not label his forgetfulness as lack of responsibility. Both felt that the emotions they expressed in the fight were preferable to the polite carefulness that had characterized their separation.

Another option that we could have used would have been to suggest a ritualized enactment of a fight. Cloé Madanes (1984) has contributed the idea of having people "pretend" to carry out problematic patterns. People may feel safer and more in control using rituals to disrupt situations with very intense emotional components if they think of themselves as pretending to be in the situation. The "pretend" enactment is a metaphor for the actual problematic pattern.

Co-creating Ceremonies

No matter which of the strategies is used in developing a ceremony, it will fit better if it is created by the therapist and client together. In a very real sense, all rituals are co-created because they come out of the thinking that occurs in the therapeutic relationship. However, utilizing the uniqueness of the client system and being receptive to responses and modifications offered by that part of the therapeutic mind will take the process even further. Many of the examples we have already given in this chapter are examples of co-creating ceremonies. This separate section emphasizes the importance of co-creation.

We use two basic strategies, and sometimes a combination of the two, in co-creating ceremonies:

— Suggest the structure and give a reason for the ritual. Encourage clients to modify it and flesh it out so that it works for them, or be open to counter-proposals.
— Find the seed of a ceremony in something a client is already doing or planning to do. Use the therapeutic interaction to nurture and shape the seed as it grows, so that it blossoms into a meaningful ritual.

Suggest the Structure for the Ritual; Encourage Clients' Modifications and Counter-proposals

Using this strategy, a therapist outlines a basic form or idea for a ceremony, leaving some of the details unspecified. This is sometimes referred to as closed and open parts (van der Hart, 1983;

Whiting, 1988). Clients fill in gaps, make modifications, or suggest different ideas.

Gary and Maureen agreed that things were bad at their apartment when he came home at night. The kids rarely had their chores done. They were watching television instead, and everyone always seemed to be in a bad mood. Gary suggested that, if Maureen were providing some supervision for the kids instead of staying in the bedroom, everything would be fine. Maureen countered that the whole problem was that Gary came home every night in a bad mood, yelling. She would go into the bedroom to avoid the crossfire, and the kids watched television as a way of avoiding him. She believed that if Gary came in talking, instead of yelling, things would be different.

I(JF) suggested a ritual in which they could follow Maureen's suggestions one time a week and Gary's suggestions one other time each week. The night before each of these two experiments, one of them would give instructions to the other.

They agreed, and when I asked them to choose two nights, Gary said, "How about when we go home tonight?"

I asked if they had the same difficulty when they arrived home together. The answer was no, and that seemed significant to both of them. Gary then suggested they short-circuit the whole pattern with a different ritual. Every evening when he arrived at home, he would ring the bell from the downstairs porch. Maureen would come downstairs, they would greet each other privately, and then they would go upstairs together and join their kids. It would be as if they always arrived home together.

That marked the beginning of a new pattern that continued beyond the ritual, not of meeting on the front steps, but of both enjoying being home more, with Maureen spending more time out of the bedroom and Gary yelling less.

Nurture and Shape the Seed of a Ceremony
Found in Something a Client Is Already Doing or Planning to Do

Using this strategy, the therapist utilizes something that is already going on and builds it into a ritual.

Frances and Bernie came to therapy after Frances had consulted a lawyer about divorce. Frances experienced herself as having tried to be a good daughter-in-law for years while being ignored and insulted by Bernie's parents, who lived far away but made frequent contact by telephone and letter.

Three months before their first therapy session, Frances had severed ties with her in-laws. Bernie, who usually visited his parents a couple of times a year, had gone to see them three times in the three months after Frances' action. Frances felt that, in visiting so frequently, Bernie chose his parents instead of supporting her.

At the point in therapy the example is concerned with, Frances' anger had been defused and she believed that Bernie was choosing her again. She and Bernie were enjoying each other and planning to stay together, although they were both still feeling insecure in the relationship. Frances still hadn't reconnected with Bernie's parents.

Bernie's parents had extended an invitation for Ray, Frances and Bernie's son, to visit them. The couple agreed that their son could make the visit and had agreed on a deadline date by which Bernie would set the time of the visits and make travel arrangements. For Frances, having specific plans in advance represented Bernie's closing a "window of vulnerability" she experienced in regard to his parents. She wasn't sure he would do it, and in fact bet him $100 that he wouldn't. (She later said that the bet was to motivate Bernie to come through.)

From behind the mirror, Gene recognized the $100 bet as something we could utilize to develop a ceremony.

After consulting with Gene, I(JF) asked a series of questions to both Frances and Bernie about what it would mean if Bernie made the deadline and won the bet. They agreed that it would have very positive implications for their relationship. I wondered if it would mean such positive things that they might want to celebrate. It did. I then suggested that if Bernie won the bet, they use the $100 to celebrate their new relationship. They enthusiastically agreed, and Frances suggested that the celebration include going to a concert and hearing the same music they had heard on their first date!

The couple, in fact, did win the bet by Bernie's making the deadline. They could not find a concert playing the same music, which may have been fitting, since they were in a new phase, but they did have a dinner and concert celebration acknowledging the joy and progress in their relationship.

Summary

We have given you examples of eight different strategies for designing therapeutic ceremonies. For each strategy we have attempted to acquaint you with the thought processes we go through in applying it.

Our list of ceremony-construction strategies is not exhaustive and we certainly don't mean to imply that ours are the only ways of thinking about rituals. We do believe that it is useful for therapists to know and employ several kinds of ceremonies and several ways of coming up with them.

Practice makes perfect, or at least moves us closer to perfection, and we suggest that you practice designing rituals. We hope that you will pick the strategies from our list that you are least familiar with and work to make them your own. You may also find exercises XIV, XV, XXII, and XXVII from Chapter 4 to be useful in expanding your skills.

III

The Therapeutic
Interaction

8

METAPHOR IN THE OVERALL CONTEXT OF THERAPY

ALTHOUGH WE DO NOT believe that people need to do a particular kind of therapy to use metaphor, we do believe that metaphor should make sense within the context of the therapy used and that it should be used congruently, naturally, and with nonverbal behavior that affirms its importance.

In this chapter, we offer both some specific ideas for integrating metaphor into your work and some general guidelines for how to conduct psychotherapy in a way that values and supports the effectiveness of metaphor. We start with our most specific suggestions and end with more general ones.

Guidelines for Stories

Keep Your Clients and the Therapeutic Relationship in Mind

In teaching therapeutic storytelling, we are often asked if clients will not think it's strange or that we're completely off task when we launch into stories about things other than what they came to accomplish. There are two parts to the answer to this question, both of which are important.

First, it is essential to communicate nonverbally — through eye contact, facial expression, voice tone, and the like — that what we are saying is important and selected to relate to the particular people with whom we are talking at that moment in time and to their specific goals. This requires that therapists congruently believe in the value of a metaphoric approach.

Second, one should keep clients in mind when choosing the subject matter of stories. It's best to avoid subjects that may elicit strong responses having nothing to do with our purpose in telling them. For example, telling a single mother who works two jobs to put her kids through school stories about sunbathing on a yacht between Greek islands may arouse feelings of resentment and ideas about injustice rather than a state of comfort. We also avoid subjects likely to hold no interest for a particular person.

Generally, using the strategies we have described leads to finding appropriate stories. Because we look for stories during the session, as we interact with people, they are part of the therapeutic mind that discovers the stories. This helps us find appropriate stories and leads easily to rejecting any that might be offensive or inappropriate.

Still, clients occasionally do wonder why we tell all those stories. We have not found the ambiguity to be a problem, and often people make some important discoveries in wondering about what we think we are doing with stories.

Be Thoughtful in How You Use Stories About Yourself

Our strategies for finding relevant therapeutic stories encourage therapists to search their personal experience for incidents on which they can elaborate to tell a story. Such stories usually work just fine, but occasionally problems arise. One potential problem is that clients can come to feel that a therapist is so self-involved that he doesn't notice them. Another is that if the stories are all about personal successes, they can make clients feel hopelessly unsuccessful or cause them to think a therapist is a braggart.

On the positive side, stories about one's personal experience can be more engrossing and convincing than second- or third-hand stories. What's important is that you consider the potential effect of whom each story is about and adjust accordingly.

Generally, if first-person stories are not about precisely the same situation as the clients', and are not solely about achievements, they work well. Stories that happened when the therapist was in a different time of his life also have less potential for negative side effects.

If it seems wise not to tell a particular story about oneself, the same story can be used by simply telling it about "a person I know well" or "someone I once heard of." Or you can always find another story.

Tell More Than One Story

The best way to create an atmosphere in which stories are valued is to tell lots of them. This doesn't mean that you should tell irrelevant stories or stories that strain and gasp to make their point, but we do believe that one reasonably relevant story invites another.

Stories usually are more effective in encouraging small steps than large ones. It is rare for any single story, no matter how well it is designed and told, to be the decisive element in a course of psychotherapy. For both these reasons, we believe that it's better to put your energy into finding and telling several small stories than to hang all your hopes on one tale.

We oftentimes tell more than one story to come at a single purpose from different angles. For example, to access motivation we might tell a story about our friend who against great odds got a play she wrote into the hands of a famous comedian, a story about getting up very early in the morning when everything is quiet and knowing with great clarity what's ahead, and another about someone getting ideas from a book that let him believe he could do something he never before thought he could do. We wouldn't know how a particular client would use the different stories, but we have observed that redundancy can be important.

Virginia is the mother-in-law of one of our friends. She came to see me(GC) because she was losing her self-confidence and beginning to spiral into hopeless and unhappy feelings. She is a small and energetic lady in her mid-fifties who still has traces of her Appalachian Mountain origins in her accent. In her size, energy, and accent she reminded me of my grandmother at that age.

Virginia had been working at the same company for years. Although she had started at the lowest possible level, her energy and dedication had earned her several promotions. Her troubles seemed to have started when she was promoted from assembly line supervisor to a managerial position. She had never thought of herself as a white-collar type, and she was suddenly supposed to be a peer of all these young men with college educations. While most of the people she sat with in meetings were men young enough to be her sons, she was intimidated by their fancy language and stylish attire. She wasn't used to sitting at a desk or in meetings all day. She missed walking through the factory. The people that used to be her peers now treated her with deference. She just wasn't sure she was up to the job, and the uncertainty was beginning to spread into other areas of her life.

I was very conscious of being (by Virginia's definition) a college-educated young man. If I gave her direct advice or in any other way took an authoritarian position with her, I would be recapitulating an important part of the situation that had led to her problems. I needed a strategy that would let me pursue the goal of reconnecting Virginia with her obviously (to me) abundant resources while creating a context that would let me assume a low-key, non-authoritarian role.

I couldn't stop thinking of my grandmother as I sat listening to Virginia, so I decided to utilize my memories of "Granny Combs." Without explaining why, I began to tell her about my Granny Combs, telling her stories selected to have relevance to her current situation.

I told her about how happy I always was as a child when I went to stay with my Granny on her farm in the Kentucky mountains, how I went with her as she milked the cow and gathered eggs from the chickens, how much fun it was to dig worms and go sit on the creekbank and fish with her. I knew that Virginia had grown up on a mountain farm, and I used those stories to establish a connection between her and my Granny.

I told her about the death of my grandfather when Granny Combs was in her fifties, and how I imagined that was a major adjustment for her. She must have had to take over more of the administrative tasks of running the farm while mourning the loss of her husband.

I told her how two of my uncles lived on the farm into their thirties and forties, and although they had college educations and were twice her height, there was never any question about who was the boss. I described, and perhaps in my enthusiasm even invented, scenes in which she told them in no uncertain terms what to do and they did it, scenes in which they came to her for advice, scenes soon after the death of her husband in which she surmounted doubts and difficulties about her role with her sons, and particularly, scenes in which they all worked together and made decisions, each contributing a different kind of expertise.

I talked about what a great hugger Granny was, how even though she was less than five feet tall she could fill you up with her warmth. I talked about the paintings she had done as a girl that still hung on her walls. I talked about the 100-gallon tropical fish tank she had and all the various plants and fish that filled it. I described the joy I had felt eating her home-cooked Sunday dinners with meat and produce fresh from the farm. Above all, I repeatedly but indirectly stressed her similarities to Virginia while portraying her as a happy creative person who had used her interests and abilities in successfully making a difficult transition in her mid-fifties, a transition that brought new responsibilities. I spent the better part of two sessions telling stories about Granny Combs.

A week after the second session, we ran into her son-in-law, and he told us that Virginia wasn't really sure that she was getting any help from me. It seemed that I wasn't giving her any practical advice. In fact, I was hardly talking about her problems at all. She thought it strange that I had spent most of the time talking about my grandmother.

She didn't mention these feelings to me at her third session, but she did say that, although she didn't know why, she was doing better at work and that she felt better in general. Together, we decided that she had probably turned a corner, but we scheduled another visit in a month "just to see that everything was still on the right track."

As well as being a real and vibrant person, Granny Combs was a symbol that evoked many wonderful associations for me. I had tried to select some experiences that I thought would be useful to Virginia and tell stories about Granny Combs that would lead Virginia to identify with her. I thought that if I was successful, Virginia would then have access to those experiences, and through them associations to her own experiences of being a resourceful person. When she was worried about her new responsibilities she might remember how another Appalachian woman had coped. When she felt intimidated by the educated young men she now worked with, the story of Granny Combs and her two sons might remind her of similar experiences in her own life. When she was tired she might find her equivalent of a creekbank and "fish" for a while.

Given the feedback we had gotten from our friend, we weren't so sure that the plan had worked. We wondered how Virginia would be at her one-month visit.

Well, she was super. She talked about her work with interest and enthusiasm. She smiled and laughed and told me how much she'd enjoyed my stories about Granny Combs, how they'd reminded her of some of the good things about her hillbilly heritage. She said she wasn't sure what had happened that had helped so much, but she sure was glad to be feeling so much better.

The next time we saw our friend, he confirmed what Virginia had told me and added this detail: Virginia bowled on a team with some of her co-workers. When they bought new shirts, what Virginia had written on the back of hers in the place for her name was "GRANNY."

We usually tell stories about a wide range of subjects, not about just one person. We include this case here because we think it is clear how unlikely a single story of Granny Combs, even a long, complicated one, could have brought forth the variety of resources and ideas that Virginia used in adjusting to her new situation. We probably could have achieved the same result with similar stories about a variety of people, but this approach had the additional benefit of creating a multidimensional symbol that could guide Virginia in her new role.

Integrate Stories into the Rest of Therapy

We have noticed that beginning students of storytelling tend to carefully mark out a story as an event separate from the rest of therapy. This may entail giving an introduction such as, "Now I'm going to tell you a story," and waiting expectantly after the story for a response to it.

Marking out a story in this way tends to invite listeners to analyze it for meaning or sometimes to expect an explanation from the therapist. If we are using stories as multidimensional metaphors to bring forth new associations and facilitate clients' developing many maps, we defeat our purpose when we collaborate with clients in reducing a story to a single meaning. Sometimes people do pick out a single meaning that is helpful and important. Sometimes we want to convey a very particular meaning. This can be effective, but since a major purpose of stories is to communicate with other-than-conscious dimensions of people, it is usually better to integrate stories smoothly into the flow of the therapeutic process.

We do this all the time in casual conversation. If you overhear a conversation in a restaurant, half of its content will be in the form of "yesterday I did so-and-so" or "you'll never believe the incredible thing that you-know-who is doing now." People are used to hearing stories in the natural flow of a conversation. They need no introduction or commentary about meaning.

We have even found that, given a therapeutic relationship in which we have good rapport, we can tell stories whose content is extremely different from the matter at hand. Clients assume, in the context of our relationship, that these stories must be meaningful, and they search to find meaning.

However, it can aid the natural flow of conversation and put therapists at ease to find some way to introduce stories that do not seem to naturally relate to the conversation. Phrases such as, "As you were talking I thought of . . . " and "This may not be exactly what you were meaning, but . . . " can be used to integrate a story into the conversation.

Let Clients Find Their Own Meanings in Your Stories

At least since the time of Aesop, stories have had morals. Our story construction strategies encourage therapists to find stories that suggest specific ideas or elicit specific resources. It can feel quite natural in telling such a story to end it by overtly stating its "moral," that is, specifying the idea or state you want to convey.

More often than not, telling the moral of a therapeutic story undermines its effectiveness, because it stops people from searching for meaning relevant to them. There are exceptions to this rule, such as when a series of stories is told to prepare a foundation for a direct suggestion or when a person's nonverbal behavior indicates he or she may have interpreted the story in a very unhelpful way. But we usually use stories as part of a stochastic process, and directly stating their purpose weakens their ability to elicit a creative "random" response.

I(JF) learned this lesson well when one of our therapy rooms had a common wall with a neighboring optometry office. They must have had their lens grinding machine just inches from that wall, and it sounded like the world's loudest vacuum cleaner. I was doing some hypnotic work with a woman named Marilyn one day when the machine came on. I wanted to suggest the idea that she had natural processes that could shield her from any disturbance, especially the noise, so that she could continue the hypnotic work in which she was engaged. I quickly told a story of a caterpillar inside a cocoon, going through wonderful transformations inside that cocoon and oblivious to what was going on outside. She seemed undisturbed by the noise, so we continued the work.

At the next session Marilyn declared that the story about the caterpillar in the cocoon was all that she remembered from the hypnotic work, and that it was the most meaningful story I had ever told her. She went on to say that we both knew she had been stuck, but that I was right. She was not doing nothing. She was doing some very important things inside that cocoon. She was preparing to take off and fly!

And in fact, she had ventured out in some ways very new for her after hearing that story and realizing that she did have wings. She went on to talk about new behaviors she had begun since the previous session.

Guidelines for Ceremonies

Construct Ceremonies as Experiences, not as Models

It is important, both in planning ceremonies and in suggesting that families or individuals do them, that therapists understand

and communicate that ceremonies are for facilitating experience. In describing the Milan systemic approach, Karl Tomm (1984, p. 266) writes that " . . . the ritual is not intended to become part of their usual pattern of daily activity. The ritual is offered in the sense of an experiment, a trial, a symbolic gesture or a transitory rite. There is no implication that 'this is the way things should be done' in the course of regular family living." In ceremonies, what is important is what clients experience, what clients learn, and the meaning that clients make. Instructions in what clients should do on a day-to-day basis would not have the metaphorical nature of a ceremony.

Ceremonies can occur both in the session and outside of it. Our bias is to suggest that people do ceremonies outside of therapy sessions. In this way therapy extends beyond the office and may have greater significance simply by virtue of including more than one context. Outside-the-office ceremonies also seem to be more memorable because clients are responsible for seeing that they occur; also, they go through them again by talking about them at the following session.

However, meaningful rituals can also occur in the office. Particularly when dealing with very threatening issues, clients may feel more secure carrying out a ceremony in the presence of a therapist. In addition, individuals doing rituals alone may value the presence of a witness.

Accept and Utilize All Client Responses

A frequent question from workshop participants is "How do you get clients to do a ritual once you have designed it?" The simple answer is that we don't.

When we suggest that people do ceremonies, we communicate that we think the ceremonies are important and valuable. We attend to verbal and nonverbal responses and are open to modifying our ideas, dropping them, or explaining them until clients congruently agree. At the same time we are aware of maintaining the ambiguous and metaphorical nature of the tasks.

In presenting a ritual we do what we know how to do to make it seem intriguing or helpful or whatever else it must be to appeal to the clients at hand. We believe that it will be valuable and we convey our belief. We don't assign rituals unless we genuinely believe they will be valuable.

We do this within the context of a relationship with a particular client system, so we naturally alter our communication to fit with the clients', as we do in all relationships. If, for example, we think a particular family may find our suggestion strange, we say, "You may find this suggestion strange, and we think it can be helpful." We may tell a story of how another family did a similar ceremony and benefitted from it. Above all, we are open and pleased to coevolve ceremonies with clients. We find that the more people participate in designing ceremonies the more likely those ceremonies are to fit for those people.

However, sometimes people don't perform ceremonies.

We have been intrigued to discover that sometimes, when people don't do ceremonies, the result is still somehow as though they had. That is, we might develop a ceremony with the intention of bringing forth a particular resource in a family. We will not have mentioned that our hope is to access that resource. The family members then sometimes come back having not done the ceremony, but with much evidence that they are now using the resource.

Our understanding of this phenomenon is that some people do the ceremony in imagination as it is being described or negotiated and reap the same benefits as they would in actually doing it. We routinely check for this possibility when people don't actually carry out a ceremony. What is important, of course, is the learning, not the doing.

Other times failure to do a ceremony provides us with information. Sometimes we have assigned too much too fast or misunderstood the needs of the client system in some way. We hypothesize and talk with clients about these possibilities, altering the next ceremony we suggest or use other kinds of interventions, depending on the feedback we get.

Also, people sometimes appreciate support and time in doing important rituals. When clients don't carry out a ritual between the session in which it was suggested and the next one, it does not necessarily mean the ritual should be dropped. Clients' attitudes about a ceremony, particularly as expressed nonverbally, can provide clues about whether to drop the ceremony or to support them in doing it at a later date.

Sharon identified the problem that brought her to therapy as "low self-esteem and everything that goes with it." She specified a number of problem areas and how they would be different when she felt good about herself. At the point in therapy we are concerned with here, she had reached several of her goals and was feeling better about herself.

She very eloquently communicated how she was doing in her report of a dream she had: "In the dream I discovered some uncut diamonds. I didn't know if they were mine. I was confused. I put some in my change purse. I put others in a box full of junk jewelry where I didn't think anyone would notice them. Funny, what I once thought was junk is in style now.

"Then Columbo was taking me out to dinner. You *know* he wouldn't have been there if he didn't know about the diamonds, but they must have been mine, because he didn't take them.

"Then I woke up. I knew it was important because I felt good."

Although Sharon was feeling better about herself there were still a number of areas she wanted assistance with. One situation that Sharon found very distressing was how her brother, Fred, was managing some property that they had co-inherited. She had agreed to the arrangement initially, but was now disturbed by her lack of control. He was managing the property on his own and had not listened to Sharon's ideas or made the financial records available to her when she requested them.

I(JF) knew from our earlier work that Fred, who was 12 years older than Sharon, had sexually abused her when she was three or four. Although I believed that Sharon was genuinely disturbed by her current relationship with Fred, I also heard the way she talked about the current situation as a metaphor for the past sexual abuse.

Earlier, we had worked directly with the sexual abuse and now I saw an opportunity to work with it metaphorically, in a ceremony. We only referred to the inheritance, never overtly to the sexual abuse, in connection with this ritual. I suggested that Sharon write a letter telling Fred who she was now. I specifically suggested that she stand up for herself in a way that would let him know she was taking charge of her life, and would not let him control it anymore.

Sharon wrote a many-page letter, going into great detail about just that. She cried and screamed and laughed while she wrote, and felt that it had been tremendously helpful. However, it felt to her like a private letter that she did not want to share with Fred.

We talked about whether it would be helpful for her to write another letter that she could mail to Fred. She very congruently indicated that it would. However, she came to the next session without the letter. She said she still intended to write it, but she came to the following session and the one after that still without the letter.

At first I wondered if she had accomplished what she wanted to with the huge letter that she kept. She said no, she thought it was important to write a letter she could actually send to Fred, but it was scary. I did not want to be pushy or controlling or to in any way recapitulate aspects of the problematic relationship with Fred, but it seemed that the ritual of writing and sending the letter was important.

I tried to be supportive but not pushy. We talked about using a session to write the letter, but Sharon said she wanted to do it on her own. I began to wonder if she would ever actually write to Fred, but continued to feel it would be good if she did. I did my best to quietly and consistently convey that feeling. Finally, four sessions after I suggested it, Sharon brought a second letter, ready to be mailed to her brother:

Dear Fred,

I am still very angry and hurt about what happened. The incident [a disagreement about the property is what she is overtly referring to] brought to the forefront my need to let people know that I am no longer to be used or abused. My struggle to have self-esteem has been difficult and I will allow no one to diminish the progress I have made, but I am willing to allow a dialogue that has mutual respect for all concerned.

In regard to our financial relationship as co-inheritors of the property, at a minimum, I need to see the books, so I can know what is coming in and going out, in order to determine what I may owe you and your wife and what you may owe me. We also need to arrange a way for me to be treated as an equal partner.

To begin this process I'd like Margaret [Fred's wife] to bring me the books the next time she comes to the coffee shop [run by their sister]. If you have any difficulty with this or would like to arrange it in a different way, please let me know before then.

Sincerely,

Sharon

Sharon felt tremendous relief after mailing the letter. Suddenly, all the things that she wanted to accomplish seemed easy. Therapy ended on a very positive note one session later. A follow-up call three years later indicated that Sharon had recently married, was happy, and "felt really good about" herself.

Amplify and Extend Meaning with Interventive Questions

Both before and after people do a ritual, questions can be used to amplify and extend its meaning. We developed the kinds of questions we use in this process as we studied the work of the Milan team (Selvini Palazzoli et al., 1980), Peggy Penn (1982), Karl Tomm (1987), and Michael White (1988a,b).

In the process of developing and suggesting a ritual, a question like, "What do you think you will discover in doing this ceremony that you might not have known if you were not doing it?" invites clients to vividly imagine themselves in the middle of carrying out a ceremony and to search for any discoveries that they might be making. In a sense, they must have the internal experience of carrying out the ceremony in order to answer the question.

Encouraging clients to carry out the ceremony in imagination in this way has several beneficial effects. It lets them notice in more detail what about the ceremony does and doesn't fit for them. This information can be used to fine tune the ceremony so that it really fits the client system at hand. A custom-fitted ceremony is more likely to be carried out than an off-the-rack model.

Once people have performed a ritual in their imaginations, it feels more natural to go ahead and do it in the real world. Nevertheless, even if they never carry out the ceremony in the real world, they can learn much of what they would have learned by carrying it out through their experience in imagination. When they do follow up by actually performing the ritual, it is as if they have performed it twice, and this redundancy increases the chances that they will remember its lessons.

A similar question to the one above is, "When you look back at this ceremony, what do you think it will mean to you?" This question invites people to inhabit a slightly different perceptual position. Whereas the first question asked them to imagine themselves in the process of doing the ceremony, this one asks them to step into a time in the future after they have already finished it. From this position, they can notice how the ritual continues to affect their lives after its completion. In answering this question, people accept the presuppositions that they will perform the ritual and that its performance will have some meaning for them.

Other useful questions before a ceremony is performed are: "When you see your (wife, for instance) doing this ritual, what will you know about her that you didn't know before?" and "When your son (daughter, uncle, boss, etc.) sees you performing this ritual, what will he know about you that he didn't know before?" The first type of question asks a person vividly to imagine doing the ritual with a significant other and to perceive something new about that person. The second, related question asks a person vividly to imagine the experience from another person's perspective. The experience from that perspective offers a whole other level of redundancy and opportunity for new learnings.

Similar questions can be asked to fully utilize and bring forth all the meaning of a ritual once people have performed it. For instance:

— What does your spouse believe is the most important discovery your child made in doing this ceremony?
— Who has changed most since you did the ceremony?
— How will the discoveries you have made make a difference in your life?
— Who will the discovery make the most difference to? Who next?

—What will be your next step now that you have this new knowledge?

Questions of this type presuppose that change has occurred and encourage people to notice that change, spread the news of its occurrence, and begin to plan for a different future. In so doing, they amplify the effects of the ceremony.

General Guidelines

Utilize Clients' Style

Symbols, stories, and ceremonies can be used most effectively when their presentation is tailored to the communication and learning styles of clients. Noticing how clients express themselves, how they tend to generalize from experience, and what kinds of experiences seem meaningful to them can be helpful in tailoring the presentation of metaphors.

For example, when I(JF) was walking to the therapy room with Dana she burst out with, "I must be crazy. I keep buying all these clothes I'd never wear."
I answered, "It could be an identity crisis. The clothes are probably symbols of new identities you are trying out."
"Really?"
"Yes. In fact, I think that at least twice a week you should wear something you didn't ever think you'd wear."
"To check out a new identity?"
"Yes."

This reframe appealed to Dana. She is an avid reader of self-help books, so "identity crisis" made sense to her. She likes labels, and using her new clothes as symbols of new identities enabled her to exchange the label "crazy" that she was entertaining for the label of "identity crisis." I gave the reframe succinctly, without explanation, because that was Dana's usual manner of talking. The evidence she gave for her problem was behavioral, and I suggested a behavior to drive home the reframe.

Meg, on the other hand, had a critical internal voice that disturbed her. A variety of strategies to access positive experience in other realms had not had any impact on Meg's internal dialogue or her preoccupation with it. Neither had her attempts to shut it out or "overpower" it.

At one session Meg described her voice again at length and hypothesized about many possible negative meanings it could have. I(JF) suggested that Meg had done everything she knew how to do to deal with that negative voice. Nothing had worked so it was time to try something different. I suggested that for the following two weeks she listen to that voice as if it were a wise and loving friend. She was given many examples of what listening to such a friend might be like, along with predictions about how she would sometimes forget to listen from the new perceptual position.

When she came back two weeks later, the entire session was spent on a chronological report of her experience each time she heard her wise and loving friend—when her friend was quiet, what each little nuance meant, and how this would apply to other things. She was delighted with the helpfulness she now found in her inner voice, and also discovered that it was no longer always talking. The symbol of "a wise and loving friend" gave Meg access to a new place where she could hear new messages from an old voice.

Meg always explained things in detail with many examples. A meaningful strategy for her had to incorporate this style and provide room for her detailed report.

Approach Psychotherapy as a Ceremony

Psychotherapy itself is a ceremony. When it is successful, it can be one of the most important ceremonies in a person's life. All meaningful ceremonies, be they worship services, weddings, or wrestling matches, are constructed to create a certain atmosphere, a certain emotional and attentional context. Each of us has his or her own style of working which needs a certain context in order to produce its best results, and every client has his own style which needs to be utilized in the therapeutic context. Through ceremony we can evolve therapeutic contexts that work for each new client-therapist system.

There was a time when we sent almost every new person who came to work with us to the public library. We suggested that they wander the stacks until they found an interesting book they'd never heard of before, take it home, and read it. At the next therapy session we would talk with them about the book and the process of finding it until they realized (if they hadn't already) that they had learned something that was pertinent to their goal in therapy.

This simple ceremony (you may notice that it's an *ambiguous function* ceremony) was designed to establish indirectly some ground rules about therapy. It offered clients an active position, in charge of their own learning, and affirmed our belief in their powers of discovery. It established that much of the therapy would occur outside of the therapy session. Maybe most importantly, it established that there was not one particular right answer, that answers would emerge in the course of experience and exploration. It also oriented people to the importance of ceremony.

At the same time, the ceremony let us gather information. We could learn how each person responded to our suggestion about doing something active outside the session that, at least on the surface, was not directly related to a therapeutic goal. We could learn things about their interests from hearing what sections of the stacks had caught their attention. We could get hints about how and whether they relied on other people by listening to how they made use of librarians. Using the ceremony as a metaphor for the larger ceremony of psychotherapy, we could get a feel for each client's personal style and begin to adjust our own style in coevolving an optimal therapeutic context for that client.

We have grown wary of using a single or particular ceremony to establish therapeutic relationships, and we now strive to more carefully to tailor any task we give to fit particular people. However, the ideas involved in the "trip to the library" ceremony are important ones to be addressed in some way as we begin joining with a new client system to form a therapeutic Batesonian mind.

When we cultivate an awareness that each psychotherapy session is part of one large ceremony of transformation, it automatically leads us to an interactional style in which metaphorical communication is valued. Without having to talk about it directly, we will create a context where clients know that symbols, stories, and ceremonies are important.

Notice What the Therapeutic Process Might Symbolize

When I(JF) was in graduate school, I had an appointment with a professor after a class of hers that I was taking. The class was an experiential one and on that particular day one of the students had done some uncomfortable personal exploration. After the class, as I was walking with the professor to her office for our meeting, I noticed that particular student trailing behind us, looking very uncomfortable. I told the professor that what I wanted was just routine and that I would be glad to meet with her some other time so that she could attend to Debby, the other student. "If I drop my schedule and commitments to talk with Debby," she answered, "I would be telling her, in effect, that this is an emergency, that she can't handle her feelings herself, and that something needs to be done. I don't believe any of those things, but when I'm free I will be glad to talk with her if she still wants to."

We try to apply that kind of thought process to our communication and actions, to the client's communication and actions, and to the relationship patterns within the "mind" of therapy as it develops. This is no easy task and it cannot be accomplished on a consistent basis by conscious scrutiny. Nonetheless, it is important to remember that our communication and actions reflect and symbolize our beliefs about the people with whom we are working. It is useful to examine which beliefs we might be conveying from time to time and whether they really represent what we want to be contributing to the system.

Useful questions to ask oneself in evaluating the ongoing therapeutic process are "What does or can our process of relating symbolize?" and "How does this relate to what the person or family is here for?"

Include Some Intentional Ambiguity

An ambiguous communication generally hints at ideas or possibilities, perhaps even conflicting ones, without necessarily contextualizing or clarifying them. It's similar to a gin rummy hand that has cards that could be part of a run or could be part of three of a kind. It all depends how the player plays the hand.

This is an ambiguous communication: Trusting parents can fool you.

It is not clear whether the sentence means parents who are trusting can fool you or if it means you can be fooled by trusting your parents. Therefore, both possibilities are conveyed. Because of the uncertainty, the listener becomes actively involved in trying to discover the meaning. The involvement is heightened if both possibilities are pertinent to a situation relevant to the listener and further heightened in the context of therapy, where the client expects the therapist's words to be meaningful and helpful.

Simply by speaking generally, one can include a shade of ambiguity, and such a shade of ambiguity invites clients to examine everything that's going on as if it might have more than one meaning. When clients approach therapy with this attitude, they can find meaning in very unexpected places.

I(GC) was working with Tina, who was scheduled to have a minor surgical procedure. She was anxious about the potential pain involved and wanted help in approaching the surgery with confidence. As part of the work that we did, I talked with her about walking in the park on a sunny day in spring and all the things one could feel on such a walk. I talked about the warmth of the sun and the feeling of a cool breeze on your face. I said I'd always found it interesting to feel the warmth and the coolness at the same time. I discussed the physical sensations of walking, of sitting in the damp grass, and of standing still in the sun. I said that in each situation you could choose whether to pay attention to your hands, your face, or some other part of your body. I mentioned the feeling of the wind blowing hard enough to make your hair fly in your face and how that could be an enjoyable part of spring.

My conscious plan was to use the sensations I mentioned as metaphors for the sensations involved in her upcoming surgery. I wanted to remind Tina that she could experience many sorts of physical sensations at the same time, that the meaning she attached to each of those sensations had some effect on whether or not she enjoyed them, and that she had some choice about which sensations to focus on. However, I never directly said that she was to apply my words about spring to her surgery or only to her surgery. I simply spoke about those things as if I believed they had relevance for her, leaving the specific relevance ambiguous.

The next time I saw Tina, she told me about an experience she'd had the previous week. She was walking from her office to her car when a strong wind came along and really messed up her hair. She said that normally this would have upset her, but this time she just stood there and enjoyed the sensation of her hair flying in the wind. The experience touched off two trains of thought, one about her perfectionism and the other about her relationship with her mother, who had treated her more like a doll than a person, taking great pleasure in dressing her up, combing her hair, and showing her off. The experience came to be a vivid symbol for Tina. It stood both for a newfound ability to relax and take things in stride and for the fact that she was a person in her own right, not someone else's precious possession.

Something in the metaphors about the sensations of spring had been compelling enough that it stayed with her after the session. She probably didn't think much about it consciously, but relevant themes had been stimulated in a way that let her find two useful bits of information, information from quite different dimensions of her life, in what would ordinarily have been a slightly irritating and quite forgettable incident.

I hadn't been consciously thinking about either Tina's perfectionism or her relationship with her mother, but because I had delivered my message in metaphor, and because I had left my specific intent ambiguous, Tina was able to find those particular dimensions of meaning for herself. As I heard Tina's report, I was able to learn more about how both her perfectionism and her overpampered and underloved relationship with her mother might be involved in her anxiety, and to utilize that information in suggesting further therapeutic experiences.

If I had not already established a way of working with Tina that included ambiguous communications and encouraged her to find her own meaning in the ambiguities, she would have been less likely to treat the incident with the wind in her hair as an important and meaningful experience.

See Chapter 4, Exercise XVI for practice in using words ambiguously.

Trust Your Intuition

We find it helpful to notice and value thoughts, feelings, and pictures that come to our awareness as we sit with clients. If we have our attention focused on the person or family in a respectful way and are attending for metaphors in their communications, then ideas and images that come to us are probably not random. They quite likely have something to do with us in relation to the client system. If together we are coevolving as a Batesonian mind, then images, thoughts, and ideas that occur to us are a product of that mind.

Even when we don't fully understand their importance, sharing symbols and stories that emerge intuitively can be useful. Clients often can fill us in on how they are relevant through their responses.

I(GC) was sitting with Anne, who felt hopelessly stuck and wanted help in finding a new direction for her life. My attention kept being drawn to a book of poems on the bookshelf behind her. I redirected my attention to her several times, but it kept drifting back to the book. Then I found myself musing about a specific poem in the book. It was a poem by Rilke that begins, "Every angel's terrifying. . . . " Finally, after the third or fourth time this had happened, I took the book off the shelf and read her the poem, explaining that it kept coming into my mind, and I thought it might have some relevance for her.

She didn't like the poem at all, and could find no way in which it might be meaningful to her. I put the book back on the shelf, somewhat disappointed, and went on with the session. At least I was able to keep my attention on her once I had read the poem.

The next session, Anne brought in a book of her favorite poems.

They were beautiful poems about nature by David Wagoner. I hadn't even known that she was interested in poetry, much less that she loved to go hiking and camping. Both of these previously hidden resources were useful in helping Anne rediscover her zest for life, and I don't know when or how I would have found out about them if I hadn't read her the poem when my intuition told me to.

Similarly, if during a session an image comes to mind of a boy sailing a toy sailboat on a pond, we are likely to tell a story about a boy sailing a toy sailboat on a pond, or mention it in some way. We might have a thought, as family members talk, of their cooking a meal together. We would probably then introduce the idea in some way, perhaps by asking questions about family behavior around meal preparation, or perhaps as the kernel of a ceremony.

Communicate Expectantly

One of the things that struck me(JF) most in being with Milton Erickson, was how he would ask a question or make a suggestion and then beam expectantly at you, brimming with curiosity, as though he already knew he would be delighted by your response, and he could hardly wait to find out what it would be. The question or suggestion preceding this look was usually ambiguous, sometimes incomprehensible, oftentimes metaphorical; people would not know how to respond. They found a way, though, when they saw that look.

I(JF) was puzzled once when sitting as part of a behind-the-mirror team. We had begun to develop an idea for a ritual when the therapist said, "I couldn't ask them to do that. They would never do it." He was right. But that isn't to say that the family would not have done the ritual. They would not have done it within that particular client-therapist system, just as the therapist could not suggest it within that particular client-therapist system.

In working metaphorically, we have found that it is important to believe in people's resourcefulness and creativity and to be able to communicate that belief nonverbally and congruently. It is important to be comfortable with ambiguity. It is important to scrutinize our beliefs and how they are operationalized and to attend to what we are contributing to the system through our presuppositions. And it is really important to enjoy people!

Remember That This is Therapy, not Broadway

Symbols do not have to be aesthetically pleasing, stories do not have to be material for publication, and ceremonies do not have to be chucklingly clever to be therapeutic. In working metaphorically we are facilitating experiences for people that can bring forth resources and provide new perceptions and possibilities. Whether a therapist, her clients, and her colleagues are bowled over by how aesthetically pleasing and clever her metaphors are seems to have little correlation with how well these same metaphors facilitate therapeutic experience.

In fact, the more perfect the metaphor, the more difficult it is to allow it to change and evolve with the system.

So relax, and allow metaphors to evolve in the system. Many of them will naturally turn out to be fascinating symbols, satisfying stories, and moving rituals.

A Final Story

We wrote the bulk of this book while we were living in San Gimignano, a medieval town in Tuscany. In preparation for our extended stay in Italy, we took one night school Italian class before we left Chicago. This gave us the false impression that we knew a little Italian.

Discovering ourselves to be in error when we actually arrived in Milan, we decided to devote a little more time to studying Italian before we settled down to writing and living in Italy. We found a school in Siena that gave us a place to live and offered us intensive lessons for two weeks, so we took off for it. The class turned out to be taught by a newly-retired high school (Italian) grammar teacher, and our lodgings were an apartment in her home that was originally designed for her in-laws. We studied Italian grammar four hours a day for two weeks, mostly through paper and pencil drills, had a wonderful time in Siena, and found an apartment in a medieval house to rent in San Gimignano, where we decided to settle down.

So we arrived at our new home still having very little knowledge of Italian.

The first Sunday we were there, Carla and Franco, the owners of our apartment, who speak no English, came to visit. Gene was upstairs with Carla, trying to get an understanding of what were to us some unusual characteristics of the bathroom. I was downstairs with Franco, who asked me something that I took to mean, "Have you been walking out in the country?" I said that we hadn't, and started to ask where he suggested we go, when he said, "Why not?" I started trying to find the words to explain how little time we had been there and then realized that maybe he had extended an invitation.

Just then Gene and Carla came downstairs, so I took Gene aside and said, "If either of them brings up anything about a walk, say yes. I think I accidentally turned down an invitation."

Several minutes later, when we detected the word "passeggiata" we both immediately said, "Si!" We then went into our bedroom, threw on jeans and walking shoes, and had a bit of an uneasy conversation about whether we had really been invited on a walk.

It was only several minutes after we left our house that we noticed that Franco was in white linen pants and a stylish Italian sport-coat, and Carla wore a smart suit. We soon discovered that in that part of the country, it is a custom on Sunday afternoons to take leisurely strolls down the main street of town.

That day we began to develop a pattern that we continued to rely on in the early stages of our life in Italy: Someone would say something in Italian and Gene and I would hypothesize on possible meanings and then check out our hypothesis by responding to the statement.

Gene was much more willing to actually speak than I was. I spent a lot of time in my head correcting his endings and tenses. I have always been a good student, and I had the rules in my mind. To me it was like a puzzle. I'd have all these categories and constructions, and I'd pick the right one. The only problem was that the person I was talking to would be gone by the time I'd figure out exactly what to say!

And Gene would say to me, "When you learn to speak Italian you're going to be great, but we aren't going to be in Italy anymore."

Gene would get all the tenses wrong, all the endings wrong, some of the words wrong, but people would know what he was talking about and they would respond.

I really wanted to be part of all that too, so I began talking. And just when I thought I was really speaking well, I spent an afternoon making pasta with Carla, and her son, Francesco, said, "Stop speaking American, Mom." It seemed that Carla had adapted her sentence structure and word choice to match ours.

But by the time we left Italy we had taken trips with Italian friends, stayed up late in the night trading stories and ideas, and helped out other English speaking people who didn't know how to make themselves understood. And we can't tell you exactly how that transformation occurred.

Soon after we came back from Italy we were doing a storytelling workshop. We had set up an exercise in which some participants were being asked some of the questions we discussed in Chapter 6 by other participants, who were sitting by their side as their internal voice. As I walked around the room, at first I thought the exercise was going really well. But then I noticed that after a while many people were not doing the internal voice part. And I wondered if we had set up a bad exercise.

I told Gene what was on my mind, and he said, "Remember what was so hard for you to learn about Italian: Once you know the form you don't have to keep asking yourself what it is, you just say it."

People were not following all the directions for the exercise, but they were spontaneously telling stories. And the stories were delightful to hear.

BIBLIOGRAPHY

Bandler, R. & Grinder, J. (1975). *The structure of magic I.* Palo Alto, CA: Science and Behavior Books.

Bandler, R. & Grinder, J. (1979). *Frogs into princes.* Moab, UT: Real People Press.

Bateson, G. (1972). *Steps to an ecology of mind.* New York: Ballantine.

Bateson, G. (1979). *Mind and nature: A necessary unity.* New York: Dutton.

Bateson, G. & Bateson, M. C. (1987). *Angels fear: Towards an epistemology of the sacred.* New York: Macmillan.

Behan, B. (1981). The confirmation suit. In *After the wake.* Dublin: The O'Brien Press.

Bergman, J. S. (1985). *Fishing for barracuda: Pragmatics of brief systemic therapy.* New York: Norton.

Bergman, J. S. (1989). The family shrine. *Family Therapy Networker,* July/August, 48–51.

Bogdan, J. L. (1984). Family organization as an ecology of ideas: An alternative to the reification of family systems. *Family Process, 23:* 375–388.

Bolles, R. N. (1980). *What color is your parachute?: A practical manual for job-hunters and career changers.* Berkeley, CA: Ten Speed Press.

Capra, F. (1988). *Uncommon wisdom: Conversations with remarkable people.* New York: Bantam.

Cameron Bandler, L. (1984). Compelling Future and Present-to-Future Cause-Effect. Workshop handout.

Dilts, R. (1988). Reimprinting. Workshop handout.

Dilts, R. (1990). *Changing beliefs with NLP.* Cupertino, CA: Meta Publications.

Dolan, Y. (1985). *A path with a heart: Ericksonian utilization with resistant and chronic clients.* New York, Bruner/Mazel.

Erickson, M. H. (1927/1980). Facilitating a new cosmetic frame of reference. In

E. L. Rossi (Ed.), *The collected papers of Milton H. Erickson on hypnosis. IV. Innovative hypnotherapy.* (pp. 465–469). New York: Irvington.

Erickson, M. H. (1948/1980). Hypnotic psychotherapy. In E. L. Rossi (Ed.), *The collected papers of Milton H. Erickson on hypnosis. IV. Innovative hypnotherapy.* (pp. 35–48). New York: Irvington.

Erickson, M. H. (1954a/1980). A clinical note on indirect hypnotic therapy. In E. L. Rossi (Ed.), *The collected papers of Milton H. Erickson on hypnosis. IV. Innovative hypnotherapy.* (pp. 99–102). New York: Irvington.

Erickson, M. H. (1954b/1980). Pseudo-orientation in time as a hypnotherapeutic procedure. In E. L. Rossi (Ed.), *The collected papers of Milton H. Erickson on hypnosis. IV. Innovative hypnotherapy.* (pp. 397–423). New York: Irvington.

Erickson, M. H. (1964/1980). The "surprise" and "my-friend-John" techniques of hypnosis: Minimal cues and natural field experimentation. In E. L. Rossi (Ed.), *The collected papers of Milton H. Erickson on hypnosis. I. The nature of hypnosis and suggestion.* (pp. 340–359). New York: Irvington.

Erickson, M. H. (1965/1980). The use of symptoms as an integral part of hypnotherapy. In E. L. Rossi (Ed.), *The collected papers of Milton H. Erickson on hypnosis. IV. Innovative hypnotherapy.* (pp. 212–223). New York: Irvington.

Erickson, M. H. & Rossi, E. L. (1979). *Hypnotherapy: An exploratory casebook.* New York: Irvington.

Gilligan, S. (1987). *Therapeutic trances: The cooperation principle in Ericksonian hypnotherapy.* New York: Brunner/Mazel.

Gordon, D. (1978). *Therapeutic metaphors: Helping others through the looking glass.* Cupertino: META Publications.

Grinder, J. & Bandler, R. (1981). *Trance-formations: Neuro-linguistic programming and the structure of hypnotic experience.* Moab, UT: Real People Press.

Haley, J. (1963). *Strategies of psychotherapy.* New York: Grune & Stratton.

Haley, J. (1973). *Uncommon therapy: The psychiatric techniques of Milton H. Erickson, M.D.* New York: Norton.

Haley, J. (1976). *Problem-solving therapy: New strategies for effective family therapy.* San Francisco: Jossey-Bass.

Haley, J. (1984). *Ordeal therapy: Unusual ways of changing people.* San Francisco: Jossey-Bass.

Imber-Black, E. (1988). Celebrating the uncelebrated. *Family Therapy Networker*, January/February, 60–66.

Imber-Black, E., Roberts, J. & Whiting, R. (1988). *Rituals in families and family therapy.* (pp. 84–109). New York: Norton.

Lankton, S. & Lankton, C. (1983). *The answer within: A clinical framework of Ericksonian hypnotherapy.* New York: Brunner/Mazel.

Lankton, S. & Lankton, C. (1986). *Enchantment and intervention in family Therapy: Training in Ericksonian approaches.* New York: Brunner/Mazel.

Lessing, Doris. (1978). "Out of the Fountain." in *Collected Stories: Volume Two, The Temptation of Jack Orkney.* London: Triad/Panther Books, Granada Publishing Ltd., pp. 82–99.

Lipchik, Eve, "Interviewing with a Constructive Ear," *Dulwich Centre Newsletter*, Winter, 1988, 3–7.

Lobel, A. (1972). *Mouse tales.* New York: Harper & Row.

Madanes, C. (1981). *Strategic Family Therapy.* San Francisco: Jossey-Bass.

Madanes, C. (1984). *Behind the one-way mirror: Advances in the practice of strategic therapy*. San Francisco: Jossey-Bass.

Madanes, C. (1985). Workshop in Chicago.

Mills, S. (1985). St. Herpes. *Whole Earth Review 48* Fall, 54–58.

O'Hanlon, B. (1986). The use of metaphor for treating somatic complaints in psychotherapy. In de Shazer, S. & Kral, R. *Indirect approaches in therapy*. Rockville, Maryland: Aspen Publishers.

Papp, P. (1983). *The process of change*. New York: Guilford.

Penn, P. (1982). Circular questioning. *Family Process (21)3*, pp. 267–280.

Rilke, R. (1955). *Duino elegies and the sonnets to orpheus*. Translated by A. Poulin, Jr. in 1977. Boston: Houghton Mifflin.

Rosen, S. (1982). *My voice will go with you*. New York: Norton.

Salinger, J. D.(1955). *Franny and Zooey*. Boston: Little, Brown and Company. p. 7.

Satir, V. (1982). Workshop demonstration in Starved Rock, Illinois.

Selvini Palazzoli, M., Boscolo, L., Cecchin, G. & Prata, G. (1978). A ritualized prescription in family therapy: Odd days and even days. *Journal of Marriage and Family Counseling*, 4, 3–9.

Selvini Palazzoli, M., Boscolo, L., Cecchin, G., & Prata, G. (1980). Hypothesizing-circularity-neutrality. *Family Process, 19*, 73–85.

Tomm, K. (1984). One perspective on the Milan systemic approach: Part II. Description of session format, interviewing style and interventions. *Journal of Marital and Family Therapy (10)3*, 253–271.

Tomm, K. (1985). Circular interviewing: A multifaceted clinical tool. In D. Campbell & R. Draper (Eds.). *Applications of systemic family therapy: The Milan Method* (pp. 33–45). New York: Grune & Stratton.

Tomm, K. (1987a). Interventive interviewing: I. Strategizing as a fourth guideline for the therapist. *Family Process, 26*(1), 3–13.

Tomm, K. (1987b). Interventive interviewing: II. Reflexive questioning as a means to enable self-healing. *Family Process, 26*(2), 167–183.

Tomm, K. (1988). Interventive interviewing: III. Intending to ask circular, strategic, or reflexive questions? *Family Process, 27*(1), 1–15.

van der Hart, O. (1983). *Rituals in psychotherapy: Transition and continuity*. New York: Irvington.

Wagoner, D. (1981). *Landfall*. Boston: Little, Brown and Company.

White, M. (1988a). Saying hullo again: The incorporation of the lost relationship in the resolution of grief. *Dulwich Centre Newsletter*, Spring, 7–11.

White, M. (1988b). The process of questioning: A therapy of literary merit? *Dulwich Centre Newsletter*, Winter, 8–14.

White, M. & Epston, D. (1990). *Narrative means to therapeutic ends*. New York: Norton.

Whiting, R. (1988). Guidelines to designing therapeutic rituals. In Imber-Black, E., Roberts, J. & Whiting, R. *Rituals in families and family therapy*. (pp. 84–109). New York: Norton.

Zeig, J. (1980). *A teaching seminar with Milton H. Erickson, M.D.* New York: Brunner/Mazel.

Zeig, J. (1983). *Symbolic hypnotherapy*. Videotape. Phoenix: The Milton H. Erickson Foundation.

Zeig, J. (1985). *Experiencing Erickson: An introduction to the man and his work*. New York: Brunner/Mazel.

INDEX

news of difference, 35, 36–37
nonverbal symbols:
    recognizing, 95–96
    see also body language; communication, nonverbal

odd days/even days ritual, 216–17
O'Hanlon, B., 55, 78
one-skill-at-a-time exercises, 89–117

pacing, 46, 46n, 70, 108, 201, 202
    models of the world, 165–67, 184
    through unique metaphors, 52
pain control, 160–62
Papp, P., 51
parables, 43
pattern-interruption symbol, 73–74
patterns:
    repetitive, 71–72
    and the use of resources, 82
pattern that connects, the, xvi, 32
Penn, P., 131n, 255
perceptual positions, 57
    kinds of change in, 157
    objective, 83–84
    subjective, 57–59
persistence, 170–71
    rewards of, 214
perspective:
    changing, 56–57
    and reframing, 68
place markers, symbols as, 119
positive connotation, 47
Prata, G., 131n, 216, 255
predictions, based on minimal cues, 97
presenting situation:
    components of, 154
    metaphors for, 110–17
    prescribing in metaphor, 234–36
    as a symbol for a function, 152–53
    useful results of, 153
problematic pattern, disrupting, 228–30
problems, as metaphors, 99

process:
    mind as, 33
    symbols found in, 153
    of therapy, 44
    see also therapeutic processes; thought processes
pseudo-orientation in time, 57
psychotherapy as a ceremony, 258–60
puns, 226
purposes:
    of ceremonies, 208
    conscious and unconscious, 40–41
    for telling stories, 163–64, 183
    in therapy, 38
    see also goals

questions, 131–32
    to access stories to suggest ideas, 173–74
    comparative, 133
    future-oriented, 137
    interventive, 255–57
    therapists, 167

random, the, xviii, 215–16
    metaphor as a source of, 10
randomness:
    ambiguous function rituals and, 215–16
    balance with purposiveness, xviii
    metaphor as a source of, 11, 39
    in storytelling, 250
    see also stochastic process
reality, knowledge about, 30
recognition of stories, symbols, and ceremonies, 94–95
reframing, 66–71, 108, 257
    ceremonies for, 222–25
    with symbols, 150–59
relationships:
    client-therapist, 45–47, 164
    distinctions as, 32–33
    and the meaning of a metaphor, 100
    resource-pattern, 82–84
    therapeutic, 259
    therapeutic and information, 48